THE STRUGGLE FOR UNITY

The Integration of the Lutheran Church in the South

By Richard O. Ziehr

The

Struggle For Unity

A Personal Look

at

The Integration of Lutheran Churches

in the

South

by

Richard O. Ziehr

Library of Congress Publication -in-print Data 99-63841

ISBN 1-890683-07-8

Second Printing Year 2000

Ziehr, Richard O. 1931-

"The Struggle For Unity" A personal look at the integration of the Lutheran Churches in the Southern District of the Lutheran Church - Missouri Synod.

Editors CJH ENTERPRISES, Milton, Florida
Stacie Toups, Milton, Florida

Cover Design by: Mark Ziehr

Published by
CJH ENTERPRISES
6064 Mayberry Lane
Milton, Florida 32570-8875

Printed by

PACE PRINTERS
Pensacola, Florida

Printed in the United States of America

Acknowledgments

Special thanks to the following who have greatly assisted in the production of this book.

The Lutheran Witness and the *Southern District Supplement* for permission to use numerous quotes and pictures.

Tom Noon who supplied a number of pictures of the early history of the Synodical Conference in Alabama and other material and resources.

John Ellermann who made his extensive files available to me and provided the photo of the last meeting of the General Conference.

Cynthia Green Dean who carefully and painstakingly searched the official minutes of Immanuel Lutheran Church, Pensacola.

Al Tarvin and C. J. Holzman for their timely assistance and expeditious editing in preparing the manuscript for the printer.

Connie, my wife, for her patient forbearance in sharing the computer and her loving encouragement throughout this endeavor.

A LESSON IN NEW GRAMMAR

I talked to a black man today.
I smiled when I heard his words.
He spoke of the "peoples" of McComb.
I wondered if he had heard of the rules
    for collective nouns.

I listened to a black man today.
I wept when I understood his thoughts.
He spoke of the "peoples" of McComb.
I knew that he understood the problems
    of divisive nouns.

Eldon Weisheit, from *Excuse Me, Sir,*
© by the author
Used with author's permission

―――――――

There is neither Jew nor Greek,
there is neither slave nor free,
there is neither male nor female,
for you are
all one
in
Christ Jesus.

Galatians 3:28

iv

TABLE OF CONTENTS

PREFACE

In the late 1960s, Alabama Lutheran Academy and College hosted a "Culture in Crisis" seminar. At the opening session each participant was invited to introduce himself and tell how he related to the race issue. One white man rose to say that he had worked for ten years in black ministry and gave some of his views about it. The next man, also white, said that he had spent 22 years in black work, and he shared his experiences. Then came Charles Graeber's turn, and he said, "I have been black all my life." Instantly all the rest of us realized that he had an understanding of black work that no white person could match.

With that in mind, I find certain risks in writing this historical sketch. First, I have worked in the South for over 40 years, and served an integrated congregation for almost 30 years; yet, I certainly do not have a full grasp of what it means to be black, and as a result, some nuances understood only by black people will be missing.

When I interviewed the venerable Albert Dominick, he concluded the conversation with this word of advice: "We don't want to stir up race relations. We want to lay low; we don't want to stir up the opposition."[1] That may have come from Dr. Dominick's peace-making tendency and from a concern that putting that troublesome time on record could stir up old, unpleasant feelings. That constitutes the second risk in this enterprise.

A third risk arises because in putting together this picture of the merger I have depended to a large extent on the memory of the people interviewed. The human memory can be capricious, especially when 30 to 40 years are added to the equation. Some memories are vague, some are exaggerated, some have been sterilized to eliminate all unpleasant

1

experiences, and some may simply confuse fiction with fact. Furthermore, the years often add an element of myth to our recollections. Consequently, there is the risk that some of the memories recorded here are not exactly the way it was.

I was spurred on to put this record together because in my ministry I often noticed that many people — especially younger people — have no comprehension of what went on to bring about the merger of black and white churches. Black youth probably have a better understanding of the struggle that took place, because they, like the Jews of old, see it as part of "their story;" however, I believe that both black and white youth need to see the struggle as it was experienced by each side.

The recollections gathered here may not always be precisely accurate; nonetheless, they provide a look at the personal experiences of Lutherans in the South in the 1950s and 1960s. Even now some aspects of segregation remain, and so do the fears that some associate with integration. Thus the reader must do more than merely look at the past: the challenge is to examine the attitudes of the present.

I am grateful to all who were willing to participate in the interviews, as almost everyone contacted did so eagerly. John Ellermann and Warren Davis served as my advisors and Vera Brown and Connie, my wife, were the proofreaders. I express my warm thanks and appreciation for their assistance.

It is my hope and prayer that this record will serve as a reminder that when different people with different gifts are willing to work patiently under the guidance of the Holy Spirit, the Lord can bring about change for the good of His Church.

Richard O. Ziehr
St. Mark the Evangelist Day
April 25, 1999

FOREWORD

With increasing frequency, we are being reminded through television and in print of the anniversary in many different parts of the South of how integration took place in the schools, lunch counters, busses, drinking fountains and restrooms.

It happened also in the church.

Here is an interesting, well-documented and long overdue history of The Lutheran Church reaching out to Black Lutherans in the South. It is not one of the highlights of the Lutheran Church - Missouri Synod in Gospel outreach.

Richard Ziehr, with unhesitating truthfulness, describes the history of the Southern District and in its relationship to Black Churches in the South, and the Synodical Conference. It was a long, drawn out record of the Southern District — knowing what it should do — and, trying to do it.

There was hesitation on both sides of the color line.

Then came the time when a new set of leaders and a new day dawned. This is also the record of those days. The job ahead was to work through long-standing segregationist practices in the churches of the Synodical Conference and The Lutheran Church - Missouri Synod.

It was a time when hopes were high. Things were changing in the South. The Church, too, was changing. There was a growing recognition within the District that we (the members of the Southern District and those of the Synodical Conference) should be pushing toward that fellowship and unity in the Church that is always prayed for. That process and progression are not yet finished....

The personalizing of this historical period, with the deep feelings and hurts — some of which still remain — adds much to this record and serves as another reminder to all who read this account: The Gospel is constantly being battered, hindered, and blocked by broken relationships. But the Church, however slow and hesitant, does move onward with the Gospel, seeking to restore these broken relationships. Reconciliation is one of the greatest gifts of God which the Church possesses.

Here is the record of people and pastors who struggled to share and spread the Good News of Christ's forgiveness; their joys and heartaches; their victories and delays. Society and the Church often did not understand.

We thank Pastor Ziehr for using his retirement profitably in gathering this material, checking and rechecking for accuracy, and then using his unique style of presentation. We thank him for this "remembering" so we do not have to repeat again our hesitancy in spreading the Gospel wherever, whenever and to whoever needs it.

Rev. John Ellermann
former District President
The Southern District

When I think back on some of the sad and harsh history of our country and church, it is always refreshing to know and see God has always raised up people who whose hearts and concerns were to do His will, despite the cost. Many people in the church, and also outside the church, were compelled by love to go forward with their hearts and minds set on God to bring about changes that they knew were in accordance with God's will and plan.

It is said, "We cannot do good to others save at the cost to ourselves, and our afflictions are the price we pay for our ability to sympathize." Pastor Ziehr has made it possible for us to look back and recapture that historical period in our church and get a glimpse of God's suffering people whose hearts and souls were bent on God.

God is always looking for a man or woman whose heart is set on Him and who will trust Him to do all He desires. Furthermore, the world is still waiting to see what God can do through a consecrated soul, who is willing to grasp God's own purposes and take His power without hesitation.

That is what I see as I read the history of the Southern District of the Lutheran Church - Missouri Synod reaching out to black Lutherans in the South.

This is a golden opportunity to thank and praise God for His never failing love, abounding grace, everlasting joy and ever-present peace which moved the Lutherans of the South to work toward merger. Richard Ziehr has provided a careful and balanced record of that struggle. It is also an opportunity to express appreciation for the love, compassion, consideration and understanding that prevailed in the past and the brotherhood that is yet to exist in the future.

Rev. Arthur Bodley
Retired Pastor of
St. Paul Lutheran Church
Chicago, Illinois

The Southern District of the Lutheran Church - Missouri Synod represents the heart of the Deep South because it encompasses Alabama, Louisiana, Mississippi and Northwest Florida. The Southern District was also the last District to integrate and recognize Black Lutheran congregations (known as the Synodical Conference) as equal partners in ministry.

Richard Ziehr, a Southern District pastor during this era of transition, provides historical perspective of this contentious process by comparing events on the national scene to the resultant issues which confronted the Lutherans of the Southern District. He skillfully weaves together a narrative of District voices regarding this issue and identifies the anger, fear, theology and cultural elements which made up the attitudes of those who were involved.

As one reads through this narrative it is easy to understand what is symptomatic in our church body as a whole. Rather than let the Gospel define what we are to be doing in ministry to our surroundings, we rationalize the process of accommodation in an attempt to "fit in" with our society. It is an easy and uncomfortable truce at best.

The answer always seems to be that one person (or more) will have to take a stand in order to bring issues to a head. As we see in this excellent narrative, it sometimes brings out the best, worst and every other emotion in between with us! Martin Luther King, Jr., and a host of others, black and white, learned the method of exposing what was unjust, marshalling love into non-violence and taking their faith to the streets, courthouses and churches. That challenge to change brought about by such instructive and courageous Gospel-oriented action now speaks for itself!

Rev. Thomas Noon, Pastor
St. Paul Lutheran Church
Birmingham, Alabama

Richard Ziehr is to be commended for making the effort to address a significant part of our "Southern Lutheran History," especially during the time of integration. His contribution to the oral and written history of that time sheds additional light on the many conversations I have heard about the Synodical Conference and how the work of the Church was carried on during those challenging years.

To listen, by way of interview, to many of the people of that time express their points of view regarding the Church's response to the social upheaval, suggests that the dialogue begun in these pages should continue. We are not so far removed from the challenges of the past that a present-day dialogue would not help us as we seek to do the *work* of *the Church* today.

I recommend Pastor Ziehr's contribution to the dialogue between Lutherans of all colors, particularly in the South. The problems unearthed in his writings and the problems solved can make a great contribution to the working together that is necessary for us to be witnesses to the cause of the Gospel today.

Rev. Warren Davis, Pastor
Jehovah Lutheran Church
Pensacola, Florida

INTRODUCTION

In 1954 the entire South was solidly segregated. Every aspect of society and life - schools, restaurants, public rest rooms, and churches - was totally separated by race.

The Lutheran Church was engaged in ministry in the South at that time, but the work was entirely separated. Paul Streufert was elected as president of the Southern District of the Lutheran Church - Missouri Synod in 1954, and when he addressed the District Pastors Conference in May 1957, he aptly described the status of black Lutherans when he stated: "The Black man belongs to the Lutheran Church, but when he is asked to which Lutheran Church he belongs, he has to answer, 'I belong to none.'"[1]

Work among black Lutherans was sponsored by a federation of Lutheran churches known as the Synodical Conference, and while the Missouri Synod provided much of the manpower, black people were never allowed to meet with the churches which served as their sponsors. The few white pastors who served black congregations could belong to the Missouri Synod as "advisory pastors," but the black pastors could not. Black pastors could not attend a district convention or a district pastors conference.

However, the winds of change were beginning to be felt in the Spring of 1954. The most obvious impact came on May 17 of that year when the U. S. Supreme Court announced that all public schools had to be integrated.

Change was to come, but it did not come quickly or quietly.

Nine tumultuous years later, the black congregations of the Synodical Conference were officially received into the heretofore all-white Southern District of the Lutheran Church - Missouri Synod. The historic event took place on August 27, 1963, at the District Convention held at Immanuel Lutheran in Pensacola, Florida.[2]

What follows is a chronicle of experiences and recollections of events and developments which took place among Lutherans in those years. Authors such as Richard Dickinson in *Roses and Thorns* and Jeff Johnson in *Black Christians - The Untold Lutheran Story* have recorded some of the ecclesiastical transactions of that time period. While I will touch on some of the decisions of Synod and District conventions, my aim is to focus on the personal anguish and turmoil experienced by those who lived and worked in the South and were involved in the often traumatic events of that period. To that end I have interviewed over 60 people, pastors and laymen, and in many cases they will speak for themselves.

✠   ✠   ✠

It is impossible to review the developments within the Lutheran Church at that time apart from society. The social upheaval in the South during the 1950s and 1960s ranks as the most upsetting period in Southern history since the Civil War. Two dates serve as the bookends of the Civil Rights Movement: its beginning is set at May 17, 1954, with the Supreme Court's announcement of school desegregation, and its end is placed at April 4, 1968, with the assassination of Dr. Martin Luther King, Jr.[3]

Did the Church affect the social change of the time, or did the social change move the Church to action? No simple answer can be given, but surely a two-way street existed, and this will become more obvious as we explore the discussions which led to acceptance and the merger.

As a reminder that Lutherans of that time period were not living in a social vacuum, I will occasionally insert brief paragraphs (in italics) to note some of the events and actions which made news.[4] Most of these will be brief unvarnished statements in order to highlight the ruthlessness and cruelty of those events and actions.

✠   ✠   ✠

My arrival in the South was closely associated with the time of change. Just twelve days before the Supreme Court announcement, I received my vicarage (internship) assignment to serve at First Lutheran in Baton Rouge, LA. Since I was born and raised in central Texas, I had been exposed to the Southern way of thinking; yet I was quite naive about the intensity of feelings regarding racial separation.

Many thought the South was still very primitive. Upon learning that I was going to Louisiana, some men in my home congregation warned me to watch for the alligators which they expected to crawl across the highways. I never saw an alligator on the road, but in those days it was common for cows to walk across the road, even federal highways, because much of Louisiana was unfenced.

I grew up in a segregated town. It was well-known that the little community north of the railroad tracks was called "Nigger-Town." Their children did not attend our schools, and the fact that they didn't apparently caused no one to give it much thought. It was the status quo. The few Mexicans in our schools were nominally accepted, and that was the extent of racial mixing that I had experienced before arriving in Louisiana.

✠   ✠   ✠

While this book is titled "The Struggle For Unity - A Personal Look at the Integration of the Lutheran Church in the South," it will not cover the history of every Lutheran Church. The reader needs to keep in mind that four major segments of Lutherans were represented in the South during this period; namely, The America Lutheran Church (ALC), The Lutheran Church of America (LCA), The Wisconsin Synod, and the Lutheran Church - Missouri Synod. Of those four entities, the LCA and the Wisconsin Synod had very few congregations in the South and none of their congregations were involved in serious racial conflicts.

The ALC had several congregations in Alabama, and Grace Lutheran in Montgomery suffered serious harassment and damage in the 1950s. However, in the late 1950s the ALC withdrew from the South and turned their congregations over to the Missouri Synod. This left the Missouri Synod congregations as the largest segment of Lutherans in the South; therefore this account will deal almost exclusively with the struggle for unity in that church body.

The Lutheran Church - Missouri Synod is Germanic in background. In 1839 a company of Lutherans left Germany because of religious restrictions, landed in New Orleans and traveled up the Mississippi to southern Missouri to carve out a new beginning — hence the name "Missouri Synod." The church's central office is still in St. Louis, Missouri.

The national body of the church is divided into districts. The Southern District is one of the original districts and once stretched from Florida/Georgia to Texas. At the time of the merger, the Southern District embraced Alabama, Louisiana, Mississippi and Northwest Florida, and thus represented a very large section of the Deep South.

To further aid the reader, the national body, the Lutheran Church - Missouri Synod, elects a President. Each district also elects a President. Each district is divided into circuits for which a Counselor is elected. The Counselor serves as an assistant to the District President and often is a general trouble-shooter when problems arise with pastors and congregations in the circuit.

✠ ✠ ✠

Integration in the church did not come easily even for devout church members. I remember one scene which perhaps captures the nature of the feelings involved.

We were gathered for a Sunday School teachers workshop at the Lutheran Church of Vestavia Hills, south of Birmingham. Attending with me was a faithful teacher, a white man, a native of Birmingham. As we stood around outside the church before the meeting, I saw a black man whom I had gotten to know and introduced my teacher to the black teacher. My member reluctantly extended his hand, but intentionally looked away and refused to look at the man he was "greeting."

In the ensuing chapters we will see more of the background which produced such unwillingness of a devout Christian Sunday School teacher to engage in even the simple gesture of extending the hand of fellowship to a devout Christian Sunday School teacher of another color.

CHAPTER 1

BACKGROUND OF THE OLD SOUTH

Remnants of the Unforgotten War

The novelist Jimmy Street once described white Southerners as "those who love the South, love her as parents love a crippled child."[1] Some remnants of that rather protective and possessive thinking can still be seen in some aspects of Southern attitudes.

When I arrived in Louisiana, although 90 years had elapsed since the Civil War, the bitterness of a lost war was still very much on the minds of people. Bumper plates declaring "Forget, Hell!" were commonplace. The Confederate Flag was frequently displayed, and the University of Mississippi band marched onto the football field with a huge Confederate Flag and to the tune of "Dixie." For at least two more decades, the Dixie Flag was raised every day at the Alabama State Capitol in Montgomery. In South Carolina, the Confederate Flag was not flown at the capitol until 1962, and then it was done as a protest against the Civil Rights Movement.

I soon learned that all public conveyances — buses and street cars in the cities — were segregated, with black people either forced to sit in the back or stand. Public eating places prominently displayed a sign near the entrance with the message: "We Reserve The Right to Refuse Service to Anyone."[2] And sometimes white Southerners revealed their educational level. Bill Wedig, who began his ministry in Mississippi in 1945, remembers seeing the restrooms at a service station identified as "White" and "Collid"[3] The public bathrooms for "Colored" were often so filthy that, as one white man observed, "You wouldn't take your dog into one of those."

To come to the Deep South in the mid-1950s was an eye-opening experience, especially to be exposed to the venom and hatred that came from Southern politicians. For instance, Tom Brady, a Mississippi Circuit Judge, described the Southern white woman as the nearest thing to an angelic being on the earth; on the other hand, he wrote that "The social, political, economic and religious preferences of the Negro remain close to the caterpillar and the cockroach...proper food for a chimpanzee."[4]

Former Mississippi Senator James Vardaman once declared: "I am just as much opposed to Booker T. Washington as a voter as I am to the coconut-headed chocolate-brown typical little coon who blacks my shoes."[5]

Furthermore, it was a new and unnerving experience to learn that The Ku Klux Klan was still around and presented a very real danger.

During my first year in Louisiana I met John Nau. We young ministers were immediately drawn to Nau because he always had something to say and with a voice that never needed amplification he was hard to ignore. By then he was a Ph.D. teaching history and philosophy at the University of Southern Mississippi in Hattiesburg. Nau gave me the following account of one of his early experiences.

Upon graduating from Concordia Seminary in St Louis in 1936, he came to work in Central Mississippi where he was assigned to teach religion at the all-black Piney Woods School located about 25 miles south of Jackson. He remembers that soon upon arrival the local sheriff found him and said, "As soon as the sun goes down, you see to it that you get off that campus and go back to Jackson, or you find you a place to sleep elsewhere. Don't sleep there!"

The locals were afraid that Nau was a trouble-maker and that he was stirring up the students, but, as he explains, "I taught nothing but religion, from morning until evening." Obviously not everyone was convinced of his activities at the school, for he relates the following experience:

> So I come, one evening about 8:00 o'clock, down to the highway, which was at that time only a two-way - north and south - not a big highway like it is today - and there I stand, and all of a sudden three hooded men with rifles in their hand come toward me. And the language they used, I won't repeat. They called me the worst names they could call. And the youngest - I thought he was the youngest guy, because he was the smallest fellow - said, "Let's kill 'im!"

12

And being single I didn't care very much for my life, and I said to them, "You're going to shoot me - put it here." All they had was a flashlight.... The big fellow told the younger, "Shut up!"...and another big curse word. "Shut up!" And then he said, "What are you teachin' up there?" And I told him, "Nothing but religion - here's a Bible and three Luther's Catechisms - you see."

And they said, "Well, I tell you what, it's a good thing you're gettin' out of here, because it's gettin' pretty dark, and we don't want to see a white man up there with those black son-of-a-bitches at night."

By that time I looked down the road and I saw two lights coming. That was my bus, going into Jackson. Every evening I went into Jackson. And I said, "Look a there, there's my bus." And when I looked around they were gone, and I never saw them again.[6]

Moses Clark is a black pastor who has worked in the South many years. In the late 1950s he was working in Central Alabama. An icy chill went through me when I recorded the following account of an experience he had with the Klan:

I had checked in over there at [Pastor] Gailes, for the first Sunday of the month, and to get some wine [for communion]. But he didn't have any, so we went on to Selma, to get some wine. And coming back from Gailes' place, down on the highway...on that dirt road, when I turned on the highway, I saw a light by the church. And by the time I got down about a quarter-mile from that intersection, they ran down on me. They ran up beside me. They ran in front of me - and they stopped!

I wouldn't stop. So they pulled out way up ahead of me. So I pulled right up behind them. They started to get out. But I pulled around, and stepped on my accelerator to the floor and ran back to Lamison. And when I got to Lamison, I turned off and went up through the woods. I went up through there, and I had a member who lived over there. So I went up to her house and told her what had happened. I could not get back on the road. I stopped over there and could not get back home.

"No, you going to stay here tonight, nobody comin' here." She had a lot of bad dogs, she had a gun, and nobody mess with her. So I stayed there. The next morning I had to go down to Camden and to Arlington, to go over at service time to preach. So I stayed over there for a while. I was living by myself...I was a bachelor, down in Arlington, and because I feared they would follow me home, and if they found out where I lived, then I really would have trouble. So rather than that, I cut through toward Lamison Community, to keep them from finding out where I lived. So I spent the night, and then went back home.

But I came back for service time from Camden, and I was really scared, because it was a carload. It looked like about six of them, and they were out just to get somebody - a black-'un - I guess.[7]

John Davis is a black man of immense size and has a voice to match. As a college student he played football for Alabama A & M. Affectionately known as "Big John," he was an active member of the black Lutheran congregation in Gadsden, Alabama when I first met him and a strong leader among the black lay people of Alabama. Late in life he studied to be a pastor.

Davis tells of the efforts to get a Lutheran church organized in the Ashville-Gadsden, Alabama area. "The Klan had harassed the white pastor who started the work," he remembered, "and when he left, a missionary-at-large followed and he also was driven off." Then Davis continued:

I carried the service on, and conducted the Vacation Bible School and confirmation classes. The pastor would come up only on Sundays and carry on the preaching service and Sunday School and when he couldn't come I would prepare a message the best I could and have it read before this group. While this was going on, we were having Bible school in Haty Phillips' yard, under the oak trees. The Ku Klux Klan would be parading the street all the hour during this service. I taught Sunday School and Vacation Bible School with a double barrel shotgun...[8]

Later the Klan burned a cross in Davis' yard and, after he was accused of working with the Black Muslims, although the claim was unfounded, the Klan burned down his house. While he had fire insurance, when the insurance company learned that the Klan had been charged with the burning, his insurance was canceled.[9]

The account of the harassment which came from the Klan and other white Southerners is not complete without a reference to Antonio Gianvittorio. Gianvittorio, a former Catholic priest, came into the Missouri Synod by colloquy, and in 1952 was sent to teach at the Alabama Lutheran Academy and College at Selma. Walter Ellwanger, the president of the Selma school, wrote in a letter that Gianvittorio "had difficulties in adjusting himself as a Lutheran and to the black people," yet he was assigned to congregations in the Alabama field. In fact, he was asked to serve at St. Paul-Oak Hill and Christ-Rosebud, in the very heart of black Lutheranism in Alabama (see map on p.25).

While serving at Oak Hill, he incurred the wrath of local white folks by referring to black people as "Mr." and "Mrs." In addition he recommended that the people of the black community boycott the local white merchant. One morning soon thereafter he was found beaten and bloody, lying in a road ditch.

Pastor Ellwanger, who was also the Superintendent of the black work in the Alabama/Upper Florida Conference, immediately moved Gianvittorio to Gadsden, Alabama. There again he had a confrontation with the Klan; and Ellwanger wrote: "At Gadsden he was threatened by the KK's (sic). I decided it would be best if he would voluntarily leave the field, and I paid his transportation back to his brother...in Maryland."[10]

The Klan often influenced many outside of its membership, and perhaps the most puzzling is the way the Klan at times became linked with churches. For example, when Ben Veit came as a new pastor to Bogalusa, LA, in 1957, he soon realized that many of the local clergy offered prayers for Klan rallies.[11] Gene Kappeler, a member of the staff at the Alabama

Lutheran Academy and College, tells that in 1959 he attended a Klan rally at Selma which was being led by a well-known Methodist pastor.[12]

While some communities in the South did not welcome the Klan, in many places it was as acceptable as the Lions Club. At the approach to more than one town, I remember seeing a roadside sign which advertised the presence of a local "Klavern," as they called it. The sign was boldly posted to suggest that the Klan was in the same category as the Lions Club, the Kiwanis, and other civic organizations. The sign displayed a hooded-horseman and was

"SEE YOU IN CHURCH."

clearly marked "Ku Klux Klan." In many places in the South the Klan made little effort to stay in hiding, although in some areas it was referred to by euphemisms, such as: "The Loyal Order of the White Camellia," or "The Knights of the White Camellia."

This was the South in which the Lutheran Church was at work.

Attitudes of White Lutherans Working in the South

In the mid-50s, changes were beginning to take place. A dozen major petrochemical companies and other industries were stretched along the Mississippi River between Baton Rouge and New Orleans. This industrial migration brought many Northerners to the South. Consequently, non-Southerners made up at least half the leadership at the congregation where I served my vicarage.

The best description of the prevailing attitude in the mid-50s was the willingness to accept the status quo. When I arrived in Baton Rouge to serve as a vicar at First Lutheran, I was soon told that Calvary Lutheran some ten blocks away was the local black Lutheran congregation. Although, black people lived within a few blocks of First Lutheran, none attended there. One or two might show up for a wedding or a funeral. I do not recall that the issue of segregation was ever discussed in any church meeting.

Within a few weeks of my arrival, I met Samuel Kent, the pastor at Calvary. The members at First were invited to Calvary for their annual Mission Festival, but no return invitations were extended. The status quo prevailed in Baton Rouge.

But not everyone was satisfied with the status quo. John Nau recalls that "a changing attitude was starting to come toward the black man." He continues to describe an incident in the '40s:

> Now it took lots more time to get our own white pastors to see that [a change was coming]. They were the hardest... For instance, I think of one who was over in Metairie [a suburb of New Orleans] - a big heavy-set guy who was a football player - Hoffmann by name. He was not with the Synodical Conference; he was serving a mission station in the Metairie area that grew into what we have in Metairie now. He was dead-set against even associating with blacks.

> He's the one who at a pastoral conference - held, as we did, monthly - in the school room of St. Paul [Lutheran] parochial school at Port and Burgundy [in New Orleans],[13] who told young John Rische, who worked with his uncle as pastor to blacks in Jackson and also in Piney Woods, that he would never allow a black man to attend the pastoral conference meeting in New Orleans. He said, "Before a black man will step into this pastoral conference, I will stand at the door and throw him out!"

John Rische said, "I can no longer accept you as a brother."

Now this happened in the '40s - right after World War II. And John turned to me, because I was a good friend of John Rische, and said, "John, you're going to stay here?" And I said, "Yeah, I'm going to fight these people until they're going to have to throw me out. I will not walk out by myself." That was the attitude of some of our white pastors.[14]

When Nau was asked how widespread the anti-black attitude was, he answered: "This was more of a fray among the younger men; the older men kept themselves aloof from that. They didn't even as much as encourage or discourage us; they just kept away from it."

But some did provide a measure of encouragement. Nau continues:

George Schmidt - he was at First English [in New Orleans] - and he took me on the corner [of Port and Burgundy] after that hectic meeting, where we were threatened to be beaten up because we took the part of the black man coming there to attend a meeting. And he said, "John, don't get too excited. The Lord's mill grinds, but it grinds awfully slow at times." So that sort of cooled me down a little bit.[15]

✠   ✠   ✠

Richard "Pedo" Meyer, a native-born Alabamian, recalled an incident in Cullman, AL, which represented a minor, although brief, breakthrough in the old Southern customs. In the summer of 1955, while on furlough as a missionary in Japan, he returned to Cullman, where his father was pastor. Since the new vicar had not yet arrived, Meyer was asked to handle the youth ministry for the summer. At his first meeting with the youth, he found them happily engaged in a Sunday afternoon baseball game which included a black youth named Joe.

Since Joe was so well received at the ball game, Meyer invited him to the youth gathering at the church gymnasium the following Friday even-

18

ing. Again Joe came and was well received. Taking it a step further, after discussing it with the teacher of the youth class, Meyer invited Joe to Sunday School the following Sunday. Joe came all dressed up and ready, and Meyer escorted him to the youth class. Eager to see how it went, Meyer rushed to see the teacher at the close of the Sunday School hour. The teacher said, "Everything went well; you won't have any trouble with the youth. If you will have a problem, it will be with their parents."

After being away for a few weeks, Meyer returned to learn that a special congregational meeting had been called. In the meantime the superintendent of the county schools had visited the pastor, some parents had threatened to withdraw their children from Sunday School, and the elders of the congregation had prepared a resolution to the effect that, while we are all one in Christ, it would be best that the different races worship separately. Before the vote only one person spoke up; Mrs. Teichmiller asked, "Isn't it strange that we send missionaries to Africa to bring people to Jesus, but we won't allow a black man to worship with us?" Her comment brought a rush of guilty feelings, and after the meeting a number of people came forward to offer help to send Joe to the Alabama Lutheran Academy at Selma, and pay his way. But Joe never came back.[16]

✠   ✠   ✠

For many white pastors it was not in Lutheran thinking to become involved in social issues; for them it was simply a matter of complying with tradition and "the Southern way of life." They did not want to make waves because of a two-pronged fear: One, that outreach to the community would be hindered by social action; and two, that reprisal from the Klan or the White Citizens Council could be expected. Against that background, maintaining the status quo was the most comfortable. The fact that the Lutheran Church was an obvious minority in the South — some would say it was an "alien" church — made it even easier to justify a willingness to maintain the status quo.

Attitudes of Black Lutherans Working in the South

Black Lutherans, for the most part, had lived under paternalistic supervision from the time Lutherans began an outreach in 1877; now, attitude changes were also being manifested among black Lutherans. The following glimpses are provided by two veteran black pastors:

Albert Dominick was an affable man, always jovial, filled with laughter and good humor. However, he was no push-over for he told me that as a young pastor he confronted a man over some wrong-doing, and the incident led to fists flying. Dominick declared, "I beat him good!"[17]

Dominick was one of the pioneers in black work. The time came when his wife wanted to start a kindergarten in their church, but E. A. Westcott, superintendent of the Alabama/Upper Florida Conference from 1931 to 1945, opposed it. Dr. Dominick's daughter said that her mother was a born teacher. When Westcott voiced objections, some of the congregation members were willing to accept his advice. Anna, the daughter, added, "But Mom didn't. She said, 'Why not?'"[18]

When Dominick described the incident, he recalled that Westcott said,

> "Your wife can't teach anymore." When I told her, she hit the roof. She called him right away. She was hard to beat one-on-one. She wanted to see him right away, and insisted that "We won't have five children in this congregation if we don't. We will have no future." She talked to him, and he said, "It's all right, it's all right, go ahead!"[19]

The oppressive supervision of the black congregation and pastor sometimes took its toll. Dominick remembers a time, especially during World War II, when a number of pastors left the field. He said:

> They didn't like the set-up. When they [the Mission Board] got ready to move pastors, they just moved them without consent of the congregation.... They just moved them like men on a checkerboard. They [the black pastors] wanted to have a constitution, and without a constitution they didn't have a say-so. That's when [Peter] Hunt and them left. There were four pastors, right in a row.... And then the other pastors that were

left, they had to take those congregations and schools and carry on - with no increase in pay.[20]

John Skinner is a tall thin man whom I met at the first integrated pastoral conference. He served as a pastor in the Synodical Conference, both in Alabama and North Carolina, and in his prime was one of the best preachers in the Conference.

He referred to the supervision as "the hierarchy," speaking specifically about Westcott. He mentioned several "run-ins" with the superintendent. "I have always been a fairly easy-going fellow," he said, "until you rub me wrong." He related the ensuing incident:

> One day I had gone into Selma to shop. And so, I met him [Westcott] on the street - on Broad Street - and he was going one way and I was going the other way, and so in my courteous self, I extended my hand and said, "Pastor Westcott." And he didn't say anything. And I knew there were some people standing there, some white people.... And after that I am going to his office. And I just wanted to know why he wouldn't shake my hand. His excuse was, "You know the situation; white and black are not supposed to associate."[21]

Skinner related another experience which took place several years

Alabama Lutheran Academy and College,
Students and faculty — 1956

21

later when Walter Ellwanger was superintendent. Skinner was serving as pastor in Oak Hill, 40 miles south of Selma. Because of a shortage in staff, he was persuaded to work four days a week teaching at Alabama Lutheran Academy and College in Selma. This meant he had to leave his wife in Oak Hill and return every weekend to conduct services there. His workload at the school included teaching English, conducting the choir, and coaching basketball. It was in connection with basketball that a problem arose. Here is how he tells it:

> We had an invitation to play a basketball game out of town, in Wilcox County. Selma is in Dallas County, so we had to go to Wilcox. I didn't think it would get someone angry with me that I was trying to take authority. I did that because the coach of the other team that I was playing asked me for a return game.

> A week or two after that incident, he [Ellwanger] had to bring this up again for the entire faculty...that I was taking authority.... I had forgot that the exam dates were at the same time. I could understand that. I just wasn't thinking, but it didn't matter to him. My taking authority is what mattered.

> But at the time I didn't say any more, except "I'm sorry." But now a week or two later, after that incident, we were in faculty meeting, and he had to bring this up again, in front of the entire faculty. They weren't interested in it, or concerned about it. And he brought up that I had tried to take over. He lambasted me in front of the whole faculty. He didn't state a name, but everyone knew who he meant. And I sat there and tried to reason with him.

> Oh, no. Now here I am, away from home, away from my wife, living with my Momma, trying to help out, wasn't making no money - just a few pennies - but I was enjoying it - glad to do it, the children were cooperating with me. But the man talked and talked, so I left out of the faculty meeting, and I went into the school office, because I was fuming. I was afraid if I stayed in there, something might happen.

22

Behind me came Dr. Hunt. He knew I was upset. "I'm
going to tell the man that I'm going home. When he made me
dissatisfied, it was the worst thing he could have done, because
I was helping him out with the school and the children." Hunt
was trying to get me to change my mind about leaving. So he
out-talked me.

So he came out of the faculty meeting and went to his
office, and I told Hunt that I'm going up here trying to reason
with the man, concerning the thing I don't like - blabbing all that
stuff in the faculty meeting involving me. So I went up there,
and he was still huffing and puffing. And I said, "Dr.
Ellwanger, I came up here trying to reason with you. I tried to
do that in the faculty meeting first, and I wasn't getting the right
answer, and I left out to cool things down. Now I am here again,
trying to reason things out with you. I should not have done
that, and I do feel that I took a little presumption." And I said,
"I apologize about that."

He said, " You need to get on your knees and pray."
And I said, "If you want to pray, you go ahead and pray - and
while you are praying, I'm going to take you...and I'm going to
throw you out the window! I have been trying to reason, but you
made me mad. Nobody is going to trample on me!" So to make
a long story short, I didn't leave there, because Hunt talked me
into staying.[22]

Pastor's Wives also have Recollections

John and Elva Ellermann came to New Orleans in 1953 where he
served as pastor of Bethlehem Lutheran Church, a black congregation.
Elva recalls her feelings and experiences of that time in this compelling
account:

These years I remember clearly because they are burned
into my psyche. I had been born and raised in Iowa. I had never
seen (and at first I could not tell them apart...all I could see was
their blackness) a black person before moving South.

23

I was completely unaware of the concept of separation of the races...I knew not the restrictions or the problems. John had been slated as a missionary to India. But by graduation in 1953, they were no longer allowing Western Missionaries into India. They asked if we would be willing to serve Negro Missions in New Orleans. We received no training or special instructions of any kind. I innocently started attending and joining my husband's church. [She had been told by an older pastor that "it was no place for a white woman." In the past, it was customary, when a white pastor served a black congregation, his wife and children belonged to a neighboring white congregation.] I not only joined, but was active — sang in the choir and joined the ladies group. It never occurred to me that this was not done. Our oldest daughter, Carol, was the first white child baptized in a black congregation.

We soon found that we had broken all the codes and rules. We were almost completely ostracized by the white clergy living in the city. It was not just those in the white churches, but also all the wives of white clergy serving other black churches. I was in New Orleans with no family anywhere close, no friends, and no support. It upsets me to this day. The only people that would have anything to do with us were Bill & Nancy Wedig. We played bridge with them every Sunday evening.... It was a difficult time for me because I could not understand the white clergy's hatred and unkindness.

The members of our own church could not have any social contact with us. They told us it was not safe for *us* or for *them*. They were afraid to come out at night and all meetings took place during the day or on Sunday. The few times John did meet at night at the church we were never at ease. He would call me just before he would leave and be home as quickly as possible. Our members (a few men) would stand across the street from the church and watch for any trouble on those few occasions.[23]

When Jim Brockmann, a white new seminary graduate, came to New Orleans in 1959 to serve as Missionary at Large in the Synodical

Conference, the same social restrictions were still the policy. Pat, his wife, remembers the briefing they received in St. Louis on Call Day. Karl Kurth, the chairman of the Synodical Conference Mission Board, told the wives that they could not have membership in a black church, they could eat meals with their members, but they could not have their members eat with them.

When they left St. Louis, Pat's membership was transferred to Zion Lutheran, a white congregation in New Orleans. But as soon as they arrived, she had her membership moved to Concordia Lutheran, the black congregation which Jim served. Like the Ellermanns, they had their children baptized in a black congregation. They also entertained some of their members in their home.[24]

Accordingly some of the young workers who came to the South began to break the rules of the past, and ignored the long-held customs of their predecessors.

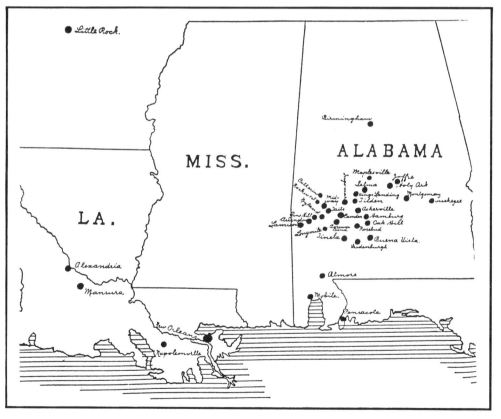

Map showing churches of the Synodical Conference - 1928

25

CHAPTER 2

MOVEMENT TOWARD MERGER

Voices of Change are Heard

The Forty-Seventh Convention of the
Southern District was held in Baton Rouge on
October 18-23, 1954, with First Lutheran the host
congregation. Dr. M. W. H. Holls, who had been
District President for 27 years, asked not to be considered for re-election. Paul W. Streufert, a relative
new-comer from Missouri and pastor of Our Savior
Lutheran in New Orleans, was chosen as the new
president.[1]

Paul W. Streufert

When the delegates gathered for that convention they did so with
the Supreme Court's decision clearly in the background. Another decision
had been made just one month after the Supreme Court decision which also
must have hovered in the background, at least in the mind of some of the
delegates.

In 1920 the black pastors and congregations which were associated
with the Synodical Conference organized the General Conference. Since
they could not attend conferences with white professional church workers,
the General Conference was created to provide a forum for study and
encouragement for black pastors and teachers. However, by 1950 all the
Districts except the Southern District had accepted black pastors and congregations within their geographic areas into membership; consequently for
black church workers outside of the South, the General Conference became
a duplication. As a result, when the General Conference gathered in Selma,
AL, in June of 1954, it voted itself out of existence.[2]

The last meeting of The General Conference - Seated front row (l. to r.) Albert Dominick, Conference Chairman; William von Spreckelson, Mission Executive, Southeastern District; Karl Kurth, Chairman, Synodical Conference Board of Missions. Back row standing: Peter Hunt, sixth from left; Walter Ellwanger, ninth from left. In middle of picture Marmaduke Carter (man in dark suit). In front of him - Miss Rosa Young, and behind his right shoulder - Andrew Schulze. John Ellermann is two to the right of Schulze

27

Pastor Albert Dominick was the chairman of the General Conference at its demise, and its dissolution was a hard blow for him and the other black pastors of the South. They were orphaned from their black brethren in other parts of the U. S. and had as yet no assurance of being received into the Southern District. *The Missionary Lutheran* reported that Rev. W. H. Hafner, First Vice President of the Southern District, was present at that final meeting and "stated his district is not opposed to taking over the supervision [of] the Negro missions within its geographical boundaries, but said that it would take time and planning to work matters out to the best interests of all concerned."[3]

Even though the Synodical Conference had recommended in 1946 that all black work be merged with the local Districts, no mention of it was made in the Proceedings of the Southern District until 1954.[4] The Proceedings of the 1954 Convention note that Rev. Walter Ellwanger was given the floor to report concerning the Alabama Lutheran Academy at Selma, Alabama. In his report he expressed concern over the possible break-up of the Synodical Conference and said that "such action would seriously affect our church's colored mission work."[5]

The Proceedings continue as follows: "Rev. Ellwanger then commented concerning the academy at Selma. He stated that, as we come to know the colored through the Gospel, [as] we come to know them as precious souls, the segregation difficulties disappear."[6]

Now the Southern District was on notice that changes were taking place, and that it would eventually have to wrestle with the question of how it would relate to the black congregations within its boundaries which now were left essentially in isolation. Consequently, a few minor overtures about race relations were made during that convention. For example, when Mr. Carl Wegener gave the report of the Synodical Conference, he included the following:

> We recommend that the Missionary Board of the Synodical Conference be asked to study ways and means of bringing the regular Synodical organs and supplements [*The Lutheran Witness*] containing also news on Negro missions, into all Negro Lutheran homes - also and especially in those areas where the work is still the responsibility of the Synodical Conference.... We feel that this is an essential part of the integration

program already in progress, and will promote among all members of the Synodical Conference a wider appreciation of the work of the church-at-large.[7]

Obviously, that recommendation was designed to give black Lutherans a better picture of the church-at-large. And then, apparently to make the reading more interesting for black people, the following related resolution was also adopted:

> In order that *The Lutheran Witness* [the official magazine of the Missouri Synod] be of more interest to our colored brethren, we recommend that the Editorial Board of the Southern District *Lutheran Witness Supplement* and the Executive Board of the District, together with representatives of the Synodical Conference seriously consider regularly including news items of our colored fields in the *Supplement*.[8]

The convention also heard a memorial submitted by the Pastoral Conference of the Crescent City [New Orleans], which proposed:

> That the Negro pastors living within the confines of our Southern District be invited to become advisory members of the District; and that their congregations be asked by our Stewardship and Finance Committee to bear an equitable share of the expenses of our District conventions.

The floor committee noted that this problem "requires time for thorough study" because "it is now in a state of transition," and therefore recommended "that the Board of Directors of the Southern District and the Missionary Board of the Synodical Conference enter into a discussion to solve this problem in a God-pleasing way." The recommendation was approved.[9]

It appears that the Supreme Court announcement, which had come five months earlier, was on the mind of at least some of the convention delegates because, without identifying its origin, the following resolution is listed under Miscellaneous items in the Convention *Proceedings*:

29

Whereas there is nothing in Holy Scripture which declares one race or color of man to be inferior to another in any respect (Acts 17:26a; Gal. 3:38; Col. 3:11),

And whereas to discriminate against any human being on the grounds of race or color is not in accord with the spirit of Christian love,

And whereas the Supreme Court of the United States, our highest governing body, has declared segregation in our public schools to be unconstitutional,

Therefore be it resolved that the Southern District urge its pastors and laymen to abide by the decision of the court, and to cooperate as the court gives further direction.

This resolution was referred to the Board of Directors for further study.[10]

In this manner, the 1954 Convention at least opened a discussion on the race problem and recognized that a merger process was under way. By 1950 all the other Districts, including the Southeastern District, (which after the Southern District had the greatest number of black congregations)[11] had taken the steps to include the black congregations within their areas. The Southern District stood all alone, still waiting to take that step.[12]

May 7, 1955 - Rev. George Lee, a black man, of Belzoni, Mississippi, was killed for leading a voter registration drive.

August 13, 1955 - Lamar Smith, a black man, of Brookhaven, Mississippi, was murdered for organizing black voters.

August 28, 1955 - Emmett Till, a black youth from Chicago, was murdered in Money, Mississippi, for speaking to a white woman - some said he flirted with her.

A Major Setback

By contrast, little mention is made about race relations at the 1955 District Convention held in Mobile, AL just a year later. However, the events which had happened earlier that year, may explain the skittishness that existed.

Excitement and anticipation were running high in New Orleans because the city had been chosen as the host for the 1955 International Convention of the Lutheran Women's Missionary League. The Lutheran Women's Missionary League (LWML) is the official women's organization of the Lutheran Church - Missouri Synod, and the convention would bring several thousand delegates and visitors from all over the United States and many foreign countries to New Orleans, the headquarters of the Southern District.

In the summer of 1954, Del Borcherding, a resident of New Orleans and the Mission Editor of the LWML *Quarterly,* had written to John Ellermann requesting an article to build interest for the upcoming convention. Her eager anticipation of the convention is expressed in this paragraph in a letter to Ellermann:

> There have been articles on colored mission work in other places, but never anything about our thriving work here in New Orleans. Since the L.W.M.L. will meet for its biennial convention here in New Orleans next July (1955), an article on our work here will be very appropriate, and highly interesting.[13]

However, despite the build-up and lengthy preparation, the following press release on May 6, 1955, sent a shock wave through the Synod, and especially the Southern District:

> The Convention Committee of the New Orleans Zone of the Lutheran Women's Missionary League announced today that it had withdrawn its invitation to hold the International

Convention of the Women's Organization in New Orleans, July 12-13, 1955....

> Local customs of segregation make it impossible for the New Orleans Zone to fully entertain the International L.W.M.L. in a manner characteristic of this organization.[14]

The local organizers were deeply hurt by the decision of the International Executive Board to withdraw from New Orleans; and the International leaders were greatly disappointed that no satisfactory arrangements could be provided, especially since the decision to relocate came less than two months before their convention.

The decision the Executive Board of the LWML to pull the convention out of New Orleans surely lingered in the minds of the Southern District delegates when they gathered in Mobile in the Fall for the 1955 District Convention. The only reference about race relations in the Proceedings is this brief paragraph under the Board of Directors' report:

> In the matter of Negro work, Dr. K. Kurth [chairman of the Synodical Conference Mission Board] felt that the time was not propitious at present for the Southern District to take up this work. Rather, he suggested that two regional committees be established to supervise Negro work in this area, with the District officially represented on each committee.[15]

December 1, 1955 - Rosa Parks was arrested for refusing to give up her seat on bus to a white man. The bus boycott in Montgomery, Alabama was started on December 5.

August 25, 1956 - The home of Robert Graetz, a white pastor with the American Lutheran Church in Montgomery, was bombed.[16]

November 13, 1956 - Supreme Court bans segregated seating on Montgomery buses. On December 21, 1956 - The bus boycott in Montgomery ended.

◇　◇　◇

Sometime in the Spring of 1957, when the Lutheran pastors of New Orleans met for their circuit conference, Paul Bretscher, of Redeemer Lutheran, announced that a student octet from Concordia College, River Forest, IL, was scheduled to give a concert at Redeemer. He extended the invitation for all the pastors to invite their congregations, and this included Vic Moritz who served Mt. Zion, a black congregation. Upon second thought, Bretscher decided that since a voters' meeting (the governing body of the congregation) was scheduled, he should check it out with them. The voters' agreed unanimously.

Since the invitation was given to all pastors, some members from Mt. Zion attended the concert. No problems occurred the evening of the concert. Bretscher was on vacation at the time, but when the next Voters' Assembly was held (this time with an attendance of 36 while the earlier meeting had an attendance of 8), the constitution was amended to prohibit any Negro from ever setting foot in Redeemer Church.

The reaction of the voters is illustrative of the growing intensity felt by white people about the race issue, because in the 1940s, when John Nau served Redeemer congregation, black people had worshiped there without incident.[17]

Years later when the Civil Rights workers came South, many more congregations adopted resolutions designed to keep black people out; one such measure gained a certain degree of popularity and was known as "The Zion Lutheran Plan."

Bretscher was one of the first pastors to have to struggle with such a racist resolution. As he recalls, he was "filled with dismay in mind and heart of the meeting itself and the impossibility of being heard." Although rebuffed by the voters, his response was, "I could not 'quit' my pastorate over it, no more than Jesus 'quit' His. They have not yet heard the Gospel."[18]

◇　◇　◇

January 10, 1957 - Robert Graetz's home was bombed again. Four black churches in Montgomery, also bombed.[19]

◇   ◇   ◇

In 1957 Some Steps Taken

While the Southern District was taking some very tentative steps toward including black congregations, the Missouri Synod at its national conventions had taken several slightly more positive steps, starting in 1953. At the 1956 Convention, the following policy was adopted:

> "That all congregations of Synod regard all persons regardless of race or ethnic origin living within the limits of their respective parish, and not associated with another Christian church, as individuals whom God would reach with the Gospel of His saving grace through the ministry of the local congregation."[20]

It should be noted that already in 1946 the Synodical Conference had adopted a resolution which urged black congregations to seek membership in the geographic districts in which they were located. The following year the Missouri Synod approved the recommendation of the Synodical Conference and requested all its districts to accept black congregations into its fellowship.[21]

In the meantime, since the General Conference had passed out of existence in 1954, the black congregations of the South found themselves in increasing isolation. Only the relatively small Alabama/Upper Florida and Louisiana Conferences remained.

Along with its more positive statements about race relations, the Missouri Synod promised to provide financial assistance (subsidy) for the Districts which took over the black work in their geographic area.[22] That took away one of the excuses which may have been held by white Lutherans in the Southern District.

◇   ◇   ◇

34

January 23, 1957 - Willie Edwards, Jr., a black man in Montgomery, Alabama, was killed by the Klan.

◇ ◇ ◇

District President Streufert came from Missouri and had already experienced the merger of black and white congregations in that area. During his presidency, the first full-time District worker was called. Pastor O. H. "Sam" Reinboth, a former military chaplain and Executive Director of the California-Nevada District, accepted the Call and arrived in August of 1956. Reinboth, likewise, came with experience of the integration of his former District.

One month earlier, after completing my final year of seminary study, I had returned to the District with my first Call as pastor. It was to St. Mark Lutheran of North Baton Rouge, which had been organized as a new mission while I was on vicarage.

With Reinboth's arrival, the District set out on an expansion program, which included opening at least a half dozen new mission congregations every year for the next ten years.

Under the leadership of Streufert and Reinboth, the race question was placed as the major item on the agenda of the 1957 Louisiana Pastors Conference. (At that time, two separate district pastors conferences were held: the Louisiana Conference and the Gulf States Conference, which included Alabama, Mississippi and Northwest Florida.) The Louisiana Conference was held April 29 to May 2, 1957, at Percy Quinn State Park in Southern Mississippi.

Four position papers were presented at that Conference.[23] All four presenters were pastors in New Orleans: Paul Bretscher at Redeemer, John Ellermann at Bethlehem (a black church), Paul Streufert at Our Savior, and the fourth who wished to remain unidentified (he later repudiated his paper and withdrew it).

The discussion prompted by the four papers was the first significant attempt to take a serious look at the racial issue; for that reason, I will give the highlights of each man's arguments. (The same four papers were given to the Gulf States Conference the following year.)

35

John Ellermann was the first to be heard. He is a man who has never shied away from a confrontation. A native of St. Louis, he had already made a study of race relations while a seminary student. Upon graduation in 1953, he came to serve a black congregation in New Orleans.

My first impression of Ellermann came during my vicarage. In the Spring of 1955, he was invited to speak to an LWML Zone Rally held at First Lutheran in Baton Rouge. He spoke forthrightly, declaring that blacks were to be treated as equals. Most of the ladies at the Rally probably blinked at his strong statements, and my "Bishop's" wife, a native Southerner, found me immediately after the Rally and stormed, "How dare he talk to us like that!?"

Ellermann gave no title to his paper, but it could have been: "Anthropology, History and the Church." He listed nine "Fictions" about black people, followed with equivalent "Facts." These facts and fictions, by the way, were what so outraged the lady at the LWML Rally.

Under the heading "THE HISTORICAL DEVELOPMENT," he had these paragraphs:

> One cannot live in the South and escape its reverence of the past. It is a people facing backwards with worshipful regard to its own sectional history.

> Somewhere in the past, then, will be found the key to the (problem) of today. At least six (sic) [seven] areas of historical Southern life must be examined if this key is to be discovered: Slavery, a lost war, a vengeful peace, poverty, politics, religion, and emotionalism.

He had this pertinent paragraph on how the South came to be as it was:

> While the Negro vote was being taken away, there were parallel moves toward establishing "Jim Crow" [laws].... The Jim Crow laws, which did not appear until the late 1880s, enforced it [segregation] in public conveyances and waiting rooms. When Negroes sued in protest, the Supreme Court turned them down cold. In the Plessy vs. Ferguson decision of

1896, the court decreed segregation was constitutional if "separate but equal facilities" were provided for Negroes. This decision set the pattern for the South....

White Southerners looked to the 14th Amendment ["No State shall make or enforce any law which shall abridge the privileges or immunities of citizens of the United States," adopted in 1868] as the basis for their argument that States had the right to determine the kind of schools they wanted. On that point Ellermann wrote:

> The 14th Amendment, like all parts of the Constitution, is open to interpretation by the Supreme Court. As the Court interprets, so goes the law.... Thereupon the Court too began to change. From the late 1930s onward, it handed down a series of decisions which chipped steadily away at segregation in the schools. On May 17, 1954, the ultimate was reached...[that] segregation in public schools does violate the 14th Amendment and must end.

In conclusion, under the heading "THE NEED FOR REPEN-TANCE," he pleaded: "This is a man-made problem we have created. It is a problem which each of us must deal with as an individual in the light of truth and fact, at the foot of the cross. Let us not allow this barrier to stand between us and the cross."

Paul Bretscher had a tremendous grasp of the Scriptures, and probably was the best theologian in the Southern District. His paper was titled "THE GOSPEL AND ITS IMPACT ON THE SEGREGATION ISSUE."

In his opening section, he seemed to argue from two contradictory views: 1) the Gospel recognizes no distinctions or classes of men before God; and, 2) this spiritual impartiality and equality, however, does not demand a classless or homogenized society. He continues: "The Christian Gospel does not abolish slavery as an institution, nor does it erect moral sanctions against the slave-holder... Though the legal-technical relationship remains, the Christian relationship of brotherhood transcends and transforms it." These two thoughts form much of his later arguments; for example, he states:

The power of the Gospel is a leaven, not an explosion. What social revolutions are wrought by the Gospel are a by-product, slow and patient, of the transformation of the human heart.... Since social change is purely a by-product of the Gospel, it must never become the purpose of the Church.

He then wrote two rather long sections under the headings: "What the Gospel does to the white man in a segregated society," and "What the Gospel does to the Negro in a segregated society."

Under the section "THE GOAL OF THE CHURCH," he gave this two-point summary: 1) The Gospel shall have "free course" and nothing shall hinder its proclamation, and 2) Love shall have free course, and no tradition or custom shall impede its free expression. Next came this paragraph:

Jesus Himself had far more important things to do than to labor over social justice. Many an ardent integrationist today, thinking that he has the Lord on his side, might be shocked to hear the Savior's rebuff: "Man, who hath made Me judge or divider over you?" Luke 12:14.

On the same page, this follows:

The application is simple: In our own day of social conflict no universal procedure can be urged, as to how churches shall conduct themselves in the face of a segregated society. If, under some circumstances, the free course of the Gospel requires peaceful conformity to a segregated pattern, the church will without shame or apology conform. Demonstrations of social equality are expendable; the Gospel is not.

In his closing paragraphs Bretscher wrote:

There are some very pressing needs at this moment - the needs of the Negro Lutheran Churches in the Southland.... We can be sure that when Christians are aware of the need, and receive the conviction from the Lord that it is their problem, they

38

will not pass it by or evade it, but that love will, as always, find a way.... Love is always, and must ever remain FREE of all law. No law can tell love specifically HOW it must respond, and WHAT ANSWER it must produce to a given need....

When it comes to the expression of love in regard to the specific problem attendant upon racial differences, no universal pattern can be set as to what love must do. Each part of the land, each congregation, and ultimately each individual must be given the high honor and trust of complete LIBERTY, to act as the Spirit moves him in response to the love and the degree of love the same Spirit has wrought in his heart.

It is not our business, nor the business of any man, to envision what kind of society Christians should labor for as the ultimate. It is our business only, a) to preach the Gospel to every creature, [and] b) to respond in Love to every need of every neighbor.

Paul Streufert probably was in his fifties at the time, but to me he presented a fatherly image. That image was fostered both by the fact he presided at my ordination, and he showed a fatherly concern for those of us who were neophytes in the ministry. His paper was titled "THE SPECIFIC APPLICATION OF THE GOSPEL TO OUR CHURCH'S PROBLEM."

He began with an overview of the history of Lutheran work among Negroes, starting with the decision of the Synodical Conference in 1877 to engage in this outreach. Then under the heading "After Eighty Years," he had this statistical summary:

God has blessed the work. According to *The Lutheran Witness* of June 19, 1956, there are 112 Negro Lutheran Churches with a membership of 17,964 in the United States. There are 32 white pastors and 46 Negro pastors serving these churches. In the four States of the Southern District, there are 24 pastors serving 50 Negro churches, 8 white pastors and 16 Negro pastors, with a combined communicant membership of 3,084.

However, he continued, when the numbers for the black Lutheran Churches within the geographic confines of the Southern District are compared with the membership twenty years earlier, a radical decline - as much as 45% - is noted. Migration to the North and long vacancies are two factors contributing to the decline. Then he added: "If this happened among 22 of our white churches we would say, 'Those churches are dying!' And we would say it emphatically."

In the next section, Streufert sought to convey the personal feelings of black Lutherans with these poignant comments:

> To the above picture must be added the negative influence of separateness. Where does the Lutheran Negro living within the geographical boundaries of the Southern District find himself today? True, he is a Lutheran. He is such by conviction. But when asked by his Baptist, Methodist, or Presbyterian neighbor, "To which Lutheran Synod do you belong?" he must answer honestly, "I belong to none. You see we have an association of Lutheran synods which appoints a Mission Board, which in turn appoints a Regional Committee, which supervises the work among us Negroes. I belong to none of those Lutheran synods, but I am being helped by them to stay a Lutheran...."

> Can the effect of such separateness on the thinking of the Southern Lutheran Negro be anything else but negative? What would be the effect on my own thinking as a white man, if I, not by choice but by compulsion, would be forced into such separateness? Let me rather say, "If there were no invitation, to come out of such separateness, from those to whom I am bound by the closest of ties of faith?" My Negro brethren are not so spiritual that they think of membership in the Lutheran Church only in terms of membership in the *Una Sancta*, - and neither am I! I would feel, "Yes, Mother Church has shared with me its pure Gospel, its pure Sacraments, its God-given faith. For this I am grateful. But, she has not shared with me all the resources of her administrative strength...."

After citing the 1953 Synod resolution which declared a willingness to assume black work in all the Districts and a readiness to provide financial support, he continued with the following steps under the heading "Solution by the Southern District":

> First, we have to convince our people that by seeking a solution to the problem of Synodical membership for our Negro brethren, we are NOT attempting to solve every problem in the area of human relations which is facing our American public, both North and South, today;...secondly, our obligation is to bring to the attention of our white churches the true situation in which the Negro churches of the South find themselves today;...thirdly, we must convince our people the problem of receiving our Negro brethren into our Synodical bond is not insurmountable; and, fourthly, we must convince our people that if step #3 is taken, it will NOT mean a sudden influx of Negro Lutherans into white congregations....

His closing question was "What is the ultimate in the Church?" In answer he wrote:

> The full expression of the faith within the Christian is by every act without...[an outward expression toward others]. Luther in his "Freedom of the Christian Man" said, "A Christian man lives not in himself but in Christ and in his neighbor. Otherwise he is not a Christian. He lives in Christ through faith, in his neighbor through love; by faith he is caught up beyond himself unto Christ, by love he sinks down beneath himself into his neighbor, yet he always remains in God and in his neighbor."

> This, and this only, is the purpose of this paper, that we might be helpful to each other, in reaching our goal. Let the actions and resolutions of our Southern District demonstrate that we are being "caught up beyond ourselves unto our neighbor." Let us live in God and in our neighbors!

The fourth paper, as noted earlier, was given by a pastor who wished to remain unidentified. When asked about it, he said, "I do not wish to be remembered for that." However, what he wrote was pertinent for the time. As a native Southerner, he was clearly sensitive to the Southern way of thinking and reflected the anguish and turmoil experienced by the conscientious Christian who was faced by the social upheaval initiated by the Supreme Court decision. Thus, herewith, some of his arguments are included.

The title of his paper was: "THE CHURCH IN IT'S (sic) RE-LATION TO THE LEGAL AND SOCIAL PROBLEMS INVOLVED IN THE QUESTION OF RACE RELATIONS."

Since he was dealing with the legal aspects of the problem, he touched on the quandary a Southern Christian faces since State laws do not agree with the verdict of the Supreme Court. Which laws was the Christian to heed? He continued:

> Where State and Federal laws conflict, the Christian ought to be sensibly mindful that the segregation policy, so deeply rooted in the folkways and mores of the South, will because of the large Negro population undoubtedly continue for many years to come. When will segregation end in the Deep South? When - and only when the Negroes are a distinct minority.... In Connecticut Negroes are 2.7% of the population, in Mississippi they are 47%. The problem is in almost every state in direct proportion to the percentages. Full integration will come, - and so will a trip to the moon. For Mississippians the trip to the moon will come first, long before![24] The proper thing for the Christian to do where there is conflict in the laws is simply to await the decision of time, guiding his own acts according to the welfare of all. There is nothing else he can do!

Still focusing on the legal angle, he went on to show that the law does not change a man's heart. He wrote:

> The Christian can see as well as anybody else the immediate results of trying to legislate that which Christian love flowing from Christian faith alone can accomplish, for where

42

else but from the attempt to legislate did the sudden revival of the Ku Klux Klan of the past two years come from if not from this?... In attempting to enforce from outside of the sinful heart those things which are contrary to the sinful heart, the law stirs up only bitterness, wrath, and violence...

Pastors who come into the South can proceed two ways, he noted. He gave examples of some who disregarded local customs and heedlessly sought to bring change only to suffer dire consequences. Others have paid attention to the Southern way of life and have not only ministered well to their flock but also enjoyed enviable positions in the white and colored communities. He ended that section saying, "Let the clergy tread lightly and watch where they tread in the South long used to a segregated society."

He spoke approvingly of private schools, saying:

I can honestly claim that this is not because of prejudice on my part, but because I fear what the vast majority of the South fears: There is too great a gap between the moral, social, economic, ethical, health, and education standards which I am determined my children must have and those of the children with whom they would in integrated education be thrown.

His "Concluding Thoughts" include the following paragraphs:

Some situations will be far beyond the control of the Southern Christians and the Lutheran Church in the South for a long time to come. We had better learn to live with it, for Scripture does not say that segregation must be abolished, nor that it must be abolished right now, nor that social separation of the races in all places is sinful, nor that it is wrong in principle.

Nor ought the individual pastor consider himself a one-man crusade for racial betterment, either in the social or in the judicial sphere, for he is a spiritual leader, and in other areas he may well endanger his chances to preach the Gospel. On the other hand he ought not dodge discussions with his people of the race problem, - for he is the logical one to lead them to new areas of Christian love and practice. He, as little as the Church, will not forget that the Kingdom of God has come wherever an individual has embraced Jesus Christ as Son of God and Savior of the world as his personal Redeemer....

Christianity in the past has made vast changes in the social relations of man, changes that those before them would surely have pronounced impossible, and that those who awaited them lost all patience expecting. Slavery, dueling, infanticide, bloody sports, the holding of women as mere chattel, - any number of examples might be cited. But these have all COME SLOWLY, and they have come only through the Gospel. Christians elsewhere, North and South, should strive to understand the differing conditions in American society in race relations, realizing that the course of action different from his own may at the same time be best both for the Gospel and for all, and therefore inevitable. Christian love must often, and with full blessing of God, sometimes express itself by following totally different courses of action. Christian love in race relations may need even to refrain entirely from speaking and criticizing when it has no first-hand knowledge of all phases of the problem as others face it.

I have given extensive attention and space to the four papers because this was an important turning point for the Southern District. It put the discussion on the front burner for the first time. Two rather distinct viewpoints were noted in the papers; namely, 1) go slowly, stick to the business of the church, preach the Gospel, and do not hinder the Gospel by creating social unrest; and, 2) go into action for the sake of equality for your fellow man. It may not have been fully obvious at the time, but those two viewpoints would become the nub of many more very heated discussions in ensuing years.

Since I was a recent seminary graduate, the 1957 Conference was my first conference experience, and I recall that the discussion was very lively. The opinions expressed covered a wide range of difference, and it was obvious that this issue was not to be settled easily. Another memory sticks in my mind, and it is of two older pastors who sat in the back of the room and who often exchanging comments with one another. At times, one of them playfully fired spit wads over the men in front of him. Whether that school-boy behavior meant disinterest or disdain for the subject I do not know. In any event, I was puzzled by the two.

As a result of the papers and discussion, the Conference drew up an overture to the District Convention which was to convene in late October of the same year. The overture, written by Conference Secretary Robert Dittmann, had this "Resolved":

> That we, the Louisiana Pastors Conference, in session at Percy Quinn State Park from April 29 to May 2, 1957, memorialize the Southern District Convention of The Lutheran Church - Missouri Synod assembled at New Orleans, La., October 28 to November 1, 1957, that it assume responsibility for the Negro mission work within the geographical boundaries of the Southern District, and that it invite the Negro congregations and pastors within these boundaries into membership with the Southern District.[25]

August 29, 1957 - Congress passed the first Civil Rights Act since Reconstruction.

September 1957 - Governor Orval Faubus of Arkansas ordered the National Guard to keep black students from Central High School in Little Rock. President Eisenhower sent in federal marshals to enforce integration.

CHAPTER 3

CONVENTION ACTIONS

The 1957 Southern District Convention

The 1957 Convention, held October 28 through November 1, celebrated the 75th anniversary of the Southern District. St. Paul Lutheran Church at Port and Burgundy in New Orleans was the host congregation.

It was the practice for Missouri Synod Lutherans always to include a theological essay on their convention agenda. For this convention Dr. Martin Scharlemann, of Concordia Seminary, St. Louis, gave an essay titled "The Church in Her Struggle for Unity." In his closing comments, he touched on the subject of justice and the effect of segregation on the Church's mission.

At the opening session, President Streufert stunned the assembly by announcing that, after a single three-year term, he was not available to be re-nominated. He gave no reasons at the time, but soon thereafter accepted a Call to Ohio.

Before the balloting for president began, First Vice President Walter Hafner, of Mobile, AL, arose to say that he did not wish to be considered for the office because of advanced age. Second Vice President William Kennell, of Warrington, FL, made the same request, stating that he wanted to devote his energies to mission work. Thus the District suddenly found itself with a leadership vacuum.

In the search for District President, the convention delegates turned to 32-year-old Edgar Homrighausen, a man with a New York accent and a severe polio-related limp. Homrighausen was senior pastor at First English

Lutheran Church in New Orleans, and Counselor of one of the New Orleans circuits, the only District office he had held previously.

Kennell did stand for election as First Vice President, and William Wedig, of St. Paul's in New Orleans, was chosen Second Vice President. All three were to serve significant roles in the process of bringing the black churches into the Southern District.

Clearly the central issue before the 1957 Convention was the Overture submitted earlier that year by the Louisiana Pastoral Conference for the District to "assume responsibility for the Negro mission work within the geographical boundaries of the Southern District, and...invite the Negro congregations and the pastors...into membership with the Southern District."[1]

As noted above, Dr. Scharlemann made a brief reference to the problem of segregation. According the Convention Proceedings,

> The Essayist then addressed himself to the problem of racial integration. He pointed out that our redemption includes the horizontal directions of our oneness with God, reaching out as we must to others. The New Testament would suggest that the major portion of the solution also to this problem lies in the area of practicing such Christian virtues as humility, subjection, love of the brethren, by which the new quality of life expected from the church is demonstrated.[2]

President Streufert used poetic language in referring to the challenge facing the Convention. In his opening address, he said,

> Between the buried yesterdays and our unborn tomorrows lies the glorious present, pregnant with opportunities. For us there is only today. The task of today was on the lips of our Lord Jesus before His dying hour, "That they may be one." Unity demands a struggle in every area of human endeavor, whether political, or economic, or social, or spiritual. The struggle is ours today![3]

Since this was the 75th anniversary Convention, Dr. John Nau delivered an essay titled "Highlights from the History of the Southern

47

District," and in it he added the following comments about work among the Negroes:

> I thought it well and fitting to bring into this story the beginning of the work of the Church among the Negroes of the South, with the hope and prayer that our congregations throughout the South will do ever more for our brethren of another color.... I hope that the day will dawn in the South when the brethren of our Negro congregation can join wholeheartedly with us in the work of the great King.[4]

The delegates obviously were aware that they would have to address the racial question. A special Open Forum was set for Tuesday evening at which "a number of pastors and laymen indicated their views on the questions involved as well as possible solutions."[5]

During the Open Forum and again when the floor committee, which was chaired by Kennell,[6] presented its resolution, many concerns were raised, some of them very emotional, which reflected "the Southern way of thinking" and a desire to maintain the status quo. The committee accurately captured the feelings of the delegates in the first WHEREAS of its resolution; namely, "Your Committee feels that in respect to a matter which is of such great importance, and so far reaching in its implications, two courses ought to be avoided — that there be unnecessary delay and that there be undue haste."[7]

The first offering of the floor committee was rejected, because the first resolve (A) was considered too vague. That resolve read:

> That this 49th Convention of the Southern District of The Lutheran Church - Missouri Synod instruct its Board of Directors to initiate discussions with the Missionary Board of the Lutheran Synodical Conference relative to Southern District supervision of Negro work within the geographical boundaries of the Southern District....[8]

The resolution was sent back to the committee with directions to clarify and strengthen the first resolve. When it was presented again, the resolve read:

48

That the Board of Directors be instructed to negotiate immediately with the Missionary Board of the Lutheran Synodical Conference, the Board of Missions in North and South America, and any other Board which may be involved, in order to make arrangements whereby the Southern District may take over the responsibility for, and supervision of, the Negro Mission program within the geographical boundaries of the Southern District...[9]

The revised resolution prompted still more debate, and as a result two amendments were made: The word "may" [take over] was stricken and replaced with "shall." Eventually the "shall" was deleted and the words "as soon as possible" were added at the end.[10] Even then, the final resolution constituted a major change from the original overture which in its resolve stated that the District "invite the Negro congregations and pastors into membership."[11]

Eventually after much anguished debate, the Convention took the challenge and adopted the resolution which stated:

A) That the Board of Directors be instructed to negotiate immediately with the Missionary Board of the Lutheran Synodical Conference, the Board for Missions in North and South America, and any other Board which may be involved, in order to make arrangements whereby the Southern District take over the responsibility for, and supervision of, the Negro Mission Program within the geographical boundaries of the Southern District as soon as possible;

B) That our Southern District congregations be requested to consider and discuss the reception of Synodical Conference churches - pastors and congregations - into membership of the Southern District - for action at the 1958 Convention;

C) That our Board of Directors furnish suitable materials outlining the problems involved as a basis for such discussion in our Southern District congregations and the congregations of the Synodical Conference;

D) That our Board of Directors be instructed to initiate discussions with the two authorized Conferences of the Negro Churches within the Southern District boundaries; namely, the Louisiana Conference and the Alabama Conference, to determine their feelings on these matters; and,

E) That immediately after the conclusion of this Convention, the President of the Southern District appoint a Special Committee to be responsible for the initiation of these resolutions, to act as a clearing house for information received as a result of the above negotiations, and to bring a report at the 1958 Convention concerning the matters involved.[12]

After the convention, President Homrighausen appointed a Special Synodical Conference Committee and chose Pastor William Kennell of Warrington, FL, to serve as its chairman.

It was a large committee, with the following members - Pastors: Paul Bretscher, New Orleans, LA; Milton Popp, Tuscaloosa, AL; Luther Loesch, Pascagoula, MS; Carl Kretzschmar, Birmingham, AL; William Wedig, New Orleans, LA; O. H. Reinboth, Executive Secretary; and Edgar Homrighausen, New Orleans, LA; and laymen: Leslie Allenstein, Gadsden, AL; Mylan Engel, Mobile, AL; Carl Wegener, New Orleans, LA; and teacher, John Remetta, New Orleans, LA.[13]

A sub-committee of Kennell, Loesch, and Wegener was appointed to draw up "Guidelines" to be presented to the Board of Directors.[14]

Many considered Kennell a wise choice to serve as chairman. Like Homrighausen, he spoke with a New York accent. More significantly, he had earlier spent a number of years serving as pastor of a black congregation in the Alabama/Upper Florida Conference and thus was personally acquainted with many of the black leaders. He also represented a cautious approach to the merger of the black and white churches.

The 1958 Southern District Convention

The 1958 Convention, October 27-31, was again held at St. Paul's in New Orleans. At that Convention, Kennell summarized the activities of the committee as follows:

50

With due deliberate speed your Committee sought to carry out the 1957 resolution. It desires to make the following report of what has been done since the conclusion of the last Convention. Two definite and distinct matters were handled:

I. Negotiations with the various Boards and Conferences involved in respect to ultimate supervision of Negro work.

II. Drawing up of "Guidelines" for presentation to white and Negro congregations relative to acceptance into the District of Negro congregations - pastors and people.[15]

The Committee reported that the following meetings were held in 1958:
>January 20 - with the Missionary Board of the Synodical Conference, and the Board for Missions in North and South America, in St. Louis;
>April 10 - with the Pastoral Conference of the Alabama/Upper Florida Field, in Bashi, AL;
>April 17 - with the Missionary Board of the Synodical Conference, in St. Louis;
>July 16-20 - with the workers of the Louisiana Conference [no location given];
>August 5-8 - with the Synodical Conference Convention, in Cleveland, Ohio.

According to the report, all the above meetings met with a fair degree of understanding and progress. The sticking point, however, was over the "Guidelines" for discussion which were to be drafted. On January 13, the sub-committee met and "a rough draft of possible 'Guidelines' was adopted." On February 24, the full committee met and "the first draft of the suggested 'Guidelines' was presented and discussed at great length" with the conclusion that "It was impossible to complete the examination of the 'Guidelines.'" On April 14, the full committee met again and at this time the remainder of the "Guidelines" was read and discussed. This time "It was the opinion of all that these 'Guidelines' eventually to be presented to the white and Negro congregations be not drawn up hastily, but that much time ought to be taken before final decisions are made." In conclusion, the committee noted, "'Guidelines' for presentation to both white and Negro congregations are still in the making. These materials are by no means ready."[16]

The committee also considered the possibility of merely supervising the black work without their congregations becoming members of the District. Thus, at its April 14, 1958 meeting, it was agreed to have guidelines drawn up for supervision of the Negro congregations; and Pastor William Wedig was appointed to serve as chairman of a sub-committee for that purpose.[17]

In its Convention report, the committee had noted that it was moving with "due deliberate speed," and the "deliberate" part was obvious in the cautious and careful manner in which the "Guidelines" for discussion were being drafted. However, at this Convention questions were raised about the "speed," for some felt that matters were moving forward too slowly.

Obviously, the 1958 Convention did not take the action which was proposed at the 1957 Convention. Instead, it adopted a resolution which 1) concurred in the findings of the committee, 2) commended the committee, 3) encouraged it to continue along the present course of its work, 4) encouraged it to produce the requested Guidelines as quickly as feasible, and 5) endorsed the committee's philosophy of going forward with due, deliberate caution because of the manifold and sensitive problems involved.[18]

At the 1958 Convention, a new voice was heard. Joseph, the middle son of Dr. & Mrs. Walter Ellwanger, graduated from the St. Louis Seminary in the spring and in July arrived as the pastor of St. Paul's Lutheran in Birmingham, a black congregation. The Ellwanger family had moved to Selma, AL, in 1945 when the father succeeded Ed Westcott, Sr., as the Superintendent of the Alabama/Upper Florida Conference.

While the father was a small man, gentle and mild-mannered, inclined to be soft-spoken, Joe was a person who was not easily ignored. Joe was a bit larger than his father with a bold voice and a full face which quickly became flushed in the heat of debate. Some would say that he spoke with the brashness of youth, and others saw him as one with the courage of his convictions. In retrospect, it can be said that he represented both.

52

In 1961, Joe Ellwanger wrote an article for the Valparaiso University Institute of Human Relations in which he described the integrationist as follows,

> The integrationist is deeply committed to a new way of life, a way of life in which every man is a man, in which every citizen can enjoy the rights and freedoms guaranteed him by the Constitution.... One must see the inherent injustice of segregation and set himself like flint against it or it is impossible to be committed to integration.[19]

Those words clearly described him. He had lived and gone to school in central Alabama, which gave him much credibility. He had frequently accompanied his father and knew all the pastors in the Conference and had worshiped at practically all the black congregations in central Alabama. Consequently he had first-hand experience and a feel for what was happening in the black congregations there.

In addition, Joe had spent his vicarage (1955-56) in a black church in Kansas City. Following his vicarage in the summer of 1956, he had served a store-front congregation which his father had started in Montgomery, AL. That summer, through Pastor Robert Graetz, of the American Lutheran Church, Joe had his first meeting with Dr. Martin Luther King, Jr.; and a relationship with King was started which was to have distinct influence on Joe in the years to follow.[20]

With the arrival of Joe Ellwanger, the lines of the debate within the District became more clearly drawn. Ellwanger espoused the view that the Gospel has social implications and that Christians must be concerned about justice and equality, while the view of others was that the Church's main goal is to proclaim the Gospel and avoid any controversial action which might inhibit the Gospel. Pastor Kennell exemplified the second view, which became very obvious in the report which he gave to the 1960 Convention.

A second new voice arrived on the Southern District scene in 1958. George Hrbek graduated from the St. Louis Seminary that Spring and was assigned to work in the white community of Selma, AL. A faint hint of a Yankee accent could be detected in his voice, although he was born in

New York City, he was raised in the South. He came from a family dating back to grandparents that was politically well informed and sensitive to the issues of racial injustices.

Hrbek was a man of action and had been arrested as a high school senior. One day as he rode the streetcar to downtown Birmingham, he found every seat filled as he boarded, and so he stood. In those days a small placard was placed on the back of the seats to designate the white and black sections. The placard could be moved in order to enlarge or decrease the white section, thereby altering the black section.

As Hrbek told the story, a white man boarded at the next stop, and seeing no empty seat, simply moved the placard back one seat, forcing two black women to get up so he could take a seat. Seeing that, Hrbek took the placard and moved it in front of the white man again and told him to get up to let the women have their seats. The white man did not take kindly to such a suggestion of courtesy and called Hrbek a young punk. An exchange of a few more words led to fisticuffs, the streetcar was stopped, the police arrived, and Hrbek's parents had to rescue him at the police station.[21]

This was the gutsy young seminary graduate who came to Selma, often considered the "Buckle" of the Black Belt of the South (and we are not talking about the color of the soil). As a clue to what might be expected during his years of ministry in Selma, he was ordained and installed in an integrated service which was held in the chapel of the Methodist Children's Village. Both black and white clergymen participated in the laying on of hands in the ordination ceremony. In 1958 such an integrated gathering in Central Alabama was extremely rare.

Hrbek and Joe Ellwanger were seminary classmates and agreed very closely in their views on social justice and integration.

April 25, 1959 - Mack Parker was taken from jail, lynched, and his body thrown into the Pearl River, at Poplarville, MS. The lynch mob included the former sheriff, a pastor, and the jailer.

February 1, 1960 - Black students stage a sit-in at a "whites only" lunch counter in Greensboro, NC.

The 1960 Southern District Convention

The 1960 Convention was also held in New Orleans, this time at First English Lutheran Church, three blocks from St. Paul's.

The special Synodical Conference Committee included several pages as a prologue to its 1960 report which conveyed the Committee's sense of caution and desire to avoid controversy. In referring to the strong Southern tradition, the Committee noted, "It is well known that segregation has been the pattern for many years in all areas of society, the church included. This is well known by white and colored alike." They were mindful of the current social condition, saying, "In spite of the many advances made in respect to the problem of race, tensions are running high. Extremists on both sides make this a difficult period. There is a reasonable element of doubt as to whether this is the proper time to carry out the program **in its completeness.**[emphasis in original] Local physical problems were noted: "It must be remembered that there are many places where white and colored could not meet together. Public meeting places often forbid joint meetings. This would be a difficult matter."[22]

Likewise, concern was expressed about the impact that integration of the church would have on the outreach of the Gospel. A series of questions were raised in the prologue:

> What effect will integrated membership have upon the work of the Church? Will it aid or hinder this work? What will be the effect upon the white people both within and outside the congregations involved? We are not so much concerned with the personal views of people as we are with the results flowing from such integrated membership as far as the progress of the Kingdom work is involved.... Is it possible for the Church to express its fellowship in Christ without social implications?[23]

Questions about the impact on black leadership were also raised: "Will Negro leadership be aided because of the association with white leadership, observance, exchange of ideas, etc.? Will Negro leadership be stifled because Negro leaders will be in the minority, whereas at present they lead their own group?"[24]

The observations in the prologue were not discussed at length; instead the main fireworks at the 1960 Convention came when the Guidelines for discussion were finally presented. The Guidelines were drafted in the form of Thirteen Theses. Theses 1 through 7 dealt with theological points such as, all humans are sinners, all are the objects of God's loving concern, and Christ made atonement for all. Those were accepted with no debate. Likewise, the theses which emphasized the mission of the church were readily accepted. (See Appendix A for full text of the Guidelines.)

However, when Thesis 8 was presented, the debate became intense. Originally that thesis stated: "The Christian congregation has the right to regulate its own affairs in keeping with its stated purpose [namely, to minister to its members and reach out to the lost, as stated in Thesis 6] so long as it violates no Word of God." After the debate the following was added: "However, it will always strive to be giving a **total living witness** which extends beyond the purely verbal sharing of the Gospel. Matt. 5:13-16, 1 John 3:18."[25]

Thesis 9 also gained a significant addition as a result of the debate. As presented, it stated: "It is a natural thing that people of varying national, linguistic, and cultural backgrounds will tend to associate with people of similar backgrounds when given the opportunity, and this applies also in church life." Examples such as Norwegian, Swedish, and German churches were given. In the final draft, the examples were deleted, and the following added: "However, Christians will seek to rise above the inclinations of the flesh and under the Spirit's guidance strive to demonstrate their unity in Christ. James 2:1-9, Gal. 6:8-10, Col. 3:10-15."[26]

Thesis 10 remained unaltered - "It ought to be the sincere desire of every Christian that the time come when any individual will be privileged to attend any church of his choice, with full membership privileges." The following Bible citations were added: John 17:19-23, Romans 12:9-10.

Thesis 11, which eventually was to become the most controversial of all, was accepted by the Convention essentially as it was presented by

56

the Committee. Originally it stated, "It is not to be considered unChristian for congregations to practice segregation when to practice integration would mean – a. the weakening or disrupting of their own congregation [and] b. the curtailment of their missionary outreach, provided no individual is thereby denied opportunity to hear the Gospel of Jesus Christ. 1 Cor. 6:12."

The opening line was replaced with the words "It is Scripturally defensible for a congregation to practice segregation when..." etc. The other change made was to replace the words "hear the Gospel of Jesus Christ" with "receive the full ministry of the means of grace." "Romans 15:1-7" was also added.[27]

A significant addition was made with Thesis 12. As submitted, it stated, "The Christian's chief aim ought to be to bring as many as possible into the Kingdom of God, and to accomplish this purpose he ought to be willing to forego privileges he might otherwise normally possess." The words "to bring as many as possible into the Kingdom of God" were replaced with "to extend and preserve the Body of Christ," and the following was added, "or experience hardship which might be necessary. Ephesians 4:1-6; 11-16."[28]

Thesis 13 was accepted almost as presented: "Christians can not take lightly the problems within the church relating to discrimination, but will seek to lessen them and eventually solve them through sincere prayer and Christian love." The only change was "can not" for "ought not."[29]

The debate over the Guidelines for Discussion spread over several sessions, and often became very intense. As noted earlier, Pastor Kennell and Pastor Ellwanger most clearly represented opposing views, and in the debate they were often like two fighters standing toe-to-toe, neither giving an inch. During these furious debates I learned that when a pastor starts his comments with "My dear brother," it does not always mean that he is feeling brotherly. Fortunately, Homrighausen was blessed with the gift of humor, which he frequently injected during the debate to relieve the tension.

The old view of status quo and acceptance of the Southern way of life was clearly on the line during this Convention, and those views were not easily surrendered. For example, one pastor cited the parable of the Good Samaritan in defense of segregation. He noted that the Levite and the priest had passed by the injured man, and finally the Samaritan (obviously the pastor understood the racial implications), came and helped the poor man who was in trouble. "But did you notice?" he said emphatically, "if you read the parable carefully, you will see that he did not take that poor man who was beaten up into his home? That would have been wrong. Instead, he dropped him off at a hotel, and said, 'You take care of him.'"

Another pastor, seeking to justify segregation, used the hand as an illustration. He pointed out that four fingers are together, and the thumb is separate. While the thumb is useful — to pick up things, to throw a ball and so on — it always remains separate. "That's the way God wants the races to be," he added. "They can be helpful to one another, but they are to remain separate."

While the views of the old South, and the related view that the role of the Church is mainly to preach the Gospel and save souls, clashed with those who were willing to take risks and become more socially engaged, it is obvious by the changes which were made in some of the Theses of the Guidelines that the debate produced a broader view of the Church's role in the issue of segregation/integration. This is demonstrated by the addition, in Thesis 8, "It [the Church] will always strive to be giving a **total living witness** which extends beyond the purely verbal sharing of the Gospel." Likewise, in Thesis 11 the idea of the Church ministry is expanded when the words "hear the Gospel of Jesus Christ" are replaced with "receive the full ministry of the means of grace." The willingness to take risks for the sake of the Gospel is illustrated by the addition of "or experience hardship which might be necessary" in Thesis 12.

After the Convention, the Guidelines for Discussion were distributed to the congregations for study on the local level. Now pastors and congregations could — perhaps for the first time — study the race issue with a Biblical basis. In the past those who adhered to the status quo of the South, often saw no Scriptural relevance to the practice of segregation. Now the Guidelines for Discussion at least provided numerous Scriptural citations for consideration and study.

Whether or not the Guidelines and the Bible references would be studied remained to be seen. Since the discussion was intense at the Convention, it was clear that a major challenge lay ahead to bring the membership in general to a readiness to accept a change in the racial picture.

A native New Orleanian told me a story which illustrates both the challenge and hope which the Church faced in those days. A young white pastor came to his parents' home for Sunday dinner; and in the course of the visit, the conversation came around to the issue of racial segregation. His father, whom he described as pure racist, said, "Well, we should take all them niggers, line them up on the river front, shoot them, and shove them into the river." When the pastor said, "Sir, don't you realize that these people have an immortal soul?" the father said, "Yeah, that's true, so line them up along the river, baptize them, shoot them, and shove them into the river."

Some months later, when a white pastor was installed at Mt. Zion Lutheran, a black congregation, the daughter in this household expressed a desire to attend the service. The father was reluctant to allow her to go alone, so he and her mother decided to accompany her. After the service. the father said, "Well, I met some colored people there; I didn't know they had colored people like that."

To be sure it was a tiny change, but it was a change nevertheless, expressed by this man of the South after having had personal contact with his fellow Lutherans in a black church. Such gradual change, in tiny increments, was also evident in the discussions of the Convention. And with that hope and a prayer for the continuous guidance of the Holy Spirit, the delegates left the 1960 Convention with the newly adopted Guidelines for Discussion.

Guidelines For Supervision

According to the Synodical Conference Committee's report, the Guidelines for Supervision were discussed in a meeting with the Missionary Board in St. Louis on February 6, 1959, and a mutually agreed upon "Sequence of Events" was developed which included negotiations with the Negro brethren and the calling of an Executive Secretary for Negro Missions in the Southern District. At the meeting of the Committee on July 20, 1959, the Guidelines for Supervision were revised and adopted.[30]

On March 18, 1960, a meeting was held in Selma, AL, which included the officials of the Alabama Conference, members of the Regional

Mission Committee, and Dr. Karl Kurth of the Synodical Conference, which resulted in the following statements:

> All representatives of Negro work felt that there would be little gained in having the Southern District supervise Negro work. While these representatives had no objection to the Guidelines for Supervision presented, they felt that there would be little interest in such supervision without membership in the Southern District.[31]

Further, in its report to the Convention it was stated:

> Leaders of the Negro congregations in the Alabama Field have gone on record in declaring they are not interested, at this time, in Southern District supervision, where such supervision does not at the same time involve District membership.[32]

Subsequent Proceedings give no further information about the Guidelines for Supervision, indicating that this idea had a brief life, and that black leaders had successfully killed the idea of supervision without membership.

CHAPTER 4

SOCIAL TURMOIL AND REACTION

Activities in The Community

Acts of violence against black people in the South had often occurred in the past without stirring much reaction from the rest of the nation. However, in 1957, when federal marshals were sent to Little Rock to protect black students at Central High, the news agencies brought the incident to the attention of the rest of the nation. Two other events were to make more national news.

The lynching of Mack Parker at Poplarville, MS, was brought to the attention of the rest of the nation because of the cold-blooded brutality with which he was killed. Parker was charged with the rape of a white woman and instantly the community was enraged. The jailer was so fearful of mob reaction that he buried the jail key in his back yard every night. A lynch mob was recruited from a prayer meeting. Three days before Parker was to stand trial, eight masked white men dragged him from his jail cell, beat him, shot him, and threw his body into the Pearl River, where it was found ten days later. The lynch mob included a Baptist preacher, the former sheriff, and the jailer (who had been persuaded, after all, to give up his keys.)

Parker's mother received so many death threats after the lynching that she fled to California within a week. Since Parker had served two years in the Army, his casket was draped in a U.S. flag. Afterward the whites raised such an uproar that the Veterans Administration, which had issued the flag, ordered Parker's sister to return it.

U.S. Attorney General William Rogers called the lynching a "reprehensible act," and sent in the FBI for a full investigation. Although the FBI came up with hard evidence, including several confessions, the county prosecutor refused to present FBI evidence to the State grand jury, and there were no indictments. Rogers called the State's action "a travesty of justice," and ordered the Justice Department to build a federal civil rights case. But the federal grand jury also refused to indict, and the lynch mob went free.[1]

When the Federal government became involved, the story of Parker's lynching played out in the national news media for a number of weeks, bringing outrage from many sections of the nation. Not only did this incident catch the attention of the nation; it certainly caught ours as well. At the time we were living in Baton Rouge, LA. I was counselor of the circuit which included Bogalusa, LA. Poplarville is less than 20 miles from Bogalusa, and the Pearl River defines the state line just outside of Bogalusa. In the language of the Southerner, this incident was "in our neck of the woods."

☒　☒　☒

The next incident which captured national news attention came in New Orleans in the Fall of 1960. New Orleans was the site of the first court-ordered racial integration of public schools in the deep South. The confrontation between deep-seated racism and the push for social change came on Monday, November 14, 1960. Two elementary schools were chosen for integration: McDonogh 19 and William J. Frantz.

When the day arrived, squads of policemen were posted at each school. As the crowds gathered, they yelled, "Are the niggers here yet?" While the officers tried to maintain a casual attitude with the hecklers, they carefully declined to answer their question. After the white children were safely inside, about mid-morning carloads of U. S. marshals arrived with three six-year-old black girls for McDonogh and one for William Frantz. After the black girls entered McDonogh 19, the white students exited, leaving the school with three black girls, all first-graders. Every morning they were greeted by a crowd of women screaming their hatred and fury.

62

The climate in which this action took place was extremely tense, having been stirred to a frenzy by Louisiana's Governor, Jimmie Davis, who was determined to close the schools rather than have them integrated. Furthermore, the section of New Orleans in which the integration took place is next to Plaquemines Parish (county) where district attorney and arch-racist, Leander Perez, ruled with an iron hand. At arousing the rabble, Perez had few equals. Shortly after the four black girls were enrolled, he addressed a New Orleans Citizens Council, saying, "Are you going to wait until the Congolese rape your daughters! Are you going to let these burr-heads into your schools! Do something about it!"[2]

Lutherans were both negatively and positively involved in the New Orleans school integration effort. On the negative side, national television daily showed scenes of outraged, screaming whites railing against the black girls and the federal marshals. Redeemer Lutheran Church is located near the William Frantz School, and some members of that congregation were identified in the angry scenes shown on TV.

On the plus side, Jack Stewart, a member of St. Paul's at Port and Burgundy in New Orleans, was at that time the principal at McDonogh 19. Stewart recalls how he received word that his school would be integrated. On November 11, a Friday, the schools were closed for Veterans Day. Early that morning he received an urgent call to report to the central service building at the school. The following are his words:

> The board attorney told us that we were sworn to secrecy and that the following Monday morning, the public schools would be desegregated, and we were the two schools that would "catch the brass ring".... On Monday morning [in the meeting] were two representatives of the State legislature, telling us to do one thing, [and] representatives from the FBI, U.S. marshal's office, city police, state police, school board officials, superintendent of police from New Orleans - and we were all drinking coffee, just like any morning - except that we knew all hell was going to break loose....

> So we had many children there that morning [Monday], and as soon as the black children came into the school, the parents came by and picked up their white children and took

them home. And so that school stayed that way the rest of the year. The faculty went through some tough times, because their salaries were cut off for a while, until early January.... We had U.S. marshals in the building...who stayed in the building the whole year. Of course, the people would gather – gather every morning and jeer and shout, and gather every evening and jeer and shout.[3]

When I asked Stewart if the ugliness affected the faculty, he said, "Not really. That faculty was a veteran faculty and many of the parents outside had been taught by those very same teachers. And so our school did not suffer a great deal of personal animosity."

When I asked him, "How did the members of your congregation respond to all that? To you personally?" He said, "Like it wasn't going on. They just ignored it." My next question was, "Not everybody in the church agreed with you, did they?" He answered, "Probably nobody. Or very few people in the church would dare to have agreed." While he had the support of his pastor, he did not receive much encouragement or support from his fellow gchurch members.[4]

Stewart did an admirable job of maintaining order at the school. He noted that the faculty drew very close to one another during that difficult year. Although of different church affiliations, they nurtured each other in Christian faith. Stewart was a positive witness of the Spirit of Christ, which gave him and the faculty the ability to endure a traumatic time of change.

Once again the racial turmoil was being played out in the national news and the nation became aware of how bitter and harsh Southerners could be in the determination to maintain "their way of life." For us personally this also was close to home — only 80 miles away. Furthermore, we lived in Baton Rouge, the State Capital, and the politicians were engaged in a furious flurry of activities to try to block the school integration.

Tension in the local churches was beginning to surface. The Baton Rouge ministerial association drafted various statements to provide Christian leadership to the community.[5] However, in the congregation which I was serving, the racial question had not yet been extensively discussed.

64

Selma, AL, was the first community in the Southern District to experience direct conflict with the Lutheran Church over the racial issue.[6] A strong Lutheran presence existed in Selma in the black community because of the Alabama Lutheran Academy and College which was established there in 1922. In the late 1950s Walter Ellwanger, the president of ALAC, began ministering to white Lutherans who wanted to worship together. In 1958, George Hrbek arrived with the Call to expand the work among the whites in order to establish a congregation.

Hrbek immediately took an active role in the community, working with various youth activities and the YMCA. He and his wife also took in foster children, and the citizens of Selma were impressed by the young energetic pastor who had come to their city. The Junior Chamber of Commerce named him as the outstanding young man of Selma. With that recognition his reputation spread beyond Selma, and he was invited to speak at various places, including the University of Alabama. Furthermore, the Alabama Bankers Association asked him to be their keynote speaker at a state-wide gathering. Since Hrbek came from Birmingham, the locals did not consider him one of those outside trouble-makers — at least not early on.

In the meantime, work was progressing to develop a congregation and build a sanctuary. On the Sunday following the dedication of the new building, Rosa Young brought a large group of black worshipers from ALAC to the service. (It should be noted here that Rosa Young was in many ways the "Mother" of the Lutheran Church in Central Alabama. She was a teacher and was instrumental in starting numerous Lutheran Schools in Wilcox County, and the surrounding area, South of Selma. At the time of the above incident she was a teacher at ALAC in Selma.)

The group which came with Miss Young was welcomed at St. John's Lutheran Church. However, partway into the worship service, a half dozen or more Selma policemen arrived, and asked "What are those Nigras doing here?" Hrbek said that they were conducting a worship service and that the policemen were invited to join them. The policemen, however, were unsure of what to do next, and left.

The next day Hrbek was summoned to the office of the Selma mayor, Chris Heinz. The mayor asked, "Are you going to let those Nigras into your church?" To which Hrbek answered, "Mayor Heinz, that's not my church; that's Jesus' church; and Jesus said, 'Come unto me all ye that labor and are heavy laden, and I will give you rest.' And if you have trouble with that, you'll have to take your argument to Jesus."

No action was taken against Hrbek at that time, since the city fathers knew of his popularity in the community and thought it unwise to do anything further.

Hrbek, though, didn't leave matters lie and said to the mayor that the city owed St. John's congregation an apology for sending police to a worship service. This the mayor could not very well do and maintain his position in the community. So Hrbek said to him, "As a sign of your apology, I want you to contribute the baptismal font for St. John's Lutheran." In a matter of weeks the font arrived, complete with a brass plate designating it as a gift from the mayor's wife.

Later, Hrbek was invited to a meeting with a local judge, Judge Reynolds, who likewise expressed disapproval of Hrbek's involvement in interracial activities. But again, the judge went no further with action against Hrbek.

In the meantime, Hrbek was involved in meetings with six others — the white Presbyterian minister and five male and one female black teachers. They held clandestine meetings at Browns Chapel in order to organize a chapter of the Southern Christian Leadership Conference. When word got out about their meetings, the Presbyterian minister was chased from his congregation. The homes of three of the teachers were fire-bombed.

Next, the White Citizen's Council turned their attention to the chairman of St. John's congregation, Charles Glass, a native Southerner. But he refused to yield to their demands, and that became a turning point for the better with the congregation.

But all was not smooth for the young Lutheran pastor in Selma. Hrbek tells of an incident with Joe Smitherman, who later became mayor of Selma. At that time, Smitherman had an appliance store, and Hrbek went there one day to buy an item. They became engaged in a conversation which quickly turned harsh, Smitherman took a swing at the pastor, and bystanders had to pull the two combatants apart. Once when he was invited to give the invocation at the local white high school, as he was walking through a passageway toward the stage, he was accosted by a man who said, "No way in hell that you're gettin' up on that stage, you Nigger-lover!" He threatened to beat up Hrbek; thus, the opposition was heading toward physical violence.

Hrbek had not exactly invited a friendly relationship with the Klan either. He told of the time when he returned from Birmingham to Selma and met some hooded Klansmen at the outskirts of the city. He stopped and asked what they were doing, and was told that they were looking for Freedom Riders, and he told them that what they were doing was ridiculous.

A small Jewish community existed in Selma, and their leaders invited Hrbek to a secret meeting which was held in the office of an auto dealer. They offered their support for Hrbek's efforts, including financial support, if it were needed. They could not offer public support for fear of repercussions against them, since the Klan had no great love for them either.

The worst was yet to come in Hrbek's years in Selma. The White Citizen's Council, which represented many of the prominent business leaders, held a barbeque picnic for local white high school students and brought in a Baptist preacher from Montgomery whose speech was titled, "Better Dead Than Mixed Blood." The content of the speech was prominently featured the next day on the front page of the Selma *Times-Journal*, and Hrbek felt compelled to write a long letter to the paper to present another view. After reading the letter, Ed Fields, the editor of the paper, made an hour-and-half-long visit to the Hrbek home, and pleaded with Hrbek that for his own safety he should withdraw the letter. But Hrbek refused, and it was printed.

Then, as Hrbek recalled, "All hell broke loose" and the phone calls really started coming. The White Citizen's Council had a letter printed in the paper aimed specifically at Hrbek, accusing him, among other things, "That he was a Judas, that he had obviously fallen under the spell of the Communists, and that for his own sake, and for the good of the community. it would be best for him to get out of Selma." The harassment and threatening phone calls continued until the Hrbeks, by their own free choice, moved to New Orleans in September of 1962.

✠ ✠ ✠

The experiences of Eugene Kappeler provide additional insights into the life and times in the deep South in the late 1950s, both in the Church and in the community.[7] Immediately upon graduation from the St. Louis Seminary he was assigned to be missionary-at-large in the Alabama/Upper Florida Conference. He was to serve four congregations in central Alabama (Arlington, Lamison, Midway, and Possum Bend). Two of those congregations he served every other Sunday. Sometimes he also preached at Thomasville and later started a black Sunday School in Meridian, MS.

In addition Kappeler was assigned to teach a variety of courses at the Alabama Lutheran Academy and College, including German.

He may be one of the few Lutheran pastors who attended a Klan Rally by choice. As he tells it, a big official of the Klan had been killed, and under the direction of a Methodist minister, a rally was held at Selma as a fund-raiser to hire a lawyer to avenge the death.

Hrbek was the pastor of the local white congregation, and Kappeler asked Hrbek's sister-in-law to go with him to the rally. They each wore a heavy coat and hat to provide some disguise. While at the rally, his companion noticed that the Klansmen were passing Kappeler's picture around. Apparently he was on their "hit list." "When I saw that they were looking at it," he recalled, "we got scared and left. But before we left, I very wisely put a little money into the hat they were passing. I didn't go home that night...I spent most of the night at George Hrbek's house, hiding out."

However, shortly before he left Selma in 1961, Kappeler learned that he had been "protected" because he had a room in a home owned by a member of the White Citizen's Council. They had checked him out and declared that he was OK and was working for the Lord and not meddling into politics. He said, "Whenever anybody was following me with a pickup truck with guns in the back racks, when I got on Tremont Street [now in the historical district] they turned away."

December 5, 1960 - The Supreme Court outlaws segregation in bus terminals.

◊   ◊   ◊

Move To Alabama

Early in 1961, I accepted the Call to be pastor of Grace Lutheran Church, in Huntsville, AL, and we moved in mid-April.

Huntsville was a dynamic community flushed with the excitement of the space industry. Just before we arrived, the Russian cosmonaut, Yuri Gagarin, made the first sub-orbital flight. Since we were in a race with the Russians, U.S. space scientists were pressing even harder to match that feat. Within weeks of our arrival, Alan Shepard made the first U.S. sub-orbital flight, and the event was celebrated with a parade through downtown Huntsville.

Regarding the race issue, Huntsville was a social island. The George Marshall Space Center, located there plus all the ancillary industries, brought people by the thousands to the city from Detroit, Seattle, Wichita, and other places. The natives who ran the city were eager for the inflow of money which came with the rapid growth and, as a result, did not insist on the strict preservation of the "Southern way of life."

This was not true of the rest of Alabama, and when we drove out of the city I often felt we were traveling in an alien country. I had no specific evidence of the existence of the Klan in the surrounding area, but I had the impression that it was never far away.

Throughout my ministry in the South, the Klan was never far away. When we were in Baton Rouge, Bogalusa (100 miles away) was the headquarters of the Klan for Louisiana. In Huntsville, we were only about 50 miles from Pulaski, TN, where the Klan was originally formed. When we moved to Fort Walton Beach, FL, we were only 45 miles from Milton,

FL, which once was the Florida State Headquarters for the Klan. Even in the 1980s, when the Cuban refugees were brought to our area here in the Florida Panhandle, the Klan had a cross-burning within a few miles of our home.

◊   ◊   ◊

May 14, 1961 - Freedom Riders attacked in Alabama while testing compliance with bus desegregation laws.

◊   ◊   ◊

The Freedom Riders' bus was attacked and burned outside of Anniston, AL, about 80 miles south of Huntsville. That happened only weeks after our arrival

"Who Do They Think We Are—Communists?!"

From *The Birmingham Post-Herald*
April 1, 1965

in Alabama, and when the picture of a burned out bus appeared on the front page of *The Huntsville Times* the following morning I began to wonder what sort of rampaging redneck country this was. It was a shocking experience which greatly influenced my view of Alabama for a long time.

The Fackler Flogging[8]

The social/racial environment of Alabama was influenced by additional terrifying events.

Shortly before we left Baton Rouge, we received word from President Homrighausen (who by then had moved to Cullman, AL) that Vicar James Fackler, at Tuscaloosa, AL, had been flogged by the Klan. Since Fackler had to be moved out of Tuscaloosa for his own safety,

70

Homrighausen considered the possibility of having him serve the congregation I was leaving.

Two incidents led to the Fackler flogging. On February 5, 1961, he hosted a meeting at the local Lutheran Church with the theme "The Church and Human Relations." Joe Ellwanger, from Birmingham, brought two black girls with him to the meeting and the discussion was good but uneventful. On March 12, during Lent, the vicar was asked to preach, and his message was on foot-washing in which he "elaborated on our Lord's foot-washing by saying, '...and how many of us would wash a Negro's feet'...as our Lord had washed His disciples' feet." As he recalls, "No negative reaction was received from either Pastor or congregation that day."

Fackler and his wife lived in a renovated garage in back of their landlord's house. On Thursday evening of that week, the Klan burned a cross in their back yard. Their landlord was supportive of Fackler and dismissed the cross-burning as "a dumb kind of thing." What happened later that night, Fackler told in an article he wrote for *The Cresset*[9] magazine under the unusual title, "The Peace That Passeth All Understanding" --

> Thursday evening, March 16, Pastor had asked if my wife and I would baby-sit his children. This was in order. We had done it before. My wife had to work until 11:00 p.m., but we would spend the night at Pastor's home. Again, nothing was different as I went to pick up my wife at the hospital except that I thought I had left a book at church, earlier, and so expected to pick it up on the way to the apartment. When I arrived at the hospital entrance my wife was not there (as usual), so I decided to go pick up the book and thus save that much time getting back to Pastor's home. I drove to the parish, turned the lights to dim, left the motor running and started toward the door. Then the "fun" began.

> Hardly was the door ajar than I was grabbed from behind by a pair of gloved hands - one over my mouth and another over my eyes - and carried to the back seat of a waiting automobile. Lying cross-wise in the back seat of a speeding auto I had many thoughts cross my mind. I had no idea that it was the Klan but naively hoped it was some of my college friends out

for fun. This last thought was squelched when my custodian said: "You ain't on no joy ride, preacher," as I attempted to get more comfortable. After many bumps, sounds, and prayers, we arrived at our destination. I prayed and I prayed and I prayed.

Following a short interval of what seemed to be a conference, I was masked, punched in the stomach, and lifted out of the automobile. Someone was holding me from behind when another fellow punched me in the stomach again. I was scared, but the Lord was there. Had He not said: I will give strength unto my people; I will bless My people with peace? I was at peace, but what about my wife?

Next I was told to lie face down on the ground and was helped to do so. Now they wanted to talk to me. Many invectives were hurled - between and during which I was flogged. "Yes, I love all people" - Negroes included. This is what Christ did. This is what I must do. "Nigger-lovers disrupt our Southern way of life." Lord Jesus Christ, give me strength. The flogging continued as a "friend" held my legs and another stood on my wrists. "Yes, I had seen the cross, but didn't know what it meant." This was America - things like that do not happen here. "Yes, I will leave town - but why haven't you warned me?" I asked. I had been warned, they said - this was final. After more floggings and invectives and prayer I was lifted to my feet and led across some railroad tracks and told to lie down again. Here they removed my mask and warned me not look up until I had counted to 100..."we have a gun." My final direction was to follow the "red lights" on the railroad track to get back to town. It was a peaceful night.

It was a peaceful night as I walked along the tracks. Sounds of the night in the swamps were everywhere. It was difficult to walk at first. My thighs were quite swollen. But so close to God, a nature-loving vicar thinks of many things. I think I sang about every hymn I knew plus a good bit of the Divine Liturgy. Not a few thoughts from the psalms came to mind. My wife was on my mind also but we had talked much about uncertainty and death. We lived by faith - I knew she was all right. My watch was gone, probably lost in the shuffle. So I had no idea of time. One pipe was broken, but I had others. It was a long walk. It was a beautiful night. God was near. This was peace.

The rest is history now. I was picked up by a very dear student friend. My automobile was found as I left it - motor still running. My wife was in good spirits. After contacting my superior my wife and I left town. We were sad of countenance but confident that we had witnessed to our Lord. It was a peaceful drive.

In his "devotional" piece, Fackler did not mention some details which he related to me in an interview, such as the fact that his back, down to his knees, was beaten so severely that it turned, as he said, "as black as my clergy clothes." Neither did he mention that about a month later his wife delivered a stillborn.

Carl Wegener of New Orleans was Fackler's father-in-law, and one of the members of the Special Synodical Conference Committee. After the incident in Tuscaloosa, the Facklers moved to New Orleans where he finished his year of vicarage as institutional chaplain.

The Fackler incident brought the Lutheran Church officially into direct contact with the Klan. President Homrighausen and Executive Secretary Reinboth went to see Robert Shelton, the Grand Wizard of the Klan (some referred to him as "The Grand Lizard") who lived in Tuscaloosa. According to Homrighausen, they contacted Shelton at a tire store where he worked, and then they went to a coffee shop to talk. As Homrighausen remembers it, the conversation went as follows:

He said, "You don't like what happened, Reverend?" And I said, "I detest what happened." I said, "Do you understand what you are doing - the burning of the cross? Do you know the meaning of the cross?" And he said, "Yeah, the cross means power and strength." And I said, "You are absolutely right, but not the kind of power and strength that you have." Then I told him about the power and strength of the cross, but it was meaningless for him. And then - he also threatened me. I can't remember the exact words. It wasn't "You're next," but it was close to it.[10]

Homrighausen also went on public TV in Birmingham and addressed the Klan. "You all hide behind your pillow cases," he said, "You can see me, you know who I am. Come out and talk with me. Debate this issue if you want to, but don't do the cowardly acts like this." When he returned to Cullman after that, and later attended the Kiwanis Club where he was a member, Homrighausen remembers that he received a very cold reception.[11]

I called Joe Ellwanger to see how he remembered the Fackler incident. He acknowledged that it was considered a "no, no" for a white man to take two black girls to a meeting. After the attack on Fackler, he received word — he thinks from Fackler — that the Klan was also out to get him and the girls. Upon hearing that, Ellwanger agonized over whether he should tell the girls of the threat. Eventually he decided to tell them, and he remembered in particular the response of Carolyn Freeman. He asked her, "How do you feel about all this? Are you scared?" She answered, "No, I am not so much afraid as I am ashamed." "Ashamed?" he asked. "What are you ashamed of?" And she said, "I am ashamed that I have suffered so little and others have suffered so much; that I have done so little and others have done so much — for the cause of freedom of my people."[12]

In this case there was no follow-up by the Klan.

CHAPTER 5

STEPS LEADING TO AN INVITATION

The 1961 Pastors Conference at Tuskegee

The Gulf States Pastoral Conference was held two weeks after I was installed in Huntsville. For the first time, the black pastors of the Alabama/Upper Florida Conference were invited as guests of the Southern District Pastors Conference. Since no white institution or hotel would host an integrated group, the Conference was held on the campus of the Tuskegee Institute in Tuskegee, AL. Tuskegee Institute was made famous by the black botanist and chemist, George Washington Carver.

I rode to the Conference with Martin Buerger of Florence, AL, and Art Gronbach of Muscle Shoals, AL. We arrived at Tuskegee in late afternoon. After finding our rooms, it was time to eat, and we decided to eat in the school cafeteria. As the three of us white men sat there, it suddenly dawned on me that we were the only white people in the place. For the first time in my life I had a distinct impression of how it felt to be in the minority.

The campus had a very formal dress code in those days. We were required to wear a dress shirt and tie during our sessions and visits to the cafeteria.

Many questions swirled in the minds of the pastors as we gathered for this history-making conference. For four years the Southern District had been discussing the proposal to assume responsibility for the congregations of the Synodical Conference. What exactly would that mean?

Black pastors were asking: Would the District supervise without providing membership? Would only the pastors, and not the congregations, of the Synodical Conference be received into membership? As full members or only as advisory members? Would they be like little fish in a big pond? Some had leadership positions; would they be swallowed up, with little or no opportunity to be in leadership? What benefits would come with belonging to the Southern District?

White pastors were asking: Will acceptance of the Synodical Conference congregations mean pulpit and altar fellowship, meaning that black people might commune at the altar of a white congregation and a black pastor might preach in a white congregation? Will black Lutherans transfer their membership to white congregations? If we meet together again in the future, where will we meet? And always the question: If we integrate, will it produce social upheaval in our local communities and, as a result, impair the spread of the Gospel?

Since we were treading on new ground, a feeling of uneasiness existed among us as we went about the business of the Conference. Underlying the uneasiness, the hard truth is that we did not believe one another or trust one another.

At the beginning of sessions on Wednesday morning, Conference Chairman Luther Loesch, of Pensacola, FL, announced that "one hour of the evening session would be devoted to a preparatory discussion of the Synodical Conference matter."

Whoever was secretary of the Conference is not identified, but he wrote extensive and careful minutes, and I am dependent on those minutes for what follows.[1]

The Wednesday evening session began at 7:00 PM, but a couple of resolutions and various questions of casuistry occupied the conference for the first hour and 25 minutes. At 8:25 PM, the minutes pick up the discussion as follows:

> W[alter] Ellwanger gave a summary impression of the attitude of the Synodical Conference toward the S[outhern] Dist[rict]. Theses on Integration stating that they are in agreement with the first theses (sic), but that they differ with the S. Dist. on the others on the basis that the sins of pride, prejudice, etc., erect the barrier against the full realization of the first thesis.

76

An impromptu statement from J. Ellwanger as to the attitude of the Alabama Conference of the Synodical Conference brethren indicated that the brethren regard the S. Dist. Theses as a positive attempt, are in full agreement with the first six, but feel that the remainder leave something to be desired. Isolation and poor communications have led to misunderstandings. Then [When] the colored have been invited to mixed gatherings they have found it hard to reply heartily because empathy has not yet been fully established, the colored often finding it difficult to understand the pressures under which the whites are operating. It is doubtful that the S. D. Theses will unite us in theory. The actuality of confrontation, beginning at pastoral conferences such as these, is sorely needed.

Insistence from the floor demanded that the colored brethren be heard out in full this evening rather than in the morning. It was moved, seconded, and carried that the time of this evening session be extended until 10:00 p.m. in order to hear the reaction of the colored contingent of the Alabama Conference to the S. D. Theses as well as a summary of their own theses pending submission to the Board of Directors of the Synodical Conference. This motion was passed as amended to extend the time as necessary to discuss the matter to its end. A brief recess followed.

Thereupon J[ohn] Skinner read from the minutes of the committee of the Alabama Conference of the Synodical Conference for the Study of the S. D. Theses. From the floor the passages used in the S. D. Theses were examined critically and their validity placed in doubt.

Thereupon, J. Skinner read the Fourteen Articles prepared by the Alabama Conference as a positive statement to parallel the S. D. Theses, stating that these are not yet official and are not to be used as such. [See Appendix B for full text of the Fourteen Articles.]

As discussion was opened O. Reinboth advised that certain references to Selma in article #2 are contradictory and segregationistic, [and] suggested that "among negroes" be deleted from article #11, and that an additional article that would expressly speak for "forbearance of the sins of the whites" be included to correspond with the concessions of a similar nature in the S. D. Theses. W. Kennell stated that not every congregation is practicing sin as the articles would imply, that the concept of the *una sancta* cannot be directly applied to the visible church without any compensation for sin. Discussion then centered on solutions for the lag created by imperfection. Forebearance (sic) was compared to the activistic course taken by Jesus and its end in His suffering and death. Against the stated fear of loss of white membership it was asked if the kingdom grows in numbers only. J. Skinner made an eloquent plea, not for mass integration, but for the lonely, stranded individual deprived of fellowship and the means of grace because of color. At this point O. Reinboth asked: "Does article #11 mean 'whole hog or none at all'?" If you concede that our intentions are honest, will you accept them with patience? Where is the starting point? At this point the secretary feels that progress was made as he sensed a rising up out of a much-frustrated patience on the part of the colored brethren under a new hope that at last some constructive action is being taken.

Statements were made as to the effect of our integration difficulties upon mission work in Africa and elsewhere. These statements were backed up by testimonials from [Varnes] Stringer, a former missionary, and from J. Ellwanger as to a recent event in Birmingham. A[lbert] Dominick summed up that our great need is for integrated hearts that say, "This is the work of the Lord," as in the case of Peter and Cornelius.

Hereafter the discussion turned to practical solutions mainly centered in the question as to how and what the introduction of Southern District administration would signify. J. Skinner spoke with deep concern as he stated that the colored people have had plenty of administration in terms of candy held out to a hungry person. O. Reinboth replied that one administration is the answer to executing those things that will prepare and lead toward the desired goals. This statement was followed by many practical suggestions from a variety of persons.

The key to the evening's discussion was provided with the very basic and hitherto unspoken question by W[illiam] Eddleman: "What is administration?" From this point on the discussion became decidedly positive and constructive. O. Reinboth replied: "Administration is coordination of total effort," not imperious directives from above as may have seemed to be the case in former dealings with colored people. Eddleman: "A conference of this type proves that it can be done." Ellwanger: Much has been done in the past seven years, not by St. Louis, but out of the S. Dist. Frenback [Gronbach]: Administration will foster more conferences such as this one tonight and will eventually come to include aly (sic) [lay] delegates. [Milton] Stohs: In Florida the whites said, "Let's not take over the administration because, the next thing, they will want us to integrate at the local level," and this is exactly what happened.

At this point the colored brethren began to see clearly that they had surmised "administration" to imply subsidy checks, reports, and little more — that as negotionations (sic) were initiated they foresaw that the S. Dist. would merely "take over" negro missions as a whole with no further eye to progress in the betterment of their situation — that by the discussion this evening they clearly understand that the Southern District is sincerely dedicated to administering a change in cinditions (sic) as soon as possible — that by this discussion they more clearly understand the pressures which prevent the consecrated whites from making the progress they do desire together with them.

J. Ellwanger stated that the future strength of the S. Dist. may well lie in the serious cultivation of the negro field, that therein God will surely bless our efforts among the whites. Here W. Kennell affirmed that one of our intentions is to continue to promote colored missions in their own communities. This was reaffirmed by several of the colored brethren who stated that their natural desire is to establish their own communities of worship and life, but with free association with the whites at circuit and district levels and with provisions being made for the negro in isolation, or the negro who may prefer to associate with the whites. These things are said with a sense of patience that work in the Southern District will continue to be both white and colored for some years to come. These statements from the colored brethren relieved much of the tension and doubts that had existed in the minds of the white brethren.

Further discussion specified that the desires of the colored were restricted to church concerns only, not to state or community concerns. W[alter] Schindehette stated that on the basis of his experience at Meridian [MS] an isolated colored person need not remain alone if he is willing to engage in a personal evangelism effort among his own people in cooperation with the pastor of the white church.

11:03 p.m. — It was moved and seconded that the conference thank the Alabama Conference brethren for their effort and cooperation. The motion was carried as amended with the addition: "toward a most wonderful and profitable discussion of a mutual concern."

John Skinner closed the evening with a devotion based on 2 Timothy 2:1-5. He gave a heart-felt and moving message. With the frank and forthright discussion of the evening and Skinner's message, the uneasiness and tension were broken. As we assembled the next morning, there was an obvious feeling, "Yes, we will be able to do this." This was a very significant turning point in the process of merging the black and white work.

At the Thursday morning session President Homrighausen made his report, and the minutes include the following paragraph:

Pre. Homrighausen clarified the position of the S. Dist. toward the incorporation of the Synodical Conference pastors and congregations: Incorporation seems probable. Missouri will buy out Selma. A plenary board is in charge of transition.

Southern District will fight to keep Selma open. Synodical Conference congregations who do not desire to be incorporated will not be forced to do so. Pastors will first receive advisory membership in the District, voting membership as soon as possible when congregations are received. A step-by-step approach will make the ultimate come true, but a total, instantaneous approach will cause an explosion. The great problem is to keep L.H.R.A.[A.] [Lutheran Human Relations Association of America] interference at a minimum.

Just before the conference closed at noon on Thursday, the minutes include this note: "Clarification was made that the 1961 District Convention will include the Synodical Conference Brethren even if the site of the Convention must be moved and that the Missouri Synod has pledged full cooperation and support in the plan to incorporate."

Even though some complaints were registered about the accommodations at Tuskegee, it was decided to hold the Conference there again in 1962.

The optimistic closing note of the Conference secretary, namely that the Synodical Conference Brethren would be included in the 1961 Convention, was premature. It did not happen; they would not attend the Southern District Convention until 1963.

Prior to 1961, District Conventions had been hosted at a church; however, for the first time, the 1961 Convention was held at a hotel, the Admiral Semmes, in downtown Mobile, AL. Pastor Albert Dominick, who for many years served Mt. Calvary Lutheran in Mobile, said, "We could pass by that [hotel] while the Southern District Convention was going on, and we couldn't come in. We had to just drive on by."[2]

Meanwhile, other developments and events were taking place which are worth noting.

The Fourteen Articles - A Response from the Synodical Conference

At the Gulf States Pastors Conference, the secretary's minutes made a brief reference to "The Fourteen Articles" (see p. 77) which had been drawn up by the Pastoral Conference of the Alabama/Upper Florida

Division of The Lutheran Synodical Conference as a response to the Thirteen Theses of the Southern District known as the "Guidelines for Discussion." The Articles were to be employed in "Southern District Negotiations," which will be explained later. The Articles were read at the May Conference, and some items were discussed at some length, however, the Conference was informed that the Articles were still in formation and subject to revision. At a meeting at St. Philip's Lutheran Church in Catherine, AL, on June 30, 1961, the Fourteen Articles were adopted in their final form and later printed in the September 1961 issue of *The Missionary Lutheran.*[3]

A comparison between the Fourteen Articles and the Thirteen Theses (hereafter abbreviated as FA and TT) is worth noting. (See Appendices A and B for a full text of both documents.)

Number I of the FA immediately touches on the unity in Christ, stating:

> In keeping with Christ's earnest prayer that all His followers be one so that the world might believe that the Father had sent Him, we deeply desire to be one in faith and fellowship with all those who recognize the lordship of Christ. We are convinced that the witness of Jesus Christ by the Lutheran Church in the South would be strengthened by the complete oneness of Synodical Conference and Southern District congregations in life, worship, and witness.

The issue of oneness does not appear in the TT until Number 9 which states "Christians will seek...under the Spirit's guidance [to] demonstrate their unity in Christ," and in Number 12 which declares that "It is the Christian's chief aim to extend and preserve the Body of Christ...."

The subject of sin is dealt with very differently. The TT states in Number 1, "All men, alike, have been born in sin...." The FA is far more direct and specific, declaring in Number II "We testify that racial discrimination and segregation is sin." Numbers III, IV, and V expand that idea as follows:

> We believe that this sin requires repentance on the same
> Scriptural teaching which requires repentance of any and all

sin... We therefore preach, teach, and witness against racial discrimination with the same earnestness and emphasis which we use against any other sin.... We hold that any sin and particularly a sin which is as prominent as racial discrimination should not be dealt with as an adiaphoron but with the same firmness and candor which any article of faith should receive in its application.

On the subject of fellowship FA, Number VI, declares "We believe that the fellowship within the communion of saints already confessed by virtue of membership in the Synodical Conference should be practised (sic)." The closest that the TT comes to the subject of fellowship is to note that every Christian should have "full membership privileges" (Number 10).

The impact of integration on the mission of the Church was seen as radically different by the two documents. The TT allowed that "It is Scripturally defensible for a congregation to practice segregation when to practice integration would mean — a. the weakening or disrupting of their own congregation, [and] b. the curtailment of their missionary outreach," (Number 11); whereas, the FA affirmed:

> We believe that Christian fellowship (pulpit, altar, and communion) when practised (sic) under adverse worldly conditions will serve under God's blessings to strengthen unity in Kingdom building rather than harm the congregation's mission extension, since teaching and practising (sic) God's Word in fulness can never be antagonistic to the growth of the Kingdom.... Christians rejoicing in the unity which they have with the Father and with one another through Jesus Christ will gladly suffer to establish and maintain this unity and to extend it to a world dead in its separation from God and from man. (Number VII)

Instead of being willing to "gladly suffer" for the mission and unity of the Church, Thesis 12 of the TT allows that "The Christian...ought to be willing to forego privileges he might otherwise normally possess or experience hardship which might be necessary."

Rights and privileges also receive different treatment. "We believe that all rights and privileges inherent in the Church are the possession, by the grace through faith in Christ Jesus, of all Synodical Conference communicants and therefore should not be denied any of these members in requests for transfers or in the acceptance of transfers," is the statement in the FA (Number VIII). Conversely, the TT notes that "The Christian congregation has the right to regulate its own affairs in keeping with its stated purpose...so long as it violates no Word of God" (Number 8).

Regarding rights and privileges FA Number IX expands on Number VIII as follows:

> We believe that all rights and privileges as well as obligations and responsibilities given to a congregation by virtue of its membership in the one Body of Christ should not be denied any Synodical Conference congregation on the grounds of racial origin or man-made discrimination patterns.

Here, as in FA Number I, the discussion is framed in the light of the oneness in Christ.

In the Church's relation to society, the two documents reach different conclusions. The TT make no specific comment on that subject, but the FA Number X states,

> We believe that the Church should testify against all evils of racial discrimination and should not attempt to excuse or justify its silence on the ground of expediency. The Church does not seek to be at peace with the Christless culture and world around it. The Church follows the example of our Lord who was nailed to a cross because He refused to make peace with it.

Article XI of the FA appears to be aimed specifically at the Southern District with the assertion: "We believe that an administration that does not seek to answer the above theses on the basis of Holy Scripture in following the example of Christ would not be blessed in Kingdom extension." No parallel expression is found in the TT.

Article XII of the FA is a proposal regarding the Synodical training system and reads as follows:

84

We believe that there would be no discrimination in ministerial and teacher training and therefore we maintain that not only existing Synodical Conference schools should be open to Negroes but that a school with adequate facilities and with full academic and professional advantages be built and maintained for the millions in the South (who would not be served by schools in the North.)

Again, there is no parallel in the TT.

Number XIII of the FA and Number 5 of the TT are quite similar. The thesis in TT is a reminder that "It is God's will that His people exercise a spirit of humility both in respect to Him and in respect to their fellow man," and Number XIII of the FA declares that "We humble ourselves in meekness, forbearance, and repentance, praying that we recognize our own sins and shortcomings in Kingdom building and that Christ the victorious and resurrected living Head of the Church, mercifully forgive us."

The final items in the two documents run along similar lines. Number 13 of TT states "Christians can not take lightly the problems within the church relating to discrimination, but will seek to lessen them and eventually solve them through sincere prayer and Christian love." Number XIV of FA expands on that saying,

We firmly believe that the Holy Spirit is still operative in the Church today and that Christ is still Head of His body and that therefore what may seem impossible to us, the complete unifying of Synodical Conference and Southern District churches, is quite possible with God. May we be enlightened and strengthened that the Word of the Holy Scripture be fulfilled in us, Phil. 1:27: "Stand fast in one spirit, with one mind striving together for the faith of the Gospel."

Therefore, by the summer of 1961 both documents were on the table for discussion and negotiation.

According to Joe Ellwanger, who was involved in the final stages of drafting the Fourteen Articles, the men who were primarily responsible for developing these theses were Albert Dominick, Walter Ellwanger, Peter

Hunt, and John Skinner. The Fourteen Articles were deliberately written in a very forthright manner, on the possibility that the Southern District would reject them, which then would give the pastors of the Synodical Conference a reason to form their own independent association. Some of the leaders of the Alabama/Upper Florida Conference were concerned that when they were taken into the Southern District they would become "little fish in a big pond" and be swallowed up.[4]

In this sense the Fourteen Articles were designed to be used as a negotiating tool. However, the Fourteen Articles were never brought to the Southern District in an official manner and thus were neither accepted nor rejected.

A comparison of the two documents clearly shows a much bolder and stronger view expressed by the Fourteen Articles, while the Thirteen Theses reveal a more cautious view. The pastors of the Synodical Conference were trying to protect their unique identity, and also present a clear witness against the evils of discrimination, while the Southern District was concerned about the social impact that integration of the church would bring.

The Thirteen Theses were to be studied in all white congregations of the District to prepare lay people for the proposed merger. Each congregation was supplied with additional documentation which showed that by comparison the Southern District had many more black congregations in its geographic area than any other District. An expanded commentary on the Bible verses also came with the congregational study package.

At Grace Lutheran Church in Huntsville, we studied the Southern District document without much controversy, and the study was helpful in preparing for the upcoming Convention. Others whom I interviewed, however, thought that The Thirteen Theses had little or no impact in the congregations.

Merger Discussions in St. Louis

The issue of the merger in the South was also being discussed in the headquarters of the Missouri Synod in St. Louis. In a meeting of Synod's Board of Directors early in 1961, the future of the Alabama

Lutheran Academy and College was debated. Should it remain in its present site, should a new site be purchased, or should it be moved to some other place such as Atlanta? These were the questions under consideration.

The way the school was run is a story in itself. From his two years of service there, Gene Kappeler remembers that the attitude of the Synodical Conference Mission Board was very paternalistic toward the school. The white Board members never fraternized or discussed anything with the student body. Kappeler summarized their approach as: "They came, they met behind closed doors, and they went on." If proposals were made to improve conditions for the students, the response was, "They already have it better than they have it out in the country."[5]

President Homrighausen recalls that when he made his first visit to the campus, he found it in a physically deplorable state. When he met with the faculty and student body, he was asked by the administrator, "What shall we do with our school?" Homrighausen gave his famous response: "Well, I think one of two things we can do — either build it or bomb it!" The students responded with a roar of applause. In the interview Homrighausen added: "And what did we do? We built it."[6]

In the meantime, negotiations were going on between the Synodical office and the leaders of the Synodical Conference. In that Board of Directors meeting of Synod, mentioned above, the decision was made to have the Synod assume responsibility for all Negro mission work which had previously been carried out by the Synodical Conference. That offer was placed before the Convention of the Synodical Conference held in Milwaukee, WI, on May 17-19, 1961.[7]

At the same time, Synod's Board of Directors gave assurance that Synod would subsidize the Districts and accept complete financial responsibility for the training of Negro pastors and teachers.[8]

As Ed Homrighausen remembers it, the assistance from Synod's office did not come without a few bumps and bruises. He and Reinboth requested an audience with Synod's Board of Directors, but first they met for several hours the evening before with Dr. John Behnken, Synod President; and apparently all agreed that accepting responsibility for the black work in the South was a good idea. But when Dr. Behnken introduced them at the meeting the next day, he said, "We have a guest here this morning. I don't exactly know what his mission is, and he'll have to explain why he's here. And he has a request to make." To which Homrighausen reportedly answered, "Dr. Behnken, you very well know, because we spent at least three hours together." Then Homrighausen added, "That's how I introduced it, so I didn't make any points with the Board of Directors. But they saw an honest person, and they eventually said, "Yes, you should become responsible for the colored work in the Southern District."[9]

When the Synodical Conference met in May 1961, the transfer of ownership of the Lutheran Academy and College at Selma to Missouri Synod ownership was approved. With that transfer the official responsibility of the Synodical Conference for Negro mission work in North America came to an end.[10]

✠ ✠ ✠

That same month, Rosa Young, the woman responsible for the start of Lutheran education in central Alabama, was recognized. Concordia Theological Seminary in Springfield, IL honored her with a Doctor of Letters, with the citation: "Dedicated, unselfish, intelligent service."

The June 13, 1961 issue of *The Lutheran Witness* included this paragraph in an editorial about Dr. Young:

> Rosa Jinsey Young, 79, Selma, Ala., missionary, educator, author, editor, and counselor, is credited with many "firsts." She was the first person of her race to affiliate with the Lutheran Church in Alabama; she organized the first 13 Negro Lutheran churches in Alabama; she was the first secretary of the Alabama Lutheran Conference, which she helped organize; the first to contribute an article to *The Missionary Lutheran*. And on May 30, 1961, she became the first woman to receive an honorary degree from a synodical institution of higher learning.[11]

Dr. Rosa Young

While Rosa Young was honored and the institution she helped found gained new life, another school of the Synodical Conference was coming to an end. The seminary in Greensboro, NC, graduated its final class. The Greensboro Seminary was started by the Synodical Conference specifically for the purpose of training black pastors because the other Lutheran seminaries would not accept black students. Among those in the Greensboro Class of 1961 who came to the Southern District were Arthur Bodley to St. Peter in Gadsden, AL; Will Herzfeld to Christ in Tuscaloosa, AL; James B. Marshall to Grace/Trinity in Montgomery, AL; and Frazier Odom to Concordia in New Orleans, LA.

✠　✠　✠

Joe Ellwanger, as noted earlier, was a forceful voice for integration both in society and in the Church. While some agreed with him, especially George Hrbek, he often was a lone voice. However, with the arrival of Herzfeld, Ellwanger gained a supporting voice, for they had, as Herzfeld said, a symbiotic relationship. The rest of the District was not to learn about this new "team" until two years later when Herzfeld and the other black pastors were received into the District.

Soon after the Synodical Conference Convention at which it was decided to turn over the black work in the South to the Southern District, the Wisconsin Synod, one of the partners of the Synodical Conference, suspended its relationship with the Missouri Synod. Thus it was reported in the *Lutheran Witness* that

Negro work in the South, a joint undertaking of the Synodical Conference since 1877, will proceed as planned at the May 1961 Synodical Conference.

The Missouri Synod will have sole ownership of the Selma, Ala., training school for pastors and teachers. Beginning January 1, 1962, Synod's Southern District will assume full responsibility for Negro work in its boundaries.[12]

And thus the stage was set.

The 1961 District Convention

The 52nd Convention of the Southern District was held August 28 through September 1, 1961. The opening service was at Grace Lutheran in Mobile, with Synod President Dr. John W. Behnken in the pulpit. Convention sessions were held at the Admiral Semmes Hotel in downtown Mobile. For this convention Rev. Waldo Werning, Stewardship Counselor of the Nebraska District, gave the essay titled, "Let None But Christ Your Master Be."[13]

In his Presidential Address, Homrighausen called attention to the racial implications faced by the Convention and said,

> The world screams with delight, when it beats the church at its own business. We are not to sit back and watch others take the lead in relation of man to man. We are to move forward with courage and conviction that the things that we do are right in the name of Jesus Christ who died for all. Some of the resolutions of this convention will weigh heavy upon the heart and soul of every individual delegate. God must speak through the conscience of the Southern District.[14]

Only three overtures on the matter of the merger were presented to the Convention: two from the District Board of Directors in favor of the merger, and one by Mt. Olive in Metairie, LA, which was opposed to it. The Whereases of the Mt. Olive overture reflected an attitude which was

90

still widespread among many Southern Lutherans. It noted that Negro congregations had been adequately cared for by the Synodical Conference for 75 years; that the Southern District was unable to meet the financial responsibilities at this time; that the Constitution of our Nation guarantees separation of Church and State, and it is still our prerogative to foster our Christian Church affairs in the Southland among the white and Negro congregations on a segregated basis; that segregation is still observed and practiced in the South; and that it would be incompatible to have Negro people in the Southern District and not be able to function because of State Laws in such things as meetings, conventions, etc.[15]

The floor committee, which handled the merger resolution was chaired by Pastor A. Lorenz (Lorry) Grumm, of Redeemer Lutheran in Warrington, FL. In essence the same arguments on both sides, which had been heard at the two previous conventions were repeated. Homrighausen appointed men who represented both sides of the issue to the floor committee, with the aim that the differences could be thoroughly discussed before it came to the Convention floor. Nonetheless when it was presented to the Convention delegates, tension was high and the debate often heated and bitter. Finally the time came to vote. A motion to vote by secret ballot was lost. The two resolutions as offered by the committee were adopted by a large majority.[16] The resolutions are here given in full:[17]

PREAMBLE TO MEMORIALS NO. 6 AND 7

We recognize that even as Christ has made us one body through His sacrificial death and the sending of His Spirit, John 17:11, 20-21, we as His visible body here on earth must strive in a sinful world to manifest that unity so that all the world may know that we are one in Christ and thereby believe in Him. It is therefore our conviction that the following memorials enable us to achieve more fully external oneness not with the constraints of the Law but by the compulsion of the Gospel. Rom. 3:22-23; Gal. 3:27-28; 1 Cor. 10:16-17; Eph. 4; Phil. 1:27, Acts 2:42.

Resolution No. 6, Re: Negro Pastors

WHEREAS in 1946 the Synodical Conference in convention assembled "suggested that the General Board (Missionary Board) petition the respective Home Mission boards of the constituent Synods of the Synodical Conference to supervise such of the Negro Missions under the General Boards as are located within the given District"; and

WHEREAS all of said work has, pursuant to such action, been undertaken by our Districts with the exception of the Southern District; and

WHEREAS the Board of Directors of the Lutheran Church - Missouri Synod has urged the Southern District to assume its responsibility in this field; and

WHEREAS the Southern District in Convention of 1957 resolved to become responsible for the Negro work within the Southern District; and

WHEREAS the Board of Directors of the Lutheran Church - Missouri Synod recommends that the Southern District invite the pastors serving Negro congregations to seek membership with the District; and

WHEREAS the Board of Directors of the Lutheran Church - Missouri Synod recommends that the Southern District and the congregations involved work toward full voting membership in the District as early as possible; therefore be it

RESOLVED that the Southern District in Convention assembled in Mobile, Alabama, in 1961 invite the Negro pastors serving congregations within the confines of the Southern District to apply for (advisory) membership into the Southern District upon completion of transfer of the Negro work into the Southern District.

Resolution on Memorial No. 7, Re: Negro Congregations

WHEREAS neither the pastors nor congregations engaged in the work among the Negroes through the Synodical Conference have membership in any Synod; and

WHEREAS the Board of Directors of the Lutheran Church - Missouri Synod recommend that the Southern District and the Negro congregations within the Southern District work toward full voting membership in the District as early as possible; be it

RESOLVED that these congregations be urged to prepare constitutions in conformity with the Handbook of the Lutheran Church - Missouri Synod and apply for membership in the Southern District; and be it further

RESOLVED that the spirit of this resolution shall be so interpreted as not to place any congregation in a position which will precipitate the break-down of good order and reason in the matter of transfer and acceptance of members; and be it finally

RESOLVED that each congregation continue to exercise its right and responsibility in regulating its own affairs on the basis of God's Word and shall proceed in the spirit of Christian love, wisdom and discretion, seeking the advice and counsel of District officers. I Cor. 14:40 (cf. Chpts. 12, 13 and 14.)

Thus, after a vigorous and sometimes bitter debate, it was done. The District was on record to move toward a merger of the congregations and their pastors of the Synodical Conference with the Southern District.

Almost immediately after the decision was announced, a violent thunderstorm broke loose and, even though we were assembled in an enclosed conference room, we were all aware of the fierce lightning and crashing thunder on the outside. Comments were made that the Lord was taking note of what we had just done. It was, indeed, a monumental step for the Southern District, a step which was marked both by courage and fear.

September 25, 1961 - Herbert Lee, voter registration worker, killed by white legislator, Liberty, Mississippi.

Following the Convention, Executive Secretary Reinboth wrote an open letter to the members of the District which reflects both the tension and the hope which was evident at the Convention. He penned these lines:

> With the Mobile convention over, your Executive Secretary is anxious to use this column to express his personal appreciation to the pastors and delegates for their dedicated support of the District program.
>
> Especially do I feel that way about the overwhelming approval given the resolution of the Board of Directors on the question of membership to Negro pastors and congregations. Such action did not come easily in some cases.
>
> Many of our folks are deeply steeped in Southern tradition and find any changes in the social pattern difficult to adjust to. — Still, men placed Christian principles and the will of God above personal likes and dislikes. They honestly faced up to the question of Saul, "Lord, what do you want me to do?" They listened when God spoke through His Word. They saw the challenge of open doors. They knew that the Negro was their responsibility and that to work with him successfully meant giving him the rights and obligations of full membership.
>
> Once this became plain there was little hesitation. The love of Christ constrained them. They did what needed to be done as Christian people.... Now let's get on with our great task — in God's name![18]

CHAPTER 6

ADJUSTING TO A NEW REALITY

Growing Racial Turmoil and Violence

Racial tension and acts of violence had been part of the Southern scene from before the Civil War; however, starting with 1962, the next few years would see the tension and violence rise to a veritable firestorm.

The Southern District was to have a taste of violence very soon. On January 4, 1962, Robert Faga, a white pastor temporarily serving Grace Lutheran Church in Montgomery, AL, a parish in the black community, was attacked by four unidentified white men as he was unlocking the church door for an evening midweek service.

The Lutheran Witness reported "he was found lying dazed at the door of the church, bleeding from the mouth and ear, according to the police."[1]

Ironically, Faga was serving temporarily in Alabama while waiting to leave for his permanent assignment as missionary to Nigeria, where he served faithfully for many years.

April 1, 1962 - Civil Rights groups join forces to launch voter registration drive.

April 9, 1962 - Cpl. Roman Ducksworth Jr, was taken from a bus and killed by police, in Taylorsville, Mississippi.

◇　◇　◇

The 1962 Pastors Conference in Pensacola

Although we left the Tuskegee Campus after the 1961 Gulf States Conference with the assumption that the next Conference would be held there also, this did not happen.

According to the minutes of Immanuel Lutheran, Pensacola, Lorenz (Lorry) Grumm approached the Church Council of Immanuel with the report that a conflict of dates would prevent the District Pastors Conference from being held at Tuskegee, and with the request that Immanuel host the Conference. The minutes note that "the members of our congregation would not be responsible for providing meals or lodging, but meals and lodging would be on a separated status." At that meeting, the Council agreed to host the Conference to be held May 7-10.[2]

The minutes of April 12, 1962, shed further light on the arrangements for the Conference, as follows:

> The chairman directed a question to Pastor [Luther] Loesch concerning the status of the preparation for the Pastoral Conference.... Pastor replied, "Nearly all the necessary arrangements have been completed. Housing will be either at the San Carlos [Hotel] or the Holiday Inn and the Anabelle Motel Apartments."[3]

Obviously the black and white pastors would not be housed together, since the Anabelle Motel Apartments was a black establishment. The sessions, which this time included pastors from both the Gulf States and the Louisiana Conferences, would be held in the Immanuel sanctuary. The minutes noted that this would include "70 white and 20 Negro pastors."[4]

The decision to host the Conference was a major breakthrough for the Immanuel congregation, for just a year earlier the Council had adopted "The Zion Lutheran Policy" with regard to seating black people in their church. The minutes of the April 20, 1961, meeting provide a detailed

96

explanation of this policy, which showed up in a number of congregations during those years. The secretary wrote the following:

> Whereas Pastor Loesch presented the Zion Lutheran Church, New Orleans, La., procedure on ground rules for considering the attendance of colored people in its worship service, it is hereby resolved that this ground rule be adopted, as an emergency measure pending voters approval at a later date. The rule was summarized as follows: The usher stationed at the entrance door is to stop any colored people who are about to enter and he would ask them if they had come to worship with us; if answer is an unqualified "Yes," then he would suggest to them that they be seated in the area in which we want them to be seated. If they state that they wanted to sit in some other area, they would then be permitted to do so. If when asked whether they came to worship they would answer, "that they came to observe," or "we came so that we can report what we saw," they would then be informed that our service is confined to attendance by those who come to worship only, and they would not be permitted to enter.[5]

It is interesting to note that the minutes make no mention of disagreement or opposition to either the adoption of "The Zion Lutheran Policy" or the willingness to host a mixed pastors' conference.

St. Mark, Ackerville, Alabama

Attending an integrated meeting in a white church was a learning experience for me in more ways than one. On the trip to Pensacola, I rode with Ron Reinhardt of Decatur, AL, and we picked up Joe

Ellwanger in Birmingham. At that time Interstate 65 did not exist, so Ellwanger suggested that we travel through Selma. Ellwanger related many of his experiences of growing up in Selma, filling us

Hope Lutheran, Kings Landing, AL

in with information about work among the black congregations. We stopped to see what once was St. Mark Lutheran at Ackerville. In 1962 the typical frame church/school which was built by the Synodical Conference was already abandoned.

We also drove through a corn field to get to the still-active Hope Lutheran at Kings Landing. Nearby stood a now dilapidated three-story mansion. Black children were playing under the trees; obviously their family was now living in the rundown building. Ellwanger explained that the mansion was formerly the home of William Rufus King, who in 1852 was

King's Mansion - 1962

elected Vice President of the United States to serve under President

Franklin Pierce. However, King was ill when he was elected and died before his term began.[6]

✠   ✠   ✠

Dr. Richard Caemmerer of Concordia Seminary, St. Louis, was the main essayist for the Conference and Joe Ellwanger led a daily Bible Study. Holy Communion was celebrated at the opening service on Monday evening, and since there had been no Communion at the Tuskegee meeting, this was the first time the Southern District celebrated a racially integrated Communion. Wilfred Schrader, whose father was Pastor Emeritus at Immanuel at the time of the Conference, remembers that Peter Hunt said, "Pastor Schrader, I prayed for this happening, that happened tonight. I prayed this would happen, but I never realized that it would come in my lifetime."[7]

✠   ✠   ✠

By 1962, Homrighausen had served almost five years as District President, and his years of service were parallel to the years in which the District wrestled with the proper steps to bring about the merger. During these years the eyes of the nation were on the South to see how the entire racial issue would be resolved. Likewise, the eyes of the Missouri Synod were on the Southern District to see how it would work out the merger.

Homrighausen's *alma mater,* Concordia Theological Seminary in Springfield, IL, apparently was making its own observations, and at its May 30 commencement ceremonies conferred the honorary Doctor of Divinity degree upon the Southern District President. The citation read, "For his serious and practical efforts to relate the Gospel to race relations." At age 37, Homrighausen was the youngest pastors ever so honored.[8]

✠   ✠   ✠

Conditions of Life - Lingering Paternalism

"Paternalism" was the word frequently used in describing the way the pastors and congregations of the Synodical Conference had been treated. According to some accounts, when Walter Ellwanger became the Superintendent of the work, he brought a more evangelical approach, but much of the paternalistic mode remained.

Homrighausen recalled that, when he and Reinboth made visits to the mission stations, it was hard to describe how some of the black pastors lived. He said, "You talk about shanties and shacks, outdoor plumbing, and the whole works!"

Parsonage, St. Philip, Catherine, AL in 1928

He cited one visit as illustrative of the changes that were under way. After a meeting with the pastor at the church, the pastor said, "You are coming to the house, aren't you?"

> And I said, "I'd love to come to the house, love to meet your wife, but just don't have the time." And I found out later that they were extremely disappointed with my visit, that I didn't go to the house, because the pastor's wife spent two days cleaning and scrubbing and having everything ready for the *inspection* of the Superintendent. It was enough to break your heart.[9]

Apparently the old ways of living under a paternalistic system died slowly. When Jim Pape became the Stewardship Executive of the District in 1965, he also found similar reactions when he did not come to *inspect* the home.[10]

Getting Used to the South - Learning to Work in the South

At the same time as the turmoil in the South was escalating, many new congregations and mission stations were being established. Many of these were served by seminary graduates, and a major effort had to be exerted to prepare them for work in the South. Feelings ran so high in those years that sometimes newly assigned candidates were ready to jump into the fight "and change the South overnight," while others balked at the very idea of coming South.

Homrighausen remembers that he often had to plead with new graduates to come to the Southern District. His advice to them was, as he put it, "Do me a favor, come, keep your mouth shut for one year. Just listen and look. But don't get boisterous." After they had themselves ingrained in the congregation, then they could do good work. He was criticized for that approach by some, but he says that those who came and stayed told him later that it was the right advice.[11]

When Bill Wedig became the Mission Executive in 1964, he followed the same practice of advising newcomers to pay attention for a year before jumping into the racial issue.

Bernie Ansorge, who came to Jackson, MS, in the summer of 1963, recalls a new workers' orientation at which the briefing was given by Les Allenstein, a lay member of the District Board of Directors. This is how he recalls Allenstein's coaching:

> You guys are from the North. You have to understand us Southerners. We have important things to talk to you about, but first we are going to talk to you about the weather, we're going to talk to you about our family, and then we're going to talk to you about the football game that happened last Saturday - and if you are still listening we will get down to tell you about the important things. Some of you are going to come into very sensitive and highly charged circumstances. I'd advise you to listen first and then speak. And after you've got done listening,

then decide to listen some more. And when you think you're done listening, then finally listen a little bit more, and then people will respect you when you do have something to say, because they will know that you listened to them first.

It's sort of like getting drawn offsides. Don't get drawn offsides. Let the other guy move, and you stand pat. Let him move again, and you stand pat. And finally, then you make your move.[12]

Eldon Weisheit, who came in 1962 to start a new mission in McComb, MS, related the unique orientation to the South which he received. McComb is a relatively small town in South Central Mississippi. This is the account which he gave:

There was a library in town, it was a private library. For one dollar you could buy a lifetime membership, and only white people belonged. This is how they did stuff. Mrs. Lyons was the head librarian. Carolyn [Weisheit's wife] had gone in first, and then I went into the library because I was doing my "getting acquainted." She [Mrs. Lyons] was a very educated, sophisticated woman, and she said, "I can understand how you feel, and I understand that." Then she said, "Before you judge us, understand that we were taught to be this way, by our families, by our churches, by our government. And you have to be very careful before you start in saying that you don't believe in these three things. You have to be very careful."

Then she asked me to do something; she put me into a reading program. She said, "Before you condemn, find out how we were taught." Then I read *Lanterns on the Levee,* I re-read the whole Civil War history from a different point of view. I re-read a lot of things.

She was the first one to introduce me to this concept of "Cross-cultural ministry." We didn't know the terms, but we knew what it meant. And she may have saved my life, and I am not being overly dramatic.[13]

102

✠   ✠   ✠

Also on the subject of getting used to the South, Mission Executive Reinboth wrote the following in the Southern District Supplement of *The Lutheran Witness:*

A Word of Welcome.... WHY TO THE SOUTHERN DISTRICT? — WHY IN 1963?

Could a new worker be blamed too much if he were to ask these questions? After all, there are more than 400 vacant pulpits throughout Synod, and the majority of the 34 Districts in North America use at least some workers for starting their missions. Why then did God call me to the Southern District? And why this year?

These are times that try men's hearts. In addition to all the other problems that confront the church daily and make the task of the Gospel ministry trying, our decade has been confronted with the racial crisis. The answers don't come easily, nor are solutions typed. At such a time it is good to remember the words of Paul written as the Holy Ghost inspired to another young pastor. "God hath not given us the spirit of fear, but of power and of love and of a sound mind." (2 Tim. 1:7)

Perhaps our age can once more say, "Be thou partaker of the afflictions of the Gospel according to the power of God" (v. 8). God has called all of you (pastors, teachers, deaconesses) into the work, even as all the baptized ones of the church are also called to serve the Lord. And in the Word of God and the sacraments He has given us the Spirit of power. In this power stand. In this power advance.

Welcome to the Southern District in the name of the Lord! We thank God that you have come; yes, that you have come in 1963.[14]

✠   ✠   ✠

After Will Herzfeld came to Tuscaloosa, AL, in the summer of 1961, he quickly became involved in local racial issues. He was the founding pastor of the Tuscaloosa chapter of the Southern Christian Leadership Conference, and they set about integrating lunch counters in the city. On one occasion he and his group entered a lunch counter where Robert Shelton, the Imperial Wizard of the Klan, was having lunch. They did not speak to each other; only looks were exchanged. But after that the Herzfelds had crosses burned on their lawn, and he received a long phone call from Shelton. Neither man changed his mind as a result of the conversation.

The threatening phone calls continued for most of the summer, and during this time Herzfeld and his wife often slept under armed guards. One of those guards, incidently, was Samuel Cosby who later became a Lutheran pastor and served as an Air Force Chaplain.[15]

For the summer, Art Hanes, the mayor of Birmingham, ordered all parks to be shut down rather than open them for blacks.[16]

The February 20, 1962, issue of *The Lutheran Witness* carried an article titled "Interracial Marriage." The author, Frederic Schumann, pointed out some of the perils of such a marriage, gave counsel on how all marriages should be entered, but did not close the door to interracial marriages.

Two letters to the editor illustrate the strongly held feelings of that time. A woman from Houston wrote:

> In connection with racial agitation, King, CORE, NAACP, etc., you would do well to know that the promotion of racial agitation in America was adopted as a program by the Communist International in 1928 at Moscow. The program has never changed, and "civil liberties" is but a false term to mislead the uninformed.

A man from Dallas wrote,

> "I think it is a sin to marry into other races. Why should I change God's order of color? If you say it is not His order, why does it exist? I think it is high time to teach that it is God's order and that no racial intermarriage should be allowed. Period."[17]

Developments at Vestavia Hills[18]

Mission Executive Reinboth had a keen eye for identifying growing communities where a new mission should be started. One such area was south of Birmingham, an upscale suburb known as Vestavia Hills. The idea of another Lutheran Church in the area was not welcomed by everyone, especially by some at First Lutheran. First, the mother church, had already seen Trinity Lutheran on the west side organized a few years earlier and more recently Concordia in northeast Birmingham. St. Paul's and Pilgrim in the city and Zion in Bessemer were the other Lutheran churches in the area, but they were black and represented no competition for First; however, another white church on the south side did cut in on their territory.

James Pape, two years out of the seminary at the time, was called to be the mission-developer for Vestavia Hills. Homes were canvassed, services were started, and a congregation was formed. While he was getting acquainted with the community he received an unexpected bit of hospitality; he was given a membership application to join the Ku Klux Klan. Since other clergymen belonged to the Klan, apparently the offer was meant as a friendly gesture.

By the beginning of 1962, construction was started on a very modernistic first unit, a worship area with attached classrooms. Dedication was set for mid-June that year. Pape's recollection of the events surrounding the dedication is indicative of the racial climate and the community tension which existed at that time. Here is how he re-told it:

Dedication day was coming, and the question was raised at the Church Council - "Whom do we invite to this dedication?" It's traditional that you invite your sister congregations to join in that day, and that's when Vestavia Hills got into it real thick. "Do we do this?" "What's the community going to say?" Vestavia Hills was a very affluent area. "What will that do to our image?"

With considerable discussion at three or four different meetings - voters' meetings, etc., some of which Sam [Reinboth] came to - finally a vote took place. And you have been around long enough to know when a church decides really important things, it's often a *tie vote!* So our president - God bless him, he's in heaven - his name was Bob Lemmer...

The constitution said, "If there is a tie vote, the president has to break it." Oh, that man sweat bullets! He was on the right side, but he said, "If I'm gonna make this decision, it's gonna split the congregation." And we took a recess, and he came back into the room and, with tears rolling down from his eyes, he said, "I've got to vote this way, that we allow - invite - anyone to come to our dedication."

They had planned another event for the community before the dedication, and this is how Pape related that experience:

The building was done, and it was kind of an outstanding and attractive building, and at two o'clock in the afternoon [on the designated day] we were going to invite the community to come tour [the building], and we'll sing a few hymns and give a cup of coffee. It wasn't the actual dedication; it was like an Open House.

At the strike of two o'clock, when it was all supposed to happen, there was the loudest boom! Right away we thought, "Oh, bomb! Here we go!" And it was a bolt of lightning that hit the cross out in front of the church. Shattered it! And the exegetes obviously had different interpretations: "God is trying to tell us something. You've done something wrong." Others said, "God is blessing this church, and He is so happy with what you've done." So you could get all kinds of interpretations; but that's the kind of climate we were in.

Regarding the invitations which went out for the dedication, Pape tells how he tried to deal with classmate Joe Ellwanger at St. Paul's.

> I went to Joe and said, "Now we have made real progress here - new ground has been plowed." And I said, "Joe, do me a favor, please don't overdo this thing, or I'm going to lose the whole thing. If you send 50 people up there, that's going to scare the heck out my folks." Joe didn't send 50, but he did get a delegation to come, and all went well.

Such was the give and take among pastors and congregations in those days. While some took small tentative steps, others wanted to take bolder action. It was like walking a tightrope, with uncertain and potentially dangerous consequences all around.

September 30, 1962 - Riots erupt when James Meredith, a black student, enrolls at Ole Miss. Paul Guihard, a European reporter, was killed during the riot at Oxford, Mississippi.

Selma ALCA, 40th year

On November 11, 1962, the 40th anniversary of the founding of the Alabama Lutheran Academy and College was celebrated. Rev. P. D. Lehman of Los Angeles, CA, a member of the first faculty at the academy, was the speaker. Dr. Rosa Young, another founder of the academy, was present, and Rev. Walter Ellwanger and John Moss spoke at the service.

The enrollment that year was 27 in junior college, 101 in the senior high school, and 70 in the junior high school. Of the 1962 graduating class, five were enrolled at Concordia Teachers College in Seward, NE, and three at Concordia Seminary in Springfield, IL.

In its report to the Synodical Convention in Cleveland, Ohio that summer, the Board for Higher Education noted that "the wretched and hazardous conditions" at ALAC "dictates emergency measures in providing for even minimum standards of health and safety."[19]

The Debate: To Join or Not to Join

At its 1961 Convention, the Southern District opened the door for the black congregations of the Synodical Conference to come into the District. It was not a foregone conclusion, however, that everyone among the black people was uniformly ready to accept that invitation. A number of factors figured into their consideration.

One of their concerns was their identity. Even after the General Conference went out of existence, they still had their own Conferences — the Louisiana and the Alabama/Upper Florida Conferences. Though these were small groups, they were, nevertheless, their own groups where they could relate to one another on common ground. If they entered the District they would be "a little fish in a big pond," and not have much voice in the decision making. As a small minority, would they be swallowed up and only get the leavings?

Some individuals stood to lose more than others if they came into the District. In the 1940s Peter Hunt, for example, left the parish ministry and took up secular work because of the harsh conditions imposed by Superintendent Westcott. Later, Superintendent Ellwanger was instrumental in bringing Hunt back into the field, and he served as a pastor again.[20] He was soon recognized for his leadership ability and elected the Chairman of the Alabama/Upper Florida Conference.

Furthermore, Albert Dominick had served as Secretary of that Conference since 1931, all but one year of his ministry, and had very deep roots in the Conference and was closely identified with it. One pastor remembers that Dominick once said, "I'd rather eat bread and drink water than go into the Southern District."[21] For Hunt and Dominick to come into the Southern District meant giving up important leadership roles of long-standing.

One pastor observed that the discussions between the Synodical Conference congregations and the Southern District did not start correctly from the beginning, because they did not meet as equals. He believes that it was Hunt's view that, because two bodies were coming together, they should have sat down at the table and worked out the strategy as to how the merger was going to take place, rather than for the Synodical Conference pastors and congregations to give up everything they had and come over into another group.[22]

Some talked about forming a Black District, something akin to the non-geographic English District in The Lutheran Church - Missouri Synod. But two obstacles stood in the way of that route: one, that idea was essentially squelched by the 1946 decision of the Synodical Conference which urged black congregations to affiliate with the geographic Districts in which they were located; and, two, there was always the question, where would the money come from?

At this time John Davis, of Gadsden, AL, had not yet entered the seminary and was a very active layman in Alabama, and widely known when the debate was taking place. He maintained that Reinboth and Walter Ellwanger felt it was important to round up support among the laymen to endorse entry into the District. Davis told of a meeting of laymen which was held at Mt. Calvary in Mobile (Dominick's church) where he gave a speech urging entrance into the District. Leaders of the District and representatives from Synod were present. Davis claims that after the meeting Rosa Young came forward and told him, "That's the best I ever heard, and things will change as of tonight."[23]

Others, however, have said that lay people had very little influence in the black church, and that the pastors led the congregations. Will Herzfeld, Charles Graeber, John Skinner and Brice Thompson were among the pastors who most strongly favored going into the District. At the 1961 Pastors Conference, Skinner made himself known as a strong advocate for entering the District. When Herzfeld arrived later that same year, he added his voice as another strong supporter of the merger.

Some of the black pastors were genuinely apprehensive about the merger. Many of the black pastors in the South held conservative views, both theologically and socially, and did not always agree with the integrationists. They, like many white Southerners, did not want to upset the social order. They wondered, for example, what would happen if there was a pulpit exchange and a black pastor went to a white congregation.

According to Joe Ellwanger, his father was in favor of the merger, but he also had misgivings about it. For one, he was not much inclined to take risks; and for another, he was troubled by a concern that after the black pastors were brought into the District they would be expected to be carbon copies of graduates from Concordia Seminary, St. Louis and not be allowed to use their own unique gifts and cultural background.[24] James Wiggins remembers that Superintendent Ellwanger wanted the merger to go forward for the benefits that would be gained, but he wanted the black people to get fair treatment.[25]

Just what benefits were they to gain by coming into the District? It is certain they were in need of benefits. Johnny Brown succinctly stated their needs saying, "We had no benefits. We had no insurance, no retirement; we had nothing!"[26]

Simply getting a clear picture of the benefits to be gained was not always easy for the pastors in the Synodical Conference. The first meeting in which the benefits were explained was held at Bashi, AL, in 1958, but often the communication was inadequate since it was across a cultural and economic gap. Wiggins, for example, said that he learned best about the benefits while he was still a student at Greensboro and had opportunity to talk with black pastors who had already become members of the Southeastern District.[27]

The black pastors stood to gain in monetary benefits; but the truth of the matter is that after they came into the District, in many cases for many years, they never received a salary up to the level of the District scale. While the District provided a salary scale, not all congregations could afford the recommended salary, nor could the District enforce the salary scale. The black pastors suffered from this inequity because of a "double standard" which prevailed for a long time, and in some cases, may still exist.

The "double standard" showed up in ways other than salary. Art Bodley related how he had noticed that young white pastors in his area were buying their own homes, so he and his wife started the process to buy a home, only to receive a letter from Reinboth asking, "Who gave you permission to buy a house?" Before he was granted permission to buy, another district executive was sent to "check him out" regarding his pastoral ability.[28]

Nonetheless, coming into the District offered the promise of assistance for better programs in congregational life and activities. When they worked under the Missions Committee of the Synodical Conference, the emphasis was on "supervision," and very little practical help was provided for every-day congregational ministry.

Accordingly, the debate went on for a period of years, and some say right up to the day the congregations were to be received into the Southern District at the 1963 Pensacola Convention. In retrospect, one pastor said, "If the leaders had told us more clearly what we were in for, the merger would never have taken place." Another summarized the feeling of many, saying, "Well, it can't be any worse than it is." J. B. Marshall remembers Rosa Young saying, "We ought to stay together, whatever we do, go together."[29]

On August 27, 1963, Pastor Albert Dominick, stepped forward and was the first of the black pastors to be received into membership of the Southern District. He was welcomed by President Homrighausen and District Secretary Lothar Kleinhans.[30]

Why was Dominick in the forefront at this occasion, when previously he was reluctant to participate in the merger? As one observer put it, "By then he had no choice, when he realized that the battle was over."[31] In addition he was a Christian gentleman and known as a co-operative leader.

CHAPTER 7

1963, AN UNFORGETTABLE YEAR

Assimilation Begins

If the racial turmoil and related violence was escalating in 1962, then it can be said that it hit its apex in 1963. More on that later.

With the arrival of 1963, many of the congregations of the Synodical Conference were busy working on a constitution which would have to be submitted and approved as part of their acceptance into the Southern District. At the same time, some individuals were already being assimilated into District activities. In mid-January, the District Missions Committee conducted a "Goals for Souls" conference in New Orleans, and Pastor Dominick and John Davis had already been appointed to the committee. Dr. Willis Wright, a professor at Southern University who later became the president of Alabama Lutheran Academy and College, was one of the speakers at the conference.[1]

When "Big John" Davis stood to introduce himself at that meeting, he mentioned that he and his wife were blessed with a large family. Since this was an evangelism workshop, he rolled out the "r" as he added "And that's called inter-r-r-nal growth."[2]

Birmingham Demonstrations

Early in the Spring of 1963, after the demonstrations in Albany, GA, plans were being made to conduct demonstrations in Birmingham. Fred Shuttlesworth was the president of the Alabama Christian Movement for Human Rights, the Southern Christian Leadership Conference (SCLC) affiliate in Birmingham, and this group invited Martin Luther King Jr., to come to Birmingham to help organize the demonstration.

At this time Joe Ellwanger had his second meeting with King, for when King came to Birmingham, he invited all the black pastors to come together for a meeting. As Ellwanger recalls, there were about 40 black pastors and he was the only white pastor present. Ellwanger attended because he was Vice President of the Birmingham Council of Human Relations, an inter-racial group in the city, and because he was the pastor of a black congregation. As a result of the meeting, Ellwanger was invited to be part of the "Committee of Twenty" which was a sounding board to give feedback to the SCLC.

Ellwanger relates the following experience:

> I remember the meetings at the Gaston Motel and the Sixteenth Street Baptist Church with King present...and I went to some of the open meetings. I did not participate in the actual demonstrations the first week because it was Holy Week, and I had more or less decided in my mind I was going to wait until after Easter, because there was the possibility of being in jail, and I wanted to at least make it through Easter.

> The demonstrations in Birmingham did not last nearly as long as anybody thought... In Birmingham things moved quickly. I don't recall the exact number of days, but it was something like two or three days of demonstrations and a few arrests, maybe 40 or 50 adults. And then came the children...before the fourth and fifth days children and youth began to participate, and this is what made the demonstrations in Birmingham different from the demonstrations anywhere else, and which escalated the demonstrations very quickly. On the first day there may have been 100 or so, and the next day there were maybe 300 or 400 youth, and most of them were arrested and put in jail. And the numbers just escalated, and by the third day there were something like 1500 in jail.

May 3, 1963 - Birmingham police attack marching children with dogs and fire hoses.

Ellwanger continues the recollection --

> And so before we knew it, the business community of Birmingham was saying, "Hey, we cannot take this kind of a blemish on our record." The youth were going downtown with the demonstration, and so people were not coming downtown to shop; and so the business people said, "We'll come to terms with you," and so they did come to terms, within practically a week... That was certainly my first in-depth experience with the Movement.[3]

King was arrested during the Birmingham demonstration, and wrote "Letter From Birmingham City Jail" which was published in *The Christian Century.* He wrote in response to an open letter by eight prominent liberal Alabama pastors who questioned King's methods. In his "Letter," King explained and defended his methods and made an appeal for white pastors to become involved in the Civil Rights Movement.[4]

Ellwanger's Encounter With The Police

Ellwanger became a marked man in Birmingham by his participation in the demonstrations. He was already well known at the police station, for, as Pape said, "Joe had guts enough to go down to the Police Department and complain when one of his members was beaten by the police."[5]

And yet he was to have a more difficult encounter with the law. Here is how he retold that experience:

> After the demonstrations in 1963, I picketed, along with some black pastors and some others, in front of Pizitz, or Loveman's or one of the downtown department stores. And that

apparently caused a slight furor in some quarters of business, and I never did get to the bottom of who reacted this way; but I got a call to come down to the Police Department. I was called to come down to the police and defend myself against a charge. And when I got down there, it had nothing to do with picketing, although I know that this is what really caused it.

But when I got down there they tried to charge me with attempting to sexually attack a black prisoner who was down in City Hall. They brought him in as the witness. Of course, I had never seen the guy before. The poor guy was shaking because they obviously had put him up to this. I denied this and said, "I've never seen this man before, and I haven't been in City Hall down here in weeks, and this is preposterous." And they said, "Well, he's brought charges, and we are going to stick with 'em."

When I asked Ellwanger what happened as a result of this, he said, "About three or four days later, I got a call saying, "Well, if you want to avoid facing these charges.... Like, if you leave town, we will not press the charges."[6]

This was typical of the kind of manipulation and intimidation used against protesters in those days by those in law enforcement.

Jim Pape, who by now was Circuit Counselor of the Birmingham area, also became involved in this incident. He said, "Joe called me up one day and said, 'I am in trouble.' And I said, 'What's going on?' And he said, 'Bull Conner is going to charge me with indecent exposure.'"

Bull Conner was the hard-nosed police commissioner of Birmingham who became famous, or infamous, for ordering the use of fire hoses and police dogs against the demonstrators.

Now Pape was faced with a quandary. He wanted to be pastoral. Was there some truth to the charge? Finally he asked, "Joe, are you guilty? And if you have a problem, we'll get you some counseling." After being assured that Ellwanger was not engaged in homosexual activity, Pape went to see Bull Conner and related the visit as follows:

We went to bat for him, and I remember going to Bull
Conner's office and saying, "I represent the Missouri Synod."
(A slight over-statement!) "I don't want you ever to do this
again to one of our men. He is not guilty of this, and we know
what you're doing." And Conner left that alone, and no charges
were ever filed.[7]

Synod's Witness of Events

During the years of racial conflict and turmoil, *The Lutheran
Witness* provided significant glimpses of the attitude which prevailed in the
rest of the Missouri Synod. In the May 28, 1963, issue, Reinboth provided
an article titled, "Race Relations and Lutheran Missions," in which he
argued against segregation and pointed out that segregation cannot be
eliminated by decree, but only as motives and attitudes are changed by the
Holy Spirit through the Word. At the same time, he noted that sometimes
churches must be provided in an exclusively black community. He had this
paragraph:

> While the Church speaks out against intolerance, also
> as it relates to all forms of segregation, it must not fail to serve
> men where they are as they are. *To bring the Gospel to as many
> as possible without violating the principles of Christ's love is the
> Church's prime concern in missions.* [Italics in the original] This
> can best be done by (1) desegregating all existing Lutheran
> churches by their own choice and by (2) continuing to prosecute
> a vigorous mission program in Negro communities of the North
> and South.[8]

The July 9, 1963, issue of the *Witness* had a lengthy editorial
relating to the Birmingham demonstrations titled "Another Kind of Demonstration." While the editorial supported the efforts of the black people in
their quest of basic human and legal rights pledged to them by the
Constitution, it also said that the time had come "to consolidate, to continue
legal and moral pressure — but not to antagonize."[9]

Somehow that phrase "but not to antagonize" caught the attention of those who wrote letters to the editor. One reader from Indiana demanded that "these insane demonstrations should be stopped at once." A New Orleanian wrote, "Divisions, quarreling, and strife are the very things the communists want. Let's be shrewd enough to 'outsmart' communism."

Richard Neuhaus of Brooklyn, NY, weighed in with these thoughts:

> You call for a halt to the kind of demonstration that has proven so effective in recent years lest it begin to "antagonize" the majority. It is my fervent prayer that such demonstrations continue and grow precisely in order to "antagonize" (alert, stir up, etc., would be better words). I know of no prophetic movement or righteous cause in history that did not "antagonize"...

> It is not enough that Lutherans have said the right words and experienced a generous feeling about equality or the unity of the body of Christ. We must be "antagonized" to *work* for open occupancy in our own communities, for equal educational opportunities in all schools, and against discrimination in hiring in our places of employment.

Pastor Kennell, of Montgomery, AL, submitted this letter:

> How can you as a Christian writer approve of mob actions when these are contrary to local laws and even proper court injunctions? Or do the words of Paul, "Let every soul be subject unto the higher powers" (Romans 13:1), refer only either to the laws we like or to Federal laws? Have you forgotten that the apostle Peter reminds us to be subject not alone to "the king" but also to "governors" — indicating state as well as Federal rule (1 Peter 2:13,14)? How readily you condemn local authority, judging these actions, as you put it, only for the sake of preserving a way of life, rather than preserving the peace, which is the proper function of government, both Federal and local.[10]

✠   ✠   ✠

In the Spring of 1963, the Lutheran Hour Chorus, from St. Louis, under the direction of Dr. William Heyne, made a tour through the South which included a few congregations in the Southern District. Dr. Heyne took a firm stand and refused to give a concert in a segregated church. In Montgomery, AL, the choir learned that the church where they were to perform had a segregation policy. As a result, the concert was given at the chapel of nearby Maxwell Air Force Base.[11]

✝ ✝ ✝

The 1963 Pastors Conferences

In odd years, the pastors of the Southern District met in two separate conferences — the Gulf States Conference and the Louisiana Conference. By now the pastors of the Synodical Conference were routinely invited, but in some cases it was still difficult to find places which would allow integrated meetings.

The Gulf States Conference met again in Pensacola, and this time at Resurrection, a new congregation on the west side of the city.

The Louisiana Conference had its first introduction to the facilities at the Gulfside Assembly near Waveland, MS. Gulfside was owned and operated by the Black Methodist Jurisdiction, and since it was a black establishment, white people could be invited there. Anyone who ever met there certainly had some stories to tell about the facilities at Gulfside. The meeting hall was equipped with pews and was in reasonably good condition, but the dormitories were another story. After a meeting there, Homrighausen wrote the Chairman of the Louisiana Conference complaining about the "moldy conditions," and stating he did not think it was a fit place to which to invite lay people. He wanted "the dirty and filthy" conditions corrected. And he added, "Seeing is believing" regarding any changes.[12]

I don't recall that conditions changed much with the few visits I made there. The most unforgettable about that place were the swarms of aggressive mosquitoes.

118

Adjusting to Social Change

Now that the pastors of the Southern District and the Synodical Conference were meeting together on a regular basis, it sometimes produced awkward or difficult social encounters. Simply seeing black and white riding together in a car was despised by some white Southerners. For example, Ansorge relates the following experience of a group of pastors traveling to conference.

> We were traveling down US 49 between Jackson and Gulfport [Mississippi] on the way to pastors conference. There were five or six of us and Norm Schulz was driving. We had Bill Young [a black pastor] with us. He was at St. Philip's in Jackson. We forgot to tell Norm to fill up with gas before we picked up Bill. So somewhere along US 49 Norm pulled up to a country filling station/general store. We all got out to use the bathroom. Everybody was dressed in casual clothes except Bill Young. He had on a suit with white shirt and tie, totally dressed up. The "good old boys" at the filling station really shook their heads at us all, but served us anyhow, and we all got to use the one restroom they had.[13]

Eating together in public places produced far more problems. Homrighausen tells of the time he and Dominick were traveling together, and they pulled into a drive-in and ordered hamburgers and milkshakes. But nothing was served, so after waiting awhile Homrighausen said, "Pardon me, I put in an order for two hamburgers." And they said, "We don't serve niggers." They had to resort to visit a grocery store to get something to eat.

Homrighausen tells of the time he and Dominick were in Mobile and wanted to eat in a well-known restaurant. They agreed that Dominick would serve as Homrighausen's "valet" and carry his bags in. This time they were served, but by the time Homrighausen returned home to Cullman, AL, the word had already spread that he "had eaten with a nigger."[14]

Ellwanger and Herzfeld also used the same technique when Herzfeld posed as the valet, and they were permitted to eat in segregated establishments. On one occasion Herzfeld wore a turban and posed as a visitor from India.[15]

Brockmann tells of four pastors from New Orleans who traveled to St. Louis to attend the P a r i s h Administration Institute at Concordia Seminary. It was in either 1961 or 1962 and the foursome included three white men Brockmann, Erich Wildgrube, Vic Moritz, and Ted Cooper, a black m a n . S t a y i n g overnight in a motel was out of the question, so they d r o v e s t r a i g h t through. The first time they could eat

"Ask The Un-American Activities Committee To Investigate What This Strange Flag Is Doing Down Here"

ALABAMA UBER ALLES

GOV. OF ALABAMA

© 1963 by Herblock
in *The Washington Post*
Used with permission

t o g e t h e r w a s i n F e s t u s , M O , j u s t south of St. Louis. On their one other stop to eat, Cooper was put off in a corner of the eatery so that he had to get up and move every time the cook wanted something from the refrigerator.[16]

My first encounter with this problem came as Karl Kretzschmar, a white pastor, and William Eddleman, a black pastor — both from Birmingham — and I were on our way to a meeting in New Orleans. Naively, I had not given much thought about where we might eat until we were in Meridian, MS. Without saying anything to the other two, I stopped at a drive-in. As we waited to see if we would be served, Pastor Eddleman

120

broke the suspense as he spoke from the back seat and said, "You fellows order what you want; I brought my own lunch." Suddenly it occurred to me how thoughtless I had been not to think ahead about where we would eat and how thoughtful he had been to plan ahead and bring his own meal. I should add that in this case we were served.

On one occasion, when we had a Circuit meeting at Grace Lutheran in Huntsville, Will Herzfeld was in attendance. When lunchtime came, we walked across the highway to the Holiday Inn. When the receptionist greeted us at the restaurant, I said, "We have the Ethiopian ambassador with us today." She looked a bit puzzled, but after a brief hesitation seated us; and that was my first meal with a person of another race in a public place.

In 1964 my wife and I invited Art and Barbara Bodley to have Thanksgiving dinner with us. That produced no repercussions, only because the social order in Huntsville was considerably different from the rest of Alabama.

Others had different experiences with inviting a black person to their home. Harold Hermetz tells of the time he was pastor in Greenville, MS, and he and several pastors were returning from a meeting around noontime. He invited all of them to have lunch at his home. The group included Pastor Brice Thompson, who refused to enter the house. Hermetz remembers that Thompson said, "No, I don't want to cause any trouble with your neighbors. If somebody saw me, they would think you are one of the people who is pushing integration."[17]

Eldon Weisheit tells another interesting story which also includes Brice Thompson. Here is his recollection:

> Rog Klemz [of Jackson, MS] and another fellow were driving down to [McComb, MS] to pick me up to go to a meeting. We were going to New Orleans and then a couple of days later we'd be coming back. When they were picking me up, I asked what time we'd be coming back through, and they said around 5:00 in the afternoon, or maybe 5:30. So I said, "Well, we'll have dinner here," and I told Carolyn [Weisheit's wife]. Carolyn's parents from Minnesota were there, and I said, "We'll be just in time for dinner."

When we got down there, Brice Thompson was already there and he was riding back with us. So we got into the car, and we were going home, and I said, "We're having dinner at my house." And Brice just said, "Well, that's fine," but in a way he said that he wasn't participating. And I said, "What do you mean?" And he said, "I'm not going to eat dinner at your house." And I said, "Well, you're not the one extending the invitation." And he said, "I don't have time to do a funeral on you. I won't come in your house. There just is no way."

Anyway, we got in and we had three kids and my in-laws were there. My father-in-law was a hard-headed, crusty old German, to be honest. Anyway, there is one good thing I can say about my father-in-law. We were getting around, getting everyone settled, and I told Carolyn that Brice was in the car. She fixed a plate to take out to Brice. Her father saw this plate, and so he said, "What's going on?" I tried to explain to him. Now this guy was from rural Minnesota, with not a clue about racial things. I explained and I took the plate out, and the rest of us sat down at the table and after we said the prayer Fred said, "I will not eat here when there is a Lutheran pastor out there." And he took his plate and went out and sat in the car and ate with Brice. I was so proud of him![18]

June 11, 1963 - Alabama Governor stands in schoolhouse door to stop University integration.

June 12, 1963 - Medgar Evers, Civil Rights leader, was assassinated in Jackson, MS.

The 1963 District Convention - Merger Takes Place

Segregation laws still existed in many places in the South, which meant that the first question to be settled in order to hold the Convention, was where to hold it. The choice was between New Orleans or Pensacola, but Pensacola was an unlikely site for a convention since none had ever been held there before and New Orleans had hosted many. But New Orleans was not ready to host an integrated convention in a public facility, which meant that Pensacola caught the brass ring for this honor.

Once the decision was made to hold the Convention in Pensacola, the attention fell on Immanuel to be the host congregation. Immanuel is the mother church of Pensacola among Lutherans. Its venerable Gothic sanctuary, built in 1912, stands on West Wright Street, a short half-block off Palafox, the main street of downtown Pensacola. Its only neighbor on that side of the street is Christ Episcopal Church.

Immanuel Lutheran Church
Pensacola, Florida

Immanuel had hosted the integrated District Pastors Conference in May 1962; therefore, it was not an entirely new issue for the Church Council when the request to host the Convention was placed before them at their December meeting. As Wilfred Schrader remembers it, there may have been a few frowns on the face of some of the members, but he could not recall that anyone voted against extending the invitation; and so the recommendation was forwarded to the voters, the governing body of the congregation. After a brief discussion the voters, at their meeting on

January 27, agreed. Details were to be handled by the District Board with Pastor Loesch acting as the go-between.[19]

Now another question needed to be settled: Would the sessions be held at the church or at the City Auditorium? At the April 18 meeting, Loesch reported that even at a 50% discount for a church, the fee at the auditorium was $200.00 a day. That was deemed too expensive, thus it was settled to hold the sessions in the sanctuary. Catered meals and coffee-breaks would be available next door at Christ Episcopal.[20]

Next was the question about where the opening Communion Service would be held, and here there are diverging accounts. Homrighausen recalls that there was a reluctance at Immanuel about serving Communion to an integrated gathering. As he put it, "We will have Communion and Pastor Dominick will serve with me." According to him, Immanuel did not agree to that, and in a relatively short time arrangements had to be made to hold the Opening Service at the Chapel of Pensacola Naval Air Station.

However, Schrader remembers it differently, saying that it was simply a matter of accommodating the expected attendance: Immanuel's sanctuary holds only 200 and at least 500 were expected. The convention report in *The Lutheran Witness* notes that 700 were in attendance. Furthermore, the June 6 minutes of the Council support Schrader's view, particularly about any last-minute change. At that meeting it was reported that a Mr. Collier of Resurrection Lutheran had completed preliminary arrangements to hold the opening service at Pensacola NAS.[21]

Much credit must be given to Pastor Loesch for leading the congregation through the steps to prepare for the Convention. It was a large undertaking, and still risky to have an integrated group of such size in a Southern city. Schrader cannot recall any adverse reaction from the community; but the Old South was by no means dead in Pensacola, because several years later the Klan sponsored a parade down Palafox Street.[22]

Luther H. Loesch

The minutes of the congregation's meetings provide no indication of conflict or controversy. The secretary either chose not to record such matters or there was no disagreement. Wedig, in his column in the District Supplement of the *Witness* wrote: "My citation for cooperation: the Pensacola laymen meeting with Dr. Homrighausen on May 30, for convention planning. They accepted every task suggested with willing hearts."[23]

Now the stage was set for the 53rd Convention of the Southern District. The first integrated Convention of the District began with a full house at the NAS Chapel. Rev. Walter Enge, Synodical representative and President of the Colorado District, delivered a challenging message based on Joshua 24:14, with the theme, "A Time for Decision and Action." Homrighausen was the celebrant for Holy Communion and Loesch was the officiant and host pastor.[24]

The Opening Service gained considerable attention, and an article in *The Lutheran Witness* noted:

> As hundreds of cars brought worshipers from downtown Pensacola to the Naval base, onlookers saw a thrilling demonstration of equality and unity in Christ. Both the motorcade and the "integrated" service rated radio, TV, and press coverage. But publicity was played down.

> "We don't care to publicize the things we are doing," said District President Edgar Homrighausen. "We are merely servants of the Lord who see a task to do and try to do it. We are not integrationists, and we are not segregationists. We are Christians."[25]

The next morning the delegates to this history-making Convention were welcomed by C. P. Mason, the mayor of Pensacola.[26]

On the morning of August 27 came that moment which had been much debated at countless meetings, dreaded by some, and longed for by others: The pastors and congregations of the Synodical Conference in the South were received into the Southern District. Ceremonially, it was not an eye-catching event because it took place as part of the report of the Constitutions Committee. The pastors and their lay delegates stood in a long line, each waiting to sign the Constitution of the Southern District.

At the same time it was an unforgettable scene. The large number alone was extraordinary, and the many faces of different colors left a deeply etched image in my memory. No doubt prayers of thanksgiving were rising to heaven from the delegates, and I imagine our hearts beat just a little faster as we witnessed the culmination of nine years of debate, discussion and struggle to bring the merger to reality.

Albert Dominick welcomed by President Homrighausen with Secretary Lothar Kleinhans looking on. In the background (l to r) are Arthur Bodley and Ivory Cameron

In reference to the historic event, Homrighausen had said in his Presidential Address, "At this Convention the past will merge quietly yet powerfully and inseparably into the present and the future and eternity. We will perform our work united in the only bond that can unite men; namely, the Gospel of our Lord and Savior, Jesus Christ."[27]

Those congregations formerly associated with the Synodical Conference and their pastors who were received were: (* white pastors already advisory members of the District.)

Bethlehem - New Orleans, LA (vacant)
Holy Cross - New Orleans, LA, James Brockmann,* pastor
St. Paul (Annette) - New Orleans, LA, Erich Wildgrube,* pastor

126

Trinity - New Orleans, LA, Dan Otto,* pastor
Mt. Zion - New Orleans, LA, Victor Moritz,* pastor
Concordia - New Orleans, LA, Frazier Odom, pastor
Calvary - Baton Rouge, LA, Roy Stoll,* pastor
Augustana - Alexandria, LA, Moses Clark, pastor
Christ - Tuscaloosa, AL, Will Herzfeld, pastor
St. Peter - Gadsden, AL, Arthur Bodley, pastor
Trinity - Mobile, AL, (vacant)
St. Philip - Catherine, AL, Samuel Gailes, pastor
Trinity - Selma, AL, Peter Hunt, pastor
Trinity - Montgomery, AL, Brice Thompson, pastor
St. Philip - Jackson, MS, (vacant)
Bethlehem - Prattville, AL, Charles Graeber, pastor
Mt. Calvary - Mobile, AL, Albert Dominick, pastor
Bethel - Point Clear, AL, Albert Dominick, pastor
Concordia - Montrose, AL, Albert Dominick, pastor
Pilgrim - Birmingham, AL, William Eddleman, pastor
St. Paul - Birmingham, AL, Joseph Ellwanger,* pastor[28]

C. P. Thompson and J. B. Marshall, Jr., both formerly pastors in the Synodical Conference, were also received into the District.[29] Peter Hunt, who was said to be very reluctant to enter the District, was the first black pastor elected to an office. He was chosen to serve as Counselor of the Circuit in South Central Alabama.[30]

The "Missions On Parade" was another scene which left a lasting impression on those at the Convention. Every pastor who served a congregation which received financial assistance from the District Missions Committee, carried a placard which gave the name of the congregation and the number of new members gained in the previous year. After Professor Paul Elbrecht, the Convention Essayist, saw the parade of 103 congregations, he said, "This type of thing just isn't done in too many districts. A great spirit exists in the Southern District."[31]

August 28, 1963 - 250,000 Americans marched in Washington, D.C., for Civil Rights, and Martin Luther King, Jr. gave his "I have a dream" speech.

◊   ◊   ◊

The convention ended on August 29. It was a momentous convention which brought the fulfillment of many dreams and prayers. Many delegates left Pensacola uplifted and excited, but no one could tell exactly what lay ahead and how the merger would be received back home in the congregations.

CHAPTER 8

REACTION TO THE MERGER

An Explosion!

How would the decision to receive the black churches play back home? It took only a matter of hours for one pastor to find out.

When Martin Buerger, pastor of First Lutheran in Birmingham, walked in the door of his home that evening after the drive back from Pensacola, his phone was ringing. It was the president of the congregation, who said, "There are members of the congregation who are very, very disturbed because the Negro congregations were accepted into the Southern District. So, I just want to alert you."

Thirty-one meetings later, on November 10, 1963 — Buerger remembers that it was Luther's birthday — the congregation passed a resolution that "the pulpit of First Lutheran Church, Birmingham is declared vacant," and Buerger was out.[1]

Obviously that is a story in itself and we shall return to it later; but first we will look back at the preceding months in order to provide a setting for this development.

In the Spring, demonstrations were conducted in downtown Birmingham against racial policies. The eyes of the world were on Birmingham through national TV coverage, and people saw snarling police dogs rip clothes off demonstrators and marchers knocked down by powerful fire hoses. Martin Luther King, Jr., came to help organize the demonstration and was jailed, and that drew additional national and world attention.

The Sixteenth Street Baptist Church is located near downtown Birmingham, and it served as a convenient place to organize the demonstration. As we will see shortly, in the mind of some white people this church became a symbol of the Civil Rights Movement.

As a result of the demonstrations, the white community made some concessions — lunch counters were no longer closed to black people, and the Federal courts ordered the city to open its schools to all races. (However, a local judge publicly declared that the desegregation of schools did not apply to Birmingham.) The concessions further enraged many segregationists, and they often vented their hostility by bombing the homes of ministers and leaders of the Civil Rights Movement.

Pape recalls, it was a common experience, while watching evening TV to hear, "We interrupt this program to bring you this news bulletin." And it would be another bombing. Pape explained a frequently used technique: First a small bomb went off which usually only caused minor damage; and then, when the community gathered to see what happened, a larger explosion was set to go off. The second bomb was designed to hurt and kill.[2]

It was a dangerous time. Ellwanger lived next door to St. Paul's Church in the black community, and the elders of the church often stood guard at their pastor's home with their shotguns at the ready.[3]

Pape received anonymous phone calls, such as one that said, "If a nigger ever walks into your church, I'll blow it up." "People were scared to death — on both sides," he said. He added, "There was a lot of fright that went on, and not too much rationality."[4]

It was a long hot summer in 1963, and Birmingham was sitting on a powder keg with a short fuse. There were so many acts of violence and bombings during the spring and summer that the city became known as "Bombingham."

Then, one Sunday morning --

September 15, 1963 - Addie Mae Collins, Denise McNair, Carole Robertson, and Cynthia Wesley, schoolgirls, were killed in the bombing of Sixteenth Street Baptist Church, Birmingham.

130

September 15, 1963 - Virgil Lamar Ware, 13-year-old youth killed during wave of racial violence, Birmingham.[5]

The booklet *Free At Last* describes the scene at the Baptist Church:

> It was Youth Sunday at Sixteenth Street Baptist Church... The preacher had prepared a sermon especially for the children. The youth choir would lead the congregation in music, and children would serve as ushers...
>
> In the basement ladies' lounge of Sixteenth Street Baptist Church, four girls were chatting nervously and straightening their fancy white dresses. In a few minutes, the worship service would begin. Addie Mae Collins, 14, and Denise McNair, 11, were in the choir. Carole Robertson and Cynthia Wesley, both 14, had been chosen to serve as ushers.
>
> Only a few feet away, beneath a stone staircase along the outside wall of the church, a dynamite bomb had been planted eight hours earlier. At 10:22, it exploded. The whole church shook. Plaster and debris fell around the people in Sunday School upstairs. The four girls in the ladies' lounge were killed instantly.[6]

That explosion shattered the church building and certainly the lives of four families. But it shattered much more. It shattered the illusion which many Southerners held that the race problem would somehow go away and nothing would change from the old ways. It shattered the complacency of many whites who had been indifferent and were willing to leave the problem to others. It brought people to a conscious awareness to ask, "If they can bomb a church and kill little girls, what is to keep them from doing anything else?"

Martin Luther King, Jr., added: "The innocent blood of these little girls may well serve as the redemptive force that will bring new light to this dark city.... Indeed, this tragic event may cause the white South to come to terms with its conscience."[7]

The Lutheran Church, which had largely stood on the sidelines as far as racial activities were concerned, was suddenly drawn into the vortex of the racial storm because the explosion touched two of its own.

Denise McNair and her mother were members of the Baptist Church, but, Chris, her father, was a member of St. Paul's Lutheran. Cynthia Wesley was a frequent visitor at the newly-formed Prince of Peace Lutheran Mission where John Oppliger was pastor.[8]

Denise was the only child of the McNairs. At the time of the explosion, the father was quoted in *The Lutheran Witness*, saying,

> "I firmly believe that the Gospel of Jesus Christ has the answers to our problems. [The chief need of] the culprits who committed the crime," he added, "is for repentance and Christian forgiveness. God has given man the intelligence to build a true democracy," he added, "and now it's up to us to pray that the Spirit of Christ will move the hearts of people to act wisely."[9]

Chris McNair is a man of clear and strong convictions which he expresses with an unmistakable and firm voice. In 1996, when I interviewed him he was serving as a commissioner of Jefferson County, the Birmingham area. I was ushered into his imposing office and told that I would have 25 minutes for the interview — and that was exactly the time I was granted.

During the interview, I read his quotes in the *Witness* to him, and asked if he had any other thoughts at the time. He admitted that he wasn't angry at white people in general; but, however, if he could have gotten his hands on the people who did the bombing, it might have been different, he added.[10]

☩ ☩ ☩

The day after the bombing, nine Lutheran pastors gathered in Birmingham and drew up a statement which was to be read the following Sunday. Because of the volatile reaction to the statement, it is here given in its entirety:

132

The Christian church should never dodge an issue that involves the life, practice, and the Christian confession of its people. Our community has been stunned by the loss of life through the bombing of a church in Birmingham, Alabama, on Sunday, September 15, 1963.

This act of violence is the responsibility of a man or a group of men. The guilt of such violence is also ours because we did not heed the Savior's directive that "we love one another." To the extent that we have supported forced segregation by our words or silence, we have given encouragement to such lawlessness. We must repent.

We as Lutheran Christians are compelled by the Word of God to believe that the church is not a segregated community. We are one in Christ. The members of our congregations as part of the body of Christ therefore have no right to segregate any member of that body.

The Lutheran Church - Missouri Synod has reiterated its stand on this issue in a resolution of June 1959, which reads: "It is wrong for the Christian to try to justify any kind of racial discrimination.

"We acknowledge our responsibility as a church to provide guidance for our members to work in the capacity of Christian citizens for the elimination of discrimination wherever it may exist in community, city, state, nation, and world."[11]

The statement was submitted to the Synod's College of Presidents (Synod's President, Vice Presidents and all the District Presidents) which met a week later, and they drew up a resolution which endorsed the Birmingham statement and offered encouragement and support for the pastors.[12]

In its October 1, 1963, issue *The Lutheran Witness* editorialized:

The bombing of a church during worship and Sunday school sessions is a vicious, brutal crime against God and the human heart....

There are those who protest the entry of churches into the racial question. "Lay off," they say. "This is a social issue. The churches should stick to preaching the Word of God." Also: "Why is segregation a sin today if it was not morally wrong 100 years ago?"

Part of the answer to both objections would be that only belatedly have some churches come to grasp that the Gospel of Christ has social implications.... Churches will not shape the thinking of Christians and exert an influence on society unless they identify themselves with moral issues of the day. Because segregation is high on the list, Christians must speak and act on the racial issue.[13]

The Funeral, and Controversy

A mass funeral for three of the four girls was planned, and Dr. King was asked to return to Birmingham to give the message. Since the Sixteenth Street Baptist church was unuseable, the service was held at the Sixth Avenue Baptist Church. With a seating capacity of 800 to 900, the church was packed with worshipers, while many others stood in the streets. A tiny sprinkling of perhaps a dozen white people were present. Pastor Joe Ellwanger was on the platform because he had been asked by the McNairs to read a Lesson during the service.[14]

Three other white Lutheran pastors were also at the funeral. They were Martin Buerger of First, Jim Pape of Vestavia Hills, and Harold Woodworth of Concordia. In that sense, the funeral represented a coming together among Lutheran pastors in support of integration. Buerger remembers the highly-charged atmosphere at the funeral, and the uneasiness the three felt because they were such a tiny minority in the black gathering.[15]

Homrighausen and Ellwanger often saw things from a different viewpoint in those years of racial turmoil, and the funeral produced an open disagreement between the two. Homrighausen advised Ellwanger not to participate in the funeral because by doing so he would expose himself to further threat and danger from the segregationists. Furthermore, according to the understanding of the Lutheran Church - Missouri Synod, participation would be considered unionism. But Ellwanger followed his own counsel with this response:

> I am serving as pastor of the father of one of these girls. He asked me - he and his wife asked me - to lead their family in prayer before the funeral and to participate in the funeral, and I am going there as a witness to the Gospel; and I will be there.[16]

The Fallout From the Explosion

The fallout from the explosion was almost instantaneous in the Birmingham community and affected two Lutheran congregations in particular: First Lutheran and Concordia. Since Buerger was alerted within hours after the 1963 Convention that the integration of the black churches into the District would not be well received at First Lutheran, we will follow that story first.

The First Lutheran Story[17]

First Lutheran, Birmingham

Established in 1887, First Lutheran is the mother church among Lutherans in Birmingham. When first organized it was known as Zion Lutheran, but in 1948 when Trinity on the west side was organized as the second Missouri Synod Lutheran church in the area, Zion was renamed First Lutheran. Their sanctuary is of a stately Gothic design and is located in what once was Birmingham's best neighborhood. Hans Reuter served as pastor of the congregation for 50 years. He was a feisty little man, stern and authoritarian, typically *der Herr Pastor.*

Martin Buerger, considered one of the outstanding young pastors of the District, was serving in Florence, AL, when he was called to First. After declining the first Call, he was issued the Call a second time, and this time accepted and was installed on July 9, 1961. At the 1963 Convention, he was elected to the District Board of Directors, but that was met with criticism by some in the congregation, because they felt he was too much of an up-and-coming pastor.[18] On the racial issue he was part of the large middle ground of pastors who took a moderate stance, and was not nearly as confrontational as, for example, Joe Ellwanger.

Martin A. Buerger

Nevertheless, Buerger did not ignore the race question. At the 1960 Convention the Southern District had adopted "The Guidelines for Discussion" with the intent that all congregations were to study the "Thirteen Theses" and the related sections of Scripture. Buerger introduced this study at First, but as he recalls it, the congregation went through the motions of studying the material, and then by a vote of 7 for, 67 against, and 3 abstaining, rejected the "Thirteen Theses." That vote was a portent of what was to come.

When the racial turmoil came to Birmingham as the aftermath of the bombing which killed the four girls, Buerger was still relatively new at First Lutheran. And when he read the statement that was drawn up afterwards, his standing in the congregation was immediately challenged. The reaction came swiftly, and in short order a meeting of the voters was called. The following resolution was adopted: "Pastor Buerger shall not make any social statements. He shall preach the word of God, and not delve into the political side. Therefore, every sermon of his and every public announcement shall first be looked at by the board of elders."

Ironically, Buerger was not a racial activist and was not inclined to make social statements.. Nevertheless, he considered the resolution an undermining of the pastoral office, and therefore did not consent to its constraints. Now the lines of the battle were drawn.

Very quickly Jim Pape, the Circuit Counselor, was pulled into the conflict; but he was not held in high regard at First since he had started a new congregation in Vestavia Hills and had drawn away some members of

First. As is so often the case, the congregation did not want to deal with a Circuit Counselor and wanted to "go to the top," which meant Homrighausen was called in to deal with the controversy.

As Homrighausen remembers it, by the time he visited the congregation the fury of some of the members at First was as white-hot as one of Birmingham's steel smelters. His New York accent became an issue, and he was asked, "Where were you born?" implying that since he was not a Southerner he could not understand the problem. He claims that he responded saying, "You asked the wrong question. Ask me if I am born again." His polio limp became the source of a threat as well, when one of the members said, "You limped when you came in here, and you're going to limp worse when you leave."

In another recollection, he remembers this exchange: One man said, "Let me get this straight. If we don't bring niggers into our church, you're going to kick us out of the Missouri Synod?" To which Homrighausen said, "I don't have the authority to kick you out of the Missouri Synod, but I would strongly recommend that you would seek membership elsewhere because you are not keeping in step with what the Church teaches and what Scripture teaches."

"And with that, a hymnal came flying through the air and hit me in the head," Homrighausen continued. "And I started to bleed. And Luther Loesch, mild-mannered Luther Loesch, was going to go after him. I'll never forget it!" (As Second Vice President of the District, Loesch also was drawn in to help with the controversy.)

As this was going on, Buerger was harassed with anonymous "You nigger-lover" phone calls at all hours of the night; and rumors were rampant, such as, "He has a busload of Niggers around in the bushes, and he's going to bring them all into the church." He continued to conduct services and to preach in a very Gospel-oriented way; nonetheless, the members found fault with his preaching. One woman protested, "You certainly don't preach against something that all of the members agree with."

Very soon it became obvious that Homrighausen was considered *persona non grata* at First Lutheran, and since nothing was being resolved, Roland Wiederaenders, the First Vice President of the Missouri Synod, was asked to moderate the situation. Homrighausen said that he warned

Wiederaenders about what he could expect, telling him, "They're going to tear you apart. They're going to rip you up one side and down the other." "Oh, no," Wiederaenders, the kind-hearted Texan, responded "They're going to listen."

Later, in a mailing called *Southern Official Summary* which was sent to all District pastors, Homrighausen described the meeting as follows:

> We called upon Dr. Wiederaenders for his help in the hope that if our presence was not acceptable, perhaps, the Vice President of Synod could persuade the people of First Lutheran to change their ways. Dr. Wiederaenders began with a stirring devotion on the Good Samaritan. It wasn't long before he was interrupted, heckled, and ridiculed by those attending the meeting. His devotion was interrupted several times with the same heinous reaction to the truth he was speaking. Finally, in humility and with a heavy heart, he turned to the chairman and said, "Please, I cannot go on with such behavior. Please, have respect for the Word of God." The chairman asked for order. A reasonable amount of order was restored, but it was too late. The disgracing and the despising of God's Word had taken place. Those of us who represented the District and Synod were shocked, amazed, and hurt.[19]

Later in that same mailing, Homrighausen wrote:

> During that meeting several false accusations were made against me and Pastor Buerger. When Dr. Wiederaenders asked me to speak in reply, a raucous cry came from the audience with the shouts of "No." The chairman did not give me the floor. It was nothing new. I had been denied that privilege at a previous meeting with this same congregation.[20]

Several factors were at the core of the controversy. To begin with, on the Sunday after the four girls were killed, Buerger read the statement that had been drawn up. He read it from the pulpit, not from the chancel floor as one of the announcements. According to some observers, it is a widely held impression among Lutherans that something which is read from the pulpit is considered "the Word of God," or something close to it.

138

According to John Windhorst, who was president of the congregation at the time, the gist of the conversation outside the sanctuary after the service clearly was, "We can't have that!"

A second factor was that the people in the congregation took the statement literally and personally, especially the part which stated, "The guilt of such violence is also ours because we did not heed the Savior's directive that 'we love one another.'" The response of many in the congregation was, "We are not guilty of anything; we didn't kill anybody." Another part of the statement which stuck in the craw of the members was the sentence, "To the extent that we have supported forced segregation by our words and silence, we have given encouragement to such lawlessness." Those who were segregationists at heart saw no reason to repent for their "words and silence."

A third factor was Thesis 11 in "The Guidelines for Discussion," which were adopted at the 1960 Convention. That thesis stated, "It is Scripturally defensible for a congregation to practice segregation when the practice of integration would mean — a. the weakening or disrupting of their own congregation [and] b. the curtailment of their missionary outreach...." The segregationists in the congregation saw that as a loophole and took refuge in that thesis, arguing that the congregation was autonomous and could make its own decision in this case.

Furthermore, many white Southerners, Lutherans included, did not consider segregation either wrong or evil, but saw it as an *adiaphora*, something that is morally neutral, neither right nor wrong; and therefore every congregation had the right to make its own decision.

A fourth factor was a major misunderstanding between pastor and congregation and vice versa. According to some recollections, the elders of the congregation interviewed Buerger before issuing him the Call, a practice which was highly unusual in those days. According to Windhorst, Buerger accepted the Call with the understanding that he would not upset their way of life; namely, their racial policy. Buerger insists that he never agreed to that understanding; nevertheless, when he read the statement on September 22, the leaders of the congregation felt that he had broken the agreement.

One more factor must be mentioned. At his retirement, Hans Reuter was designated Pastor Emeritus, giving him a significant role in the congregation, and he supported the segregationist view. Windhorst remembers that Reuter's counsel was, "Birds of a feather flock together" and that the colored should stay in their own place.

Consequently, after 31 meetings, according to Buerger's count, one more meeting was held — in secret — on November 10. Buerger was to learn of the meeting the next morning from the church custodian, who reported finding extensive debris on the church grounds, including empty cups and empty liquor bottles.

After that meeting the pastor was handed a resolution from the voters which stated that "the pulpit of First Lutheran Church, Birmingham is declared vacant," and "that Pastor Buerger shall be out of the church office by November 30 and that he shall be out of the parsonage by December 15." Buerger protested the action of the voters; but, after consulting with Oliver Harms, the President of the Missouri Synod, he was advised that under the circumstances he would be better off to leave instead of insisting that this was still his pulpit.

◊   ◊   ◊

November 22, 1963 - President John F. Kennedy was assassinated.

◊   ◊   ◊

Buerger remembers that he and his wife were still in Birmingham agonizing over what steps they were to take next when the news of Kennedy's assassination came. "What are we going to do? Where are we going to go?" they were asking. The Synod had offered to pay his salary, pension, and health care for three months, and he could do anything he wanted to. That day the Buergers decided that he would return to school, and they moved to St. Louis a few days later.

The saga of First Lutheran, however, does not end here. With their move to St. Louis, Buerger became a member of the Missouri District where he filed an appeal to clear his name, because his removal at First carried the implication that he was guilty of false doctrine. His appeal, however, was delayed repeatedly and eventually no decision was rendered.

After Buerger was ousted, Pastor Emeritus Reuter returned to the pulpit and served for the next 18 months.

In the meantime, on November 23, President Homrighausen suspended both First Lutheran and Interim Pastor Reuter. The matter then went to the Southern District Board of Appeals, and on the basis of a by-law technicality the suspension was ruled invalid. Homrighausen had made a statement about the situation in the *Southern Official Summary* which was sent to all pastors,[21] and that was contrary to the by-law which required silence from both parties prior to a hearing.

At the 1964 Convention the District President lifted the suspension with the understanding that negotiations between the two parties would begin again. Thereupon, Henry Schaefer, delegate from First Lutheran, was given the floor. After making reference to the priceless sovereignty of the congregation, he concluded with his pledge to work together with District officials by saying he was "happy to hear Dr. Homrighausen say that we can work out our problems and we'll gladly do that together. And I sincerely hope that this will be a step forward to bring unity in our District. There's nothing greater than to have unity in love."[22]

During the pastoral vacancy, Pastor Kennell of Montgomery was called, but declined. In April 1965, Gerald Quiram, a native Texan, accepted the Call to First. He claims that for his installation Homrighausen was still not welcome, and Vice President Loesch from Pensacola officiated. The race issue was not dormant either, because the installation service was deliberately set for Sunday morning to avoid inviting the other congregations of the area. Nevertheless, St. Paul congregation sent a black delegation but they were turned away at the door.

Sometime in 1965 or later, another turn-away at the door took place. By then Mary Lynn Buss, a Prince of Peace Volunteer was working with Ellwanger at St. Paul's. According to Ellwanger's recollection,

> She decided one Sunday morning to take a group of Sunday School children to First Lutheran, thinking that if there was any point of entry where maybe they could have gotten into First and help nurture them along a bit, it might have been that children and youth would be more acceptable than a bunch of grown-ups.

When they arrived at First, they were turned away; and that incident helped to keep the tension alive between those two congregations.

Quiram maintains that he tried to understand the thinking of the congregation and that he followed a very cautious approach by restricting his preaching to a series of sermons following Luther's Large Catechism. He avoided any mention of either integration or segregation. Nonetheless, when he ended the series on the theme of Christian love, some members inferred that he was advocating integration.

Dr. Wiederaenders, Synod's First Vice President, returned to First Lutheran several times to provide guidance and assistance for Quiram. To help him keep a balanced approach to his ministry, Quiram asked three of his schoolmates — J. C. Henning, Harold Hermetz and Ron Reinhardt — to serve as his advisors. Hermetz remembers that they met with him several times and cautioned him to go slow and work with the people and get them to study the Word. Reinhardt felt that Quiram was faced with a degree of antipathy from other pastors and congregations because he was willing to serve First Lutheran and that the advisors mainly provided him with friendship and encouragement.

Quiram cited the work of Henry Schaefer, who became a leader in behalf of an open door policy in the congregation. The discussions which Schaefer led resulted in a vote on the question of opening the door to black people. The vote was a tie, the chairman voted "Nay," and it was not passed. Despite the failure, Quiram took it as a sign of progress, because in Buerger's time the congregation had rejected the "Thirteen Theses" by a vote of 7 for, 67 against, and 3 abstaining.

Despite the progress which was made, Quiram continued to experience opposition in the congregation, as well as threatening phone calls, and the pressure began to take a toll on his health. In December 1967 he accepted a Call to Oklahoma. Quiram noted that shortly after he left, within a matter of months, three of the most ardent segregationists in the congregation died; and their death caused a shift in the racial attitude within the congregation.

Next Ron Reinhardt, of Decatur, AL, was called to First, but he declined. In June 1969, J. Mark Kuehnert came as the next pastor. When Kuehnert, who had earlier served in a black congregation, received the Call, he made clear in an interview that he could accept the Call only if the congregation had an open-door policy. By now the congregation had moderated enough to make that agreement.

Kuehnert recalls that a few were still unhappy with the policy, but they became a silent minority. He recalls only one negative flare-up which occurred about two years after he arrived. A Youth Gathering was held at First, and when one family saw that black youth were present, they left immediately and that week withdrew their membership. During Kuehnert's 23-year ministry at First, the congregation received its first black members, a black man sang in their choir, and a black woman took her turn to read Scripture Lessons from the lectern.[23]

Looking back at that troublesome time, Windhorst, a Long Island native, who moved to Birmingham in 1949, asserted that the people in the 1960s had no objections to the black people worshiping at First Lutheran, if they really wanted to worship, but they resented the pushy ones, the ones who came to stir up trouble. Such is the perception in retrospect, but the troubling question remains: How were they to discern who was pushy and who came to worship?

It is significant to note that when the Statement[24] was drafted after the church-bombing, some criticized it as a "humanistic and sociological" statement. Likewise, the congregation ordered Buerger not to make any further social statements. The irony is that the congregation was largely a reflection of society as it was seen at that time; they simply did not want their social mores changed.

Others were of the opinion that the issue was forced on First Lutheran; however, that argument has little validity, since strong opposition continued even when Quiram employed a very moderate approach. The force, if it is to be called that, came with the bombing at Sixteenth Street Baptist Church. That bombing had an impact which woke up many people — either for good or for evil.

The Concordia Lutheran Story[25]

As part of the expanding mission outreach which Reinboth promoted, a new congregation was formed in the Northeast section of Birmingham, a primarily blue-collar neighborhood, and was called

Concordia. Work began in 1957 when a new seminary graduate, Ed Schwanke, came to canvass the area. The first activities of the newly-gathered group were fellowship meetings, and at the third such meeting, the group decided to call their new congregation St. Luke. One week later they changed their mind and chose Concordia. (It is now known as Haven of Hope Christian Fellowship.) In April 1962, after the congregation was successfully established, Schwanke accepted a Call to Illinois. By that time the congregation had grown to 217 baptized members and 126 confirmed.[26]

On August 26, 1962, Harold Woodworth was installed as Concordia's second pastor. Woodworth had served previously in New Orleans and was a member of the District Mission Board and Chairman of the District Evangelism Committee. Thus he had just one year under his belt in Birmingham when the four girls were killed in the bombing. Soon after he arrived, he had a frightening introduction to life in Alabama. He tells of an experience which came after the Evangelism Committee had a meeting at the church served by Herzfeld in Tuscaloosa, AL. As he was leaving Tuscaloosa, he realized that he was being followed, and he relates what happened:

> They put a tail on me and did everything they could to try to force me off the street in Tuscaloosa, and I just would not get pulled over. And then when we got to the edge of town, I put the hammer down, and they tried every way they could to run me off the road. And I felt in my mind, knowing the history of the Ku Klux Klan in Tuscaloosa, and what they had done with Fackler, that this old boy better keep going, or I'd be the next guy hosed down out in the country. They tailed me about halfway [to Birmingham]. They ran up behind me, and they would push the car, and this was just a Beetle Bug. And they got up alongside of me and tried to force me off the side. Anyway, I got back to Birmingham, and that was a scary experience.

Woodworth kept a diary in which he recorded his pastoral experiences, and he wrote as follows:

144

The explosion that killed those children...now had aftershocks from the reading of the statement.... The members of Concordia paused long enough to leave the church quietly, but then the storm hit. Special congregational meetings were called and protests were signed and presented. The congregation was polarized and, with deep concern for the churches of Birmingham, the Synodical President, Oliver Harms, sent First Vice President Roland Wiederaenders to assist me both pastorally and as a counselor during the meetings that were being held both at Concordia and elsewhere in the city.

Woodworth faced an added tension because while this was going on he was also serving as vacancy pastor at Zion in Bessemer, a black congregation; and some members of Concordia voiced the fear that he would bring some of Zion's members to worship at Concordia. He noted another area of conflict, which he recorded in his diary —

Concordia was a subsidized congregation of the District, and because I was associated with the Mission Board which supervised the work of ninety percent of the congregations, formal efforts were made from within the congregation, aided by outside legal counsel, to remove me from office. The rationale was simple. If the segregationists could get their way into a subsidized congregation in Birmingham, then they could exercise the same control in other congregations throughout the District. There was one matter they did not contend with. Since my arrival in Birmingham I had moved the congregation to grant women the right to vote at congregational meetings. This, along with an influx of new members, saved the day. One Sunday I was voted out of office. During the week I was in New Orleans for a District Evangelism Conference. The reaction of the people while I was gone created a wave of support and a petition for another meeting the following Sunday. The women of the congregation rallied this cause, and on the following Sunday a majority vote reinstated me as pastor. At this point, the segregation members arose and left.

When the split occurred at Concordia, word circulated throughout the District that the scene of the separation at that congregational meeting was "like Judgment Day" - this one stayed and that one left. Some of those who left eventually joined First Lutheran and others apparently remained unaffiliated.

The harassment that so often occurred in racial disputes also showed up at Concordia. Woodworth remembers that a cross was burned on their lawn and they received threatening phone calls. One threat stated, "Don't get into your car, because it's going to blow up." Fortunately, it didn't. One family had donated a piano for the church, and after they severed their relationship with the congregation let it be known that "they didn't want black ears to hear any music from that piano."

In his regular column "Of such is the Kingdom of God", Reinboth, in the February 18, 1964, *Lutheran Witness Supplement,* wrote the following observations about the experience at Concordia:

> You have heard much about Birmingham and the problems of the Southern District of the Lutheran Church in Birmingham. Perhaps not enough has been said about the people of one of these churches - Concordia, which is served by Pastor Harold Woodworth. This congregation met a crisis in the race issue and reacted in a most God-pleasing manner. The majority of the congregation resolved to let its doors be open for worship to any person regardless of race or color. The fact that it was a hard decision to come by and that the congregation has suffered in membership and in financial support consequently makes it all the more noteworthy. Without going into details, and without implying that everything that was done showed no fault or weakness, this column nevertheless wants to commend Concordia, Birmingham, and its pastor for the courageous way in which it reacted when the crisis arose. In working with this congregation the undersigned received invaluable assistance from Pastor Woodworth, President Homrighausen, Counselor Pape, and Vice President Wiederaenders. A special pat on the back goes to Robert Wilson, the chairman of the congregation, who presided over a number of difficult meetings and always demonstrated Christian patience and real strength![27]

Woodworth recalls that it was no easy picnic during that time, especially for his wife. Scripture and prayer were strong resources for them, and he emphasized "it was no canned prayer!" After less than two years at Concordia, in April 1964, he accepted a Call to Wisconsin.

The congregation then extended a Call to George Hrbek, whom we met earlier when he was in Selma, but who now was in New Orleans. Hrbek declined, and Victor Schulz, of Lake Charles, LA, was called next. He accepted and was installed on December 13, 1964. Did Schulz know what he was getting into when he went there? This was his response:

> Yes, I knew what I was getting into, but I have to say it wasn't a threatening thing as far as I was concerned. I realized that there had been some real agitation at First Lutheran and Concordia. But I thought I was needed there. I really did. I realized the split had already occurred. The issue was whether the church - Concordia - should have an open-door policy, and Woody had prevailed in that. Of course, about half the congregation took off, and the membership was probably down to about 70 people when I got there. Of all the people who left, only one family - one woman, Mrs. Robert Campbell and her three children - came back.

When Schulz arrived, he found that some of the founding members of the congregation were still there, and while some of them still opposed the open-door policy, they decided not to leave. As he put it, "we just carried on Gospel ministry," and a few years later the congregation officially integrated with the acceptance into membership of Henry Bythwood and Maggie, his wife, and their two teenage boys. They had moved into the area and transferred their membership from St. Paul's to Concordia.

Mr. Bythwood was a surprising candidate to join a white church. Ellwanger, who was pastor at St. Paul's, remembers that Bythwood was part of the old way of life among black people. Although Ellwanger lived right next door to the church in a black community, when Bythwood came to see the pastor he never came to the front door, but insisted on coming to the back door.

Schulz noted that a few members grumbled over the transfer of a black family, but added, "I was happy to see that happen, because we had gone through that whole ordeal of splitting the church, (and it was all theoretical) and then finally about three years [later] we were able to officially integrate without any fanfare."

Schulz served as pastor of Concordia for almost ten years; he left in August 1974, accepting a Call to Kansas. By comparison to First Lutheran, the healing came much sooner at Concordia; and Schulz obviously had a successful ministry there because, when he left, the congregation had grown to more than 200 communicants and over 300 baptized members.

A New Orleans Cauldron[28]

During the same time that Birmingham was having its racial fireworks, New Orleans was having its own boiling pot, and it was not a dish of savory gumbo. The scene was Our Savior Lutheran Church. Organized in 1952, Our Savior congregation, with a large school, was rapidly becoming one of the prominent Lutheran Churches in the city. Until 1957 their pastor, Paul Streufert, was the President of the Southern District. The Southern District Mission Executive, Reinboth, and his wife and family, were also members there.

The story about Our Savior comes into focus in late 1962. Albert Lehenbauer, their pastor, had accepted the Call to be hospital chaplain for the New Orleans area and the congregation was calling another pastor. The Call went out to George Hrbek of Selma, who, despite the urging of Reinboth, at first declined. The Call was issued to Hrbek a second time, and again Reinboth implored him, saying, "We need a witness in New Orleans to address the racism in the Lutheran Church." Because of his forthright approach to the race issue which he had demonstrated in Selma, Hrbek could provide such a witness. This time Hrbek accepted the Call, but immediately there were complicating factors.

According to Hrbek, the congregation was ready to adopt a policy to maintain its segregated status, and he accepted the Call on the condition that the resolution be tabled and the congregation be given an opportunity

148

to study the issue on the basis of Scripture. The congregation agreed to that.

Next came the decision of whether or not to invite the black pastors of the area to Hrbek's installation. Hal Kieschnick, who was the school principal, remembers that after a lengthy discussion the church council agreed to invite all the Lutheran pastors. Two or three black pastors attended the installation and took part in the ceremony. On the Monday following, one of the members blamed Kieschnick for inviting the black pastors, assuming that he had done so since he had handled some of the office administration during the vacancy. Despite the fact that he had nothing to do with the invitations, she claimed it would be the downfall and destruction of the congregation.

Hrbek arrived in September 1962, and by the beginning of 1963 a series of study sessions were planned to look at segregation in the light of Scripture. Just how many sessions were actually held is not clear; however, the congregation was sharply divided and the sessions apparently often generated more heat than light. On one occasion, Reinboth was sharply rebuffed when he read from the Lutheran Confessions. On another occasion, when a Scripture verse was read, a member shouted, "You don't believe that stuff, do you?"

The pot was also simmering among Roman Catholics in New Orleans; and in reaction against the Pope, a Catholic woman developed a study called "The Law of Separation." A member of Our Savior invited the woman to conduct a series of studies at Our Savior congregation. Kieschnick was invited to the first session, and remembers that the woman said that she would open the Scriptures, and would do it in her own sequence, and no one would be permitted to ask questions. However, she addressed the first question to him, asking, "What exactly was on the two tables of stone?" He answered, "The Ten Commandments." She said "Exactly?" and he again said, "The Ten Commandments," to which she countered, "Well, I can dismiss you, because you don't know what you're talking about." The series of studies on "The Law of Separation" had a very short run at Our Savior.

In the summer of 1963, the already heated situation at Our Savior was exacerbated when the school received an application from a black Lutheran family to enroll their child in kindergarten. After it was confirmed that the application came from a black family, Kieschnick reported it to the other faculty members. He wanted to keep them informed, but urged them to keep it quiet until it naturally come to the board of education for a decision. By seven o'clock the evening of the day he gave that information to the faculty, the chairman of the congregation called him and said, "I will meet you at the school and you will hand me that application, because I will personally reject it."

Kieschnick refused to yield to that demand and the boiling pot heated evermore in the weeks following, and the passion and fury of the discussion increased. Hrbek remembers incredible contradictions. At the beginning of a meeting the chairman said, "Pastor, lead us in prayer," and then during the meeting the discussion became so heated, that a member cursed the pastor and said, "Goddamn you, you son of a bitch! You're going to bring those niggers into our church!" In one voters' meeting a member of the church council physically charged the pastor, aiming to hit him. Fortunately the member's wife jumped between the two. On such occasions, both piety and civility left the room.

In the meantime, the school faculty was put under pressure and some were accused of teaching an integration theology. The faculty was divided, and Kieschnick remembers the pain when even some of his close friends told him to leave. They claimed he did not understand their reasons for not accepting the black child.

While the congregation was embroiled in this conflict, their worship services were well attended, sometimes with standing room only. Many came to "defend" their church from social change. The intensity of feelings sometimes led to irrational reactions. Hrbek remembers walking down the aisle at the beginning of a worship service and a person blurted out, "Here he comes with the Bible again!" One Sunday, as he mentioned "love" in the sermon, a woman stood up and screamed "I HATE love!" On the Sunday after President Kennedy was assassinated, some of the women asked to drape the altar in black to express their sorrow over the death of the President, and this was done. Others, however, drew the conclusion that the pastor had ordered the altar covered in black because the black child's application had been rejected.

Eventually, early in 1964, the controversial resolution to keep all non-whites out of the congregation was placed on the agenda. The very well-attended voters assembly voted two to one in favor of the resolution. The following Sunday, Hrbek announced that he could not in good faith celebrate the Lord's Supper because the Body of Christ was divided.

Then the pastor resigned, and here the details become murky. According to Hrbek, he resigned as pastor of Our Savior in protest against the vote, and registered the protest with the Southern District President and the Board of Directors. Some thought he had also resigned from the ministry of the Missouri Synod. He remained in New Orleans and sold office supplies to support his family. During this time, he received a number of calls, which indicates that he was still on the Missouri Synod pastoral roster. Eventually he accepted a call to Altus, Oklahoma.

Another aspect about Hrbek's resignation needs to be noted. He wanted to discuss the grounds for his protest at a voters meeting; but the chairman of the congregation refused to call a meeting, claiming that Hrbek had resigned and there was nothing to discuss. The boiling pot had finally spilled over, and it was an ugly ending.

The congregation then called William Kennell of Montgomery as their pastor. After he declined the Call, he was called the second time. This time he accepted and served there until he retired.

In 1967 Dr. Robert Preus, of Concordia Seminary in Springfield, IL, was invited to Our Savior for a Sunday afternoon Reformation presentation. Jim Brockmann, who was serving a mostly black congregation nearby, brought two carloads of his members to the service. As he remembers it, a hush fell over the gathering as they entered. However, they were seated and welcomed, and thus, on the anniversary of the day when Martin Luther put up the 95 Theses, the racial barriers at Our Savior Lutheran came tumbling down.[29]

January 21, 1964 - Poll tax outlawed in federal elections.

The Jackson, Mississippi, Story[30]

The account of Jackson, MS, will trace the experiences of two congregations, Christ Lutheran, a white congregation, and St. Paul's, a black congregation. The two congregations were served by two long-time friends — Richard Kuehnert, Jr., at Christ and Bernard Ansorge at St. Paul's.

Both Kuehnert and Ansorge are gifted musicians and often served as the "official musicians" at district events. Kuehnert, the smaller of the two, is tense and as tightly-wound as a clock's spring while Ansorge is relaxed and easy-going. Despite the differences in personality, they both are friendly, outgoing and rarely at a loss for words.

We will first follow the happenings at Christ Lutheran because Kuehnert arrived in Jackson about a year before Ansorge. Later we will explore how the two pastors worked together to assist each other through this troublesome period.

After serving in the swamps of South Louisiana at Grace, Houma and Christ, Morgan City, Kuehnert accepted the Call to Christ Lutheran in September 1962. Christ was a mission congregation on the north side of Jackson which had been started by John Huber. When Kuehnert had the Call to Christ, he discussed the race question with the congregation and was assured that they had no problem if black people wanted to worship there.

All that changed just a year later. The racial tension in Central Mississippi continued to increase, especially with the arrival of a multitude of Civil Rights workers from the north. Kneel-ins were taking place, complete with attending photographers to record every Southern reaction to the pressure. The big downtown churches were targeted first, and the resultant publicity had the entire city in a stir. The perception grew among the members of Christ that since they were very visible on Highway 51 North they would soon be faced with a kneel-in, and they were determined that it would not happen there.

Here it is important to recall that Medgar Evers, a prominent local Civil Rights leader, was gunned down in Jackson on June 12, 1963. The assassination of Evers brought national attention to Jackson and increased the tension between the races.

A resolution not to allow black worshippers was presented to the voters at Christ Lutheran. Kuehnert proposed that the congregation study the question before voting. According to one account, a study session was held; but when the pastor began a Bible study, he was rebuffed by one member who supposedly said, "Pastor Kuehnert, you can teach us the Bible all night, but we already know how we're going to vote." And vote they did, in October 1963. By a count of 13 to 12 they passed the closed-door resolution. Kuehnert was severely disappointed — "crushed" was his word for it — by the passage of the resolution, and according to him "that hung over me like a black cloud." The one consolation was the close vote. Getting that resolution off the books became the all-consuming emphasis of his ministry for the next several years. He admits that he was so focused and absorbed by that effort that he was not a very good husband and father during those years.

On the night the resolution passed, Kuehnert told the voters that he would not rest until that resolution was removed, and he assured them that he was "going to love them through it." With a single-mindedness of purpose, he worked with the conviction that the Spirit works through the Word and changes hearts. As he recalls, he included some references in his sermons to the race issue, without over-reaching or over-stretching the point. As he put it, "it would just naturally come out of the text and the preaching, and I would make an applicable point about the nature of the church being inclusive."

May 2, 1964 - Henry Hezekiah Dee and Charles Eddie Moore, killed by the Klan, Meadville, Mississippi.

Kuehnert recalls one man, a founding member of the congregation, a staunch segregationist, who vowed that if a black person ever came into that church to worship he was going to leave the church. But he wasn't going to leave the church entirely; instead, he would sit under one of the trees in the front yard by the edge of the highway and whoever wanted to come and pray with him there could do so.

Several years later this gentleman came to the pastor and announced that he had had a change of heart and was now ready to accept what Scripture says and was prepared to say so publicly. Four weeks later he died of a massive heart attack. Many people in the congregation were not aware of the man's change of heart; nevertheless, shortly thereafter, in May 1966, the resolution was again brought to the voters. This time it was taken off the books by the same vote: 13 for and 12 against.

Six months later the congregation had black members. A Lutheran from Ghana had come to serve on the faculty at nearby Tougaloo College. He and his family were welcomed at Christ Lutheran.

Having come through the struggle over the open-door policy, Kuehnert now felt free to consider a Call to another congregation. In the Fall of 1966, he received and accepted the Call to Grace Lutheran in Huntsville, AL, the congregation I had served until March of that year. But the account of Kuehnert's ministry in Jackson is not yet finished. We will return to it later to see how he worked in concert with Ansorge. First, we will pick up the account of Ansorge's experiences.

Bernie Ansorge graduated from Concordia Seminary in St. Louis in the Spring of 1963, and was assigned to start a new congregation in a black community in Jackson. Shortly after graduation, his friend, Richard Kuehnert, gave him this reassuring perspective of Jackson saying, "Racially this is probably the best place in the South to be, because there hasn't been much of a history of racial turmoil and everybody knows how to get along with everybody else."

Weeks later, when Medgar Evers was shot and killed, the racial climate changed drastically, and the races were polarized. The black community organized to demand their rights; and the white community in response, instead of integrating, simply closed the lunch counters and drained the swimming pools.

Ansorge and his wife found the welcome to Jackson something less than warm. On their first Sunday there, they attended a white congregation, and as the local pastor introduced them, he made mention that Ansorge was a new Lutheran pastor in town. The people responded with warmth, saying they were glad that another Lutheran congregation was getting under way. When the Ansorges returned the following Sunday, the welcome had

154

turned ice-cold because word had spread that he was assigned to work in the black community.

Finding a place to live proved to be a difficult experience for them; the obstacle was the fact that he worked in a black community. After living in an apartment for the first year, they started the process to purchase a home. They put money down on a brand new house which was still in the construction stage. When they returned from a two-week vacation, a "For Sale" sign was posted on the front lawn. The realtor hemmed and hawed about how he had to sell houses, but selling to someone who worked in the black community would not be good for his business.

Perplexed, Ansorge sought out a member at Christ Lutheran, a lawyer, who had befriended him. The lawyer, a native Mississippian, investigated and told Ansorge, "You are being blackballed. You will not be able to buy a house in this community through a realtor, because your name is on the blackboard of every realtor. If you're going to buy a house, you'll have to buy it from a private owner." Ansorge remembers explaining, "This is not me buying a house, it's the Southern District." (The District Church Extension Fund was providing the loan.) But the attorney said, "I don't care who it is on the paper; it's you buying the house, and people are not going to sell a house to you." After that Ansorge asked himself, "What have I done to bring this sort of hostility to the fore?"

Following the advice of the lawyer, the Ansorges found a house for sale by an owner and put down earnest money. And then almost the same thing happened again. The seller asked, "Level with me, just who are you?" Ansorge said, "I am a Lutheran pastor." And the owner said, "I know that's what you told me, but *who are you?* What are you trying to do in this community?" "I am starting a Lutheran Church," was the answer, to which the owner said, "Well, the word is out that you are a blockbuster, and if I sell this house to you, the whole community is going down the tubes." A few days after that conversation, the owner said that he had changed his mind and was not moving out of Jackson after all, took the house off the market, and returned the down payment.

Ansorge was now even more troubled, and thought, "Is this the way it's going to be? Does the Lord really want me here in Jackson?"

About ten days later, the homeowner called to say that he had changed his mind and that the Ansorges could buy the house after all. The owner acknowledged that he had been to see his priest and confessed that he had lied about not moving. With that experience, Ansorge felt a new appreciation for the Catholic Church.

They bought the house, and now the wife of the seller wanted to go out of her way to welcome Grace, Ansorge's wife. Before they moved out, the lady invited all the neighborhood women in for a tea. At the gathering, one of the women said to Grace, "You look OK. We like you. And you can have coffee with us when you move here. But don't bring your husband." Grace's response was something like, "If you don't want my husband, you don't want me." After that the warmth of the welcome rapidly disappeared, and the Ansorges had no close friends in that neighborhood.

Living there, Ansorge remembers, was not without fear. Along with the morning newspaper, they often found the *Klan Ledger* on their front lawn. The *Ledger* spread the propaganda of the Klan and was designed to instill fear. Ansorge wondered who was throwing it on his lawn, until one day he discovered that their neighbor across the street distributed the Klan paper.

One evening, several months after they moved into the house, Ansorge noticed that as he drove into the carport a man came walking up the driveway behind him. Thinking the man was a panhandler, Ansorge engaged him in a conversation, which went as follows,

> He said, "Are you a Lutheran pastor?" And I said, "Yes." He said, "Oh, good." He said, "I'm a Lutheran." And I thought, "Here it comes." He said, "Welcome to our community...and this is *our* community." He was a member of the LCA church downtown, or so he said. And he just wanted me to know that I was welcome to the community. And then he said, "You are starting a black church, aren't you?" And I said, "Yeah," thinking maybe this guy is going to be friendly after all. And he said, "We're real proud of you." He was disarming me, and I said, "What makes you so proud of me?" And he said, "Well, you haven't brought any black people over here for meetings yet." And I said, "That's true. But how did you know that?" And he said, "We know everything about you." And he said, "'Well, I'll see you later.'" and he walked away across the

street and sat on top of the storm sewer cover underneath the light and like a hound dog just looked at our house.

Ansorge admitted that this form of intimidation contributed to an atmosphere of fear. Ansorge related a nighttime experience which is given below as he told it.

> One night Grace woke me up; it was about two o'clock. And she said, "They are shooting at our house!" And I said, "What?" And she said, "Wake up, Bernie, they're shooting at our house!" And just about this time I heard this big...it sounded like an explosion, like a shot. And she says, "Get the kids!" Well, I got down - I felt like I was in a war zone - I'm on my belly crawling through the hallway, into the kids' bedroom. They were fine. And she said, "Are you OK? Are you OK!? And I said, "Yeah." We were whispering real loud. And she said, "See who it is!" And so I looked out the front window, and I couldn't see a thing; and I looked out the carport window, and at the end of the carport I could see the tail end of a car that was on the street, and the rest was hidden by a fence. And I thought, "Oh, my gosh, somebody's parked right out there!" And I just lay down on the floor. I mean I just... Finally, I went back to bed. We were petrified. We got the kids into the bed with us. And there we were...we didn't know what was happening. Well, next morning I snuck out there, and that car was still there. And we didn't know whom to call, we just didn't know... Well, about that time a wrecker shows up, and this guy had had car trouble and it had back-fired several times. But it was just that kind of an atmosphere...

Ansorge's Call was to start a new mission in a black community, and his was the first such mission successfully started by a white pastor in Jackson by any denomination. His friendship with Kuehnert was helpful because Kuehnert had already been there for a year and had some familiarity with the power structure of the community. Together the two pastors worked to establish good public relations with community leaders, and in that way tried to alleviate the suspicion that normally arose in those days whenever a white person worked in the black community.[31]

In addition, they had a unique pipeline to the Klan. A member of Christ Lutheran, a lawyer, often represented Klan leaders. When either pastor introduced a new program in the congregation, or became involved in community activities which might be perceived as threatening, word was first given to the attorney, who, in turn, passed the information to leaders of the Klan.

June 21, 1964 - James Chaney, Andrew Goodman, and Michael Schwerner, Civil Rights workers, abducted and slain by the Klan, Philadelphia, Mississippi.

During the six years that Ansorge served in Jackson, St. Paul Congregation was established. He also served as vacancy pastor at St. Phillip's, the other black Lutheran congregation in Jackson. In addition, he served Our Savior Lutheran Church at Piney Woods, 25 miles south of Jackson; and that is a story that deserves some amplification.

Piney Woods (mentioned earlier when John Nau, the young seminary graduate, was teaching confirmation classes there) was a vocational school for black youth. The students lived in dormitories, and the school provided education for children as young as seven or eight years old up through about junior college age. George Schmidt, who for a time served as Superintendent of the Alabama/Upper Florida Conference, started the work there, and later Bill Wedig's father served there. At one time, the Piney Woods Lutheran congregation grew to 300 members. When the students left Piney Woods, they often provided the nucleus of congregations such as St. Phillip's in Jackson, as well as in many other places.

Three Sundays a month Ansorge conducted services at 8:00 AM for the entire student body, with an attendance up to 400. One Sunday a month, he returned at 12:30 PM to conduct a Communion Service for the remaining group of Lutherans still there. Eventually the Lutheran presence at Piney Woods ended, and it remains for further research to determine the reason.

In 1969, Ansorge followed Kuehnert to Huntsville, AL, when he accepted the Call to Ascension Lutheran, a predominantly white congregation.

Working it Out on the Local Level

We have seen the volatile reaction in two congregations in Birmingham following the bombing at the Sixteenth Street Baptist Church, and we have recorded the turmoil at Our Savior Lutheran in New Orleans. Furthermore, we have charted the course of the two pastors in Jackson, who while they experienced much personal anguish, not only survived their time of service there but also were able to see significant changes and successes.

During this same period of time, other congregations in the District were also dealing with the issue of integration on the local level. We will now look at several other congregations, by no means an exhaustive list, and for this survey will open the lenses for a look at a wider time span.

We have already noted the transition which took place at Immanuel in Pensacola. In a matter of months, they moved from having a resolution on the books which essentially kept black people out to a willingness to host the integrated Pastors Conference in 1962, and then the integrated District Convention in 1963. By the late 1960s, the congregation received its first black members.[32]

At Grace Lutheran in Huntsville, AL, the first integrated worship service took place in the summer of 1963. Four students from Alabama A & M, all women, called the church and asked if they could worship there; they were told that they were welcome. The issue of placing a restrictive resolution on the books never came up in that congregation, because, as noted earlier, the attitude in Huntsville about race was much different from the rest of the State. By way of illustration, when Governor Wallace "stood in the schoolhouse door" at the University, the school board of Huntsville, much to the chagrin of the governor, had already decided to desegregate.

However, when the four students came, some minor reactions were noticed. After they were seated, one member, a native of Birmingham, moved to a seat on the opposite side of the sanctuary as far away from them as he could get. Normally, as the worshipers left the sanctuary they crowded together to be greeted at the door. However, when the girls from A & M made their way out, I noticed they were surrounded by a buffer zone of three or four feet as though they were untouchables. Every Lutheran congregation claims to be a friendly church, but often the members are friendly only to each other. That morning the friendliness of the congregation took a back seat, and the students never returned.

According to John Nau, St. John's Lutheran in Hattiesburg had no serious conflict over integrating the congregation. He attributed that to the attitude provided by the academic community at the University of Southern Mississippi. By the early 1970s, the congregation received its first black family into membership.

Nau was involved when the University was to receive its first black student. Since Nau was an ordained minister and a full professor at the school, the University President asked him to serve as chaplain for the University and to work with other ministers to help maintain order on the campus. The prospective student, however, was jailed instead of admitted because when he arrived he supposedly had contraband on his person (whiskey, presumably "planted" on him).[33]

January 10, 1966 - Vernon Dahmer, black community leader, killed in Klan bombing, Hattiesburg, MS.

Ed Coyner, who was pastor at Messiah Lutheran in Vicksburg, MS, claims that the relationship between the races there was better before the Civil Rights Movement; however, when he left in 1965, the congregation ran into problems during the calling process for another pastor. Bernie Ansorge, of Jackson, MS, served as interim pastor, and he relates the following unique manner in which they dealt with the race question: When a pastor received their Call, he would write and ask, "What's the racial situation?" and the people at the voters assembly did not know how to answer that question. After a year's time, Ansorge had been invited to have a meal with virtually every family in the congregation; and during casual conversation, the individual members often made comments such as, "If it were just up to me, it wouldn't bother me at all if black people came to our church, but I don't think the congregation would accept that." After Ansorge heard that from enough individuals, he brought it up at a voters meeting after another pastoral candidate had raised the race question. He said in effect,

> If you can't answer, let me tell you how I think you would answer if you were individually writing these letters. You would accept them [black people], because you all told me that individually. So if you all told me that individually, let's just accept it, that's the position of this congregation.[34]

"They looked around at each other," Ansorge continued, " and they finally agreed that was the position of the congregation, and they wrote to the pastor and he accepted the Call."

Hal Hermetz encountered a typical situation when in early 1962 he came to be pastor of Faith Lutheran in Greenville, MS. In order to get to know the congregation, he read through the minutes of previous voters' meetings. He was surprised to find that prior to his coming the congregation had adopted a policy that stated if black people should come to their church they would be politely directed to a church of their own kind. But where would they be told to go? There was not another Lutheran Church for 100 miles, and certainly not a black Lutheran church.

Hermetz confronted the leaders and they argued that they were not prejudiced, but were afraid of what might happen to their standing in the community if they integrated their church. After considering the issue at several meetings, they changed the policy to declare that everyone was welcome at the Lord's House.

Many congregations were prompted to put a "whites-only" policy on the books because of the influx of Civil Rights Workers from the North. The congregation in Greenville was soon confronted by such visitors. A group from Detroit, which included a Lutheran, contacted the pastor and he told them they were welcome. The racially mixed group was welcomed

161

and ushered in. Hermetz remembers that total silence fell on the congregation; everything was suddenly quiet with none of the talking that usually goes on before service. Apparently the congregation was tense, wondering what would happen, or, as Hermetz said, "If lightning would strike, or something like that."

Although the Civil Rights workers did not return, Hermetz remembers that the congregation remained tense for a number of weeks, but no serious repercussions came to light.

By 1965, Homrighausen had left Cullman, AL, and returned to First English in New Orleans, and Hermetz accepted the Call to St. Paul's in Cullman. There he found that a certain uneasiness about racial mixing at the church still existed. When a black person attended a wedding at St. Paul's, sometimes the phone rang the next day with an anonymous inquiry about why black people were allowed to attend.[35]

Weisheit provided a different slant on how the congregation in McComb, MS, dealt with Civil Rights workers. On Thanksgiving morning one of the workers called for directions to the church. When the phone rang, a member, a native Southerner, a man who had left the Klan, answered and gave them directions. When the four young men and one woman, arrived they were warmly welcomed by the 15 to 20 worshipers. The Yale Divinity School students, who had expected to be kicked out, were surprised by the welcome and said to Weisheit, "Those people, didn't they know who we were?" To which the pastor responded, "No, they are so Christian that they didn't care."

Weisheit continued a dialogue with the students in the weeks following, in which they discussed the students' motivation and purpose. As a result, Weisheit later was invited to speak at Yale Divinity School, where he was met by a deep-seated prejudice against the South.[36]

In a number of congregations the racial barriers tumbled because the circuit pastors met together. Ron Reinhardt tells how that happened in Decatur, AL. The pastor's wife and some other women in the church provided a meal at the parsonage for the pastors. When the church leaders heard about that, they said, "Next time, you feed them here at the church."[37]

Weisheit had a similar experience when he came to Epiphany in Montgomery. He discovered that the circuit pastors had never met there previously. He put an item on the agenda for the church council to discuss an invitation. When the congregation chairman looked at the agenda, he asked, "What is this?" and Weisheit explained. The chairman, a native Southerner, said, "Are they Missouri Synod? If they are, we don't have to discuss this. They are invited." Thus the victory of the Gospel was celebrated quietly, and gradually doors were opened in congregation after congregation.[38]

When we moved to Shalimar, in the Florida Panhandle, in 1966, Good Shepherd congregation was already integrated and had four black members. Made up largely of military people, the congregation had declared an open-door policy at the outset.

Largely through Eleanor Reynolds, a Jewish convert to Christianity, the black people were introduced to Good Shepherd. She boldly canvassed the black "Quarters" and invited them to come with her. When the black visitors first showed up with her, however, a prominent business man who was attending Good Shepherd protested. John Ellermann, my predecessor, told him "Written in invisible ink over the entrance are the words of Jesus 'Whosoever cometh unto Me I will in no wise cast out.' — Would you be the first?" The man stopped coming. We also learned that racial prejudice is not limited to the South; the only member who left the congregation because of the integration was a native of North Dakota.[39]

The above examples are success stories in which local congregations crossed the hurdles of old racial barriers. My research is not exhaustive by any means, and surely there are many other good stories.

There was one more example, however, where a problem arose over the race issue. It took place at Trinity in Panama City, FL, and it came much later.

When Henry Storm was the pastor of Trinity, a black family came to him with interest in the Lutheran Church. They were not received into membership, however. Instead, Storm, who early in his ministry had been engaged in Negro missions in Detroit,[40] was quick to offer to work in the black community. A Vacation Bible School was held in the black community center, with a large turnout. Storm continued to work in the area as a preaching station; he baptized some children, and instructed others for confirmation. The work which he conducted became the nucleus for Redemption Lutheran Church which was organized in 1963.

In April of 1965, Pastor Storm died suddenly of a heart attack. He had served as president of the Bay County Ministerial Association and was very well known in the community. As a result several black pastors attended his funeral, and that was the first integrated gathering at Trinity.[41]

Ted Strelow of Dothan, AL, with two years' pastoral experience, was then called to Trinity. In 1962 Bob Schroeder, a new seminary graduate, had come to Panama City to continue the work in the black community and had become the first full-time pastor of Redemption. The two pastors quickly formed a strong friendship, and in their discussions of church life, they proposed to hold a joint Good Friday Service at Trinity. That was in 1967.

Prior to that, black people had been welcome at circuit events which were held at Trinity; however, those gatherings had raised some complaints among the members. When the joint Good Friday service was proposed, the "lid was blown off," and the issue was hotly discussed. In addition to the race issue, various other charges were raised against Strelow, leading to a concerted effort to remove him from the pastoral office. Several contentious meetings were held, which ultimately led to a voters' meeting during which Strelow was voted out. However, Bart Bartholomew, the chairman of the congregation, ruled that the vote was unconstitutional because no adequate grounds for removal were given.[42]

With that ruling, the faction that wanted Strelow ousted removed themselves, along with their considerable financial support, and formed a new congregation, Good Shepherd in Parker/Callaway, some 15 miles to the east of Trinity. Because of the fractious developments at Trinity, the integrated Good Friday Service was never held. Trinity congregation not only survived the split, but a year later conducted a joint Vacation Bible School with Redemption held at Trinity. Strelow left there in 1970 and accepted a Call to North Carolina. After many years of struggling, the congregation regained its size and vitality.

Reinboth Leaves the District

The name of O. H. Reinboth does not appear in this record as often, as does, for example, that of Edgar Homrighausen,. Homrighausen was District President and often made the news, while Reinboth, as Executive Secretary, worked behind the scenes and out of the limelight. However, when I interviewed Homrighausen, he said, "Anything you write with regard to this integration must have the name O. H. Reinboth."[43]

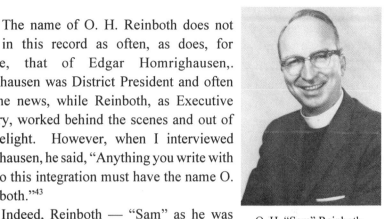

O. H. "Sam" Reinboth

Indeed, Reinboth — "Sam" as he was affectionately known — was a prime mover in the integration of the black congregations into the Southern District. When he came to the District in 1956, he came with the background of having assisted the California-Nevada District in assimilating the black congregations of that area into that District. He came to the Southern District shortly after Paul Streufert was elected President; and, while Streufert brought new thinking into the District, Reinboth was even more direct and forthright about taking on the race issue.

When Reinboth started, he assumed a five-part portfolio of responsibility, and when he left three full-time staff members had been added. He was a visionary and had a marvelous grasp of the Great Commission. He had the remarkable ability to conduct community surveys and to pinpoint locations for future churches. I had the privilege of working with him in such surveys both in Baton Rouge and in Huntsville. After a two-day visit with a dozen city officials, planners, and real estate people, on the third day he had a fully-outlined plan ready to present to local church leaders.

When he left the District in 1964, after less than eight years as Executive Secretary of Missions, his legacy was 53 new mission stations, with 47 new resident pastors. Counting the new missions and the addition of the Synodical Conference churches, the number of congregations in the District more than doubled in those years.[44]

165

Regarding Reinboth's role in the racial developments, Herzfeld characterized him as "one of the more revolutionary church leaders, because he was openly supportive and participated rather directly in our development." Ellwanger remembers him "as a forward-looking person," and felt that Reinboth was in his corner, looking ahead to the integration of the District. In J. B. Marshall's opinion, without Reinboth the merger would not have taken place.[45]

He was a courageous and innovative leader, illustrated by the fact that, upon his suggestion, the District Called Jim Brockmann to start new work in the largely black community in the Ponchartrain Park area of New Orleans. This was the first mission start-up in a black community by the Southern District, and it was done in April 1961 — four months before the vote was taken to invite the black congregations into the District, and more than two years before they were accepted. In a letter to Brockmann, Reinboth wrote: "In many respects you will become a trail blazer for us in this new program that we are about to launch."[46]   Likewise, Reinboth himself was a trail blazer.

James Wiggins perhaps gave the best picture of the true nature of Reinboth's working style. When the black congregations and pastors were waiting and wondering about the implications of coming into the District, he felt that the benefits of joining the District came across most clearly from Reinboth. Here is how he remembered him:

> I thought he was a person who tried to be fair. He went the second mile as far as the black congregations were concerned. So I felt good; I had a real relationship with him, and he took the time to find out what things were, and what your ideas and thoughts were. He was just that kind of a person.[47]

Such was the personal touch, the warm and evangelical spirit which Reinboth provided as he worked behind the scenes. Some thought that he, as well as Homrighausen, should also have been recognized with an honorary doctorate for the vital role he played in those pivotally historic years in the Southern District.

In April 1964, Reinboth accepted a position on the staff of the Board for Missions in North and South America, and moved to the

166

Synodical office in St. Louis. Bill Wedig, who was Executive Secretary for Stewardship at the time, was called to be the new Missions Executive.

Amalgamations in Central Alabama

It is well established that when Rosa Young became affiliated with the Lutheran Church, she was instrumental in starting many congregations in Central Alabama. Lutheran congregations were formed wherever there was a cluster of people, resulting in churches in many small towns or communities (see map on p. 25). With the limitation of transportation at that time, the many little churches served a good purpose.

However, when the merger took place in 1963, the population of Central Alabama had significantly decreased, and the idea of consolidating congregations was set in motion. Initial discussion of consolidation was started in early 1962 under the leadership of Mission Executive Reinboth. The amalgamation plan received a major boost from the International Lutheran Women's Missionary League, who at their 1963 Convention approved a $75,000 grant for the work in Central Alabama. Miss Hazel Gadmer of the Louisiana LWML District and Mrs. William Kennell of the Gulf States District were instrumental in bringing these needs before the Convention.[48]

Most of the original buildings of the black congregations were built according to the same pattern, a T-shaped church with a school room across the back forming the top of the T. By the 1960s, many of the old buildings were in serious need of repair.

Typical Model T Church
Rock West, Alabama

The amalgamation plan called for new buildings to be erected at central locations. To execute that plan required a study of the entire area to

167

determine which churches and schools to close and where to locate the new buildings. Reinboth conducted the preliminary study, and when he left for the Synodical office, the plan was implemented by his successor, Bill Wedig.

Ted Bussman, the District Executive for Education, also played a major role in the consolidation plan. He worked with the teachers to prepare them for the change. Hal Kieschnick was one of several white teachers who assisted Bussman, and he remembers that the training involved upgrading the curriculum and providing assistance in school administration and public relations.

Kieschnick recalls an incident which serves as a reminder that the work in Central Alabama was done in the midst of racial tension. The group of volunteers who worked with Bussman included both black and white teachers, who sometimes rode together — perhaps unwisely — from place to place; and this mixed group in cars did not go unnoticed by the locals. One Sunday they were gathered at Arlington, and while Kieschnick was teaching the Bible Class, Bussman suddenly signaled from the back of the room for him to stop, and announced, "We've got to get all the women in!" James Gildersleeve, a professor at ALAC, Selma, had driven down to Arlington with the word that he had been contacted by the white community with the message that the activities of this mixed group had been observed and that they were well-advised to get out of town and get out fast. Bussman suffered further harassment for his activities during the consoli- dation period. Since he was working with the

Congregation at Arlington, AL - 1928

black people, the white community considered him a real danger. Twice the engine of his car was destroyed after someone poured molasses into the gas tank. Once he was run off the road because they thought he was running guns to the black community. Wedig and Bussman spent much time working in the Central Alabama field under such hostile surroundings. They had an agreement to call each other every evening: if one did not receive a call from the other, he was to report it to the FBI.[49]

Despite the perils and opposition, the consolidation plan proceeded and the first new unit was built on a four-acre site at Arlington, AL. All the buildings in the consolidated churches were designed by Eldon Heck, a Lutheran architect in New Orleans. Carl Walters, a Lutheran contractor from Shreveport, served as the construction superintendent. The new units were somewhat similar to those of the old Synodical Conference churches inasmuch as the sanctuary and the classroom were connected.

The first consolidated congregation — the one in Arlington — was named Epiphany. The six congregations which were merged to form Epiphany were: St. Matthew, Arlington; St. Philip, Catherine; St. Luke, Lamison; Bethany, Nyland; St. Peter, Pine Hill; and Good Shepherd, Vineland.

On January 3, 1965, with over 300 in attendance, Epiphany Lutheran Church was dedicated. Pastor Wedig read the Rite of Dedication, Pastor Reinboth returned from

New Church at Arlington, AL - 1965

St. Louis to give the sermon, and Ted Bussman gave the children's message. Samuel Gailes, pastor of Epiphany, and Peter Hunt, Circuit Counselor, served as liturgists for the service. President Homrighausen brought greetings from the District.[50]

The following paragraphs of the dedication story in *The Lutheran Witness Supplement* give an interesting glimpse into the background of the congregations which merged to form Epiphany:

> When she [Rosa Young] taught in the Lutheran school of Mount Carmel Lutheran Church, Midway, Ala., a group came from Nyland, 9 miles distant, to request similar spiritual and secular teaching. She went there, and subsequently Pastor George A. Schmidt held the first service for Bethany, Nyland, on Feb. 8, 1918.
>
> James Scott and his wife, Sally, two Lutherans confirmed at Midway, requested a church in their town. Saint Philip, Catherine, resulted, and Mrs. James Scott subsequently willed the four-acre church site. St. Luke, Lamison, began through Fannie Steel, once a slave, confirmed at Nyland. St. Matthew, Arlington, also grew from personal efforts. Visitors to Nyland, interested by what they heard, returned home to Pine Hill to organize St. Peter, Pine Hill. Good Shepherd, Vineland, was one of several congregations begun from Bashi when Rev. Peter R. Hunt was pastor there.[51]

While the dedication of the new facilities at Arlington was an exciting occasion, the period leading up to it had also brought a profound mixture of emotions from the faithful. Some were angry about having to give up their old church and, according to John Davis, "some cried like a baby." Some felt upset because they had not been given voice on the location of the new churches. Some were simply opposed to the plan, and some members were lost because they never affiliated with the new congregations. Even years later, some registered disappointment over the new arrangement because they were told that transportation would be provided so they could get to the new sites, but the buses either never came or broke down, and no transportation was available.[52]

Whether right or wrong, the consolidation of congregations took place because the old buildings were sorely in need of repair or replacement, and something had to be done.

January 31, 1964 - Louis Allen, witness to murder of Civil Rights worker, assassinated in Liberty, Mississippi.

The 1964 Conference and Convention

For the second year in a row, the Gulf States Pastors Conference was held at Resurrection, Pensacola, and this was the fourth time that the gathering was integrated. However, the 1964 Conference was significant for two "firsts." Pastor Albert Dominick gave the sermon for the Opening Service, the first black pastor to have that honor. Dominick was an eloquent preacher, and after he was received into the District he was often asked to be the speaker for special occasions throughout the Missouri Synod. Will Herzfeld was elected Vice President of the Conference, the first black pastor to be chosen as a Conference officer.[53]

June 1964 - Over 1000 young Civil Rights volunteers came to Mississippi.

July 2, 1964 - President Johnson signed the Civil Rights Act of 1964.

The 54th Convention of the Southern District was held June 29 to July 2, 1964 in New Orleans. This was the second integrated convention, but it was not yet quite as routine as the integrated pastors conferences. The 1964 Convention was the first integrated meeting to be held in a hotel, and hotel managers were still jittery about opening their facilities for racially-mixed groups. This was doubly so in New Orleans because the memory remained that in 1955 the International Lutheran Women's Missionary League had pulled out of New Orleans over the racial issue after booking a convention there.

171

However, Charles Genella, the Director of Sales at the Jung Hotel, was willing to take a chance with the Lutherans, and the hotel agreed to host the Convention.[54] For the first time black and white delegates not only met together in a public place but also were housed together. Two limitations, however, were established. Black delegates were asked to refrain from going to the bar and from using the swimming pool. President Homrighausen felt those limitations were an acceptable compromise for the opportunity to meet in a hotel. Others were critical, claiming that it was a case of giving in to old "Jim Crow Laws."[55]

Since the decision to merge with the Synodical Conference took place in 1961, and the black pastors and congregations were officially received at the 1963 convention, it might be assumed that the issue was settled. It was not. The 1964 Convention heard heated debate over the wisdom of accepting the black congregations into the District. Some voiced the fear that black people would come in large numbers to white congregations. During one such heated discussions over a resolution, Pastor Dominick went to a microphone and, with his indomitable sense of humor, said,

> Our white brothers are afraid that if you pass this resolution, that all of us black people are going to start coming to your churches in droves. Well, I got news for you. They are not going to come to your churches in droves, because we are not coming to our churches in droves!"[56]

The laughter broke the tension.

Eldon Weisheit also contributed a bit of humor at another tense time. He typed the following "resolution" and sent it to the podium,

> Whereas, our Lord has said that He will be coming soon, and
> Whereas, His promised coming will have great effect on the church, and
> Whereas, we have not had time in 2000 years to prepare for this proposed event, be it therefore
> Resolved that we petition Him to postpone it for three years, and be it further
> Resolved that we appoint an executive secretary on eschatology.[57]

Homrighausen read the "resolution" and once again humor helped to overcome a tense moment in the Convention.

Two actions of the Convention are relevant to this history: One, the District lifted the suspension of First Lutheran, Birmingham, and Pastor Reuter;[58] and, two, the following congregations, which were formerly in the Synodical Conference were received: (* Pastors already members of the District)

Berea - New Orleans, vacant
Antioch - Ashville, AL, Arthur Bodley,* pastor
Zion - Bessemer, AL, Carl Agerstrand,* pastor
St. James - Buena Vista, AL, James Wiggins, pastor
Holy Cross - Camden, AL, Johnny Brown, pastor
St. Timothy - Selma, AL, W. C. Sowell,* pastor
Redemption - Panama City, FL, Robert Schroeder,* pastor
Jehovah - Pensacola, FL, George Miller,* pastor[59]

July 11, 1964 - Lt. Col. Lemuel Penn killed by the Klan while driving North, Colbert, Georgia.

February 26, 1965 - Jimmie Lee Jackson, Civil Rights marcher killed by State Trooper, Marion, Alabama.

CHAPTER 9

CONTINUING PROTESTS

To March or Not to March - Selma, 1965

By the beginning of 1965, many changes had taken place in the racial climate of the South. In 1964, the U.S. Government had outlawed the poll tax in federal elections and had passed the Civil Rights Act. Both of these actions offered hope for black people, but at the same time caused many white Southerners to harden in their resistance. The purpose of the poll tax was designed to keep black people from voting, but now that the tax had been rescinded, many still could not vote because they were not registered. The next hurdle to cross was to get black voters registered.

Getting registered in Alabama was no simple matter; it was an ordeal which tested both a person's endurance and patience. Only a very limited number of days were made available by the registrar, making it impossible to simply walk in on any weekday and register. When we went to register after we moved to Alabama in 1961, we found ourselves standing in a line of several hundred people just to obtain the papers to fill out. Next we had to take — and pass — a civics test to prove that we understood the United States Constitution. Altogether, it took us the better part of half a day to register. The system was clearly designed to discourage voting.

Voter registration was the push that brought hundreds of protesters from the North to Alabama, with most of the attention focused on Selma and Dallas County. For weeks the protests went on in Selma, with a rising level of hostility and resistance from the white community and the police

174

force. Eventually the campaign culminated in the Selma-to-Montgomery March.

Here it is important to note that Sheriff James "Jim" Clark of Dallas County represented the core of white power. As a demonstration of the power and authority of his department, the sheriff's deputies, dressed in full uniform and on horseback, paraded through downtown from time to time, usually on Saturdays. The parade was designed to keep minorities in their place and, according to one observer, such a parade was held "as often as it was needed."

As the registration efforts wore on, the number of protesters increased and the number that had been jailed also multiplied. Now Pastor Joe Ellwanger entered the picture. He was President of the Birmingham Council on Human Relations and as such he organized a group of about 60 to 70 white people, mainly from Birmingham, to go to Selma on Saturday, March 6. They called themselves the Concerned White Citizens of Alabama, and their aim that day was to read a statement on the steps of the Dallas County Court House.

Meanwhile, as the protests in Selma escalated, President Homrighausen received threatening phone calls implying danger to the students at Alabama Lutheran Academy and College.[1]

This led to a skirmish among Lutherans. Earlier Homrighausen and Ellwanger had disagreed regarding Ellwanger's participation in the funeral for the four girls killed in the Birmingham church bombing, and now they disagreed regarding methods of protest. Homrighausen believed he could work more effectively by personal contact with community leaders instead of marching in the streets, and therefore did not participate in the march.

Furthermore, the question arose, did Ellwanger represent the Lutheran Church? Homrighausen declared that he did not. Mindful of the threatening phone calls regarding the students at ALAC, what was Homrighausen to do? After consulting with Synod President Oliver Harms, he sent a telegram to Sheriff Clark, stating in part,

> The demonstration being led today in Selma by the Reverend Joseph Ellwanger does not have the official endorsement or sanction of The Lutheran Church - Missouri Synod. In no way does the Reverend Joseph Ellwanger represent the

church in an official capacity. He appears in his role and right as a citizen.[2]

The statement which Ellwanger read declared that white citizens also were ready to speak out against the events which had happened in Selma; that they considered "it a shocking injustice" that some counties in Alabama still had no Negro voters; that this was "a tragic retreat from the American principle of 'no taxation without representation;'" that they were horrified at the brutal treatment by police of peaceful demonstrators; and that they were "sickened by the totalitarian atmosphere of intimidation and fear...purposefully created and maintained" by the officials.

Furthermore, the statement requested that

> the governor...and all elected officials...use their power...to see to it that all open and subtle intimidation of persons seeking to register to vote be removed...[that] state and local officials...inform them [potential voters] that they are welcome and that they are encouraged to register and vote...[that] the current 'college test' type of registration form [be eliminated]...[that] assistance be made available for white and Negro citizens who are unable to fully understand or fill out the form, and [that they] plead for Federal help in terms of laws and registrars if these injustices are not removed forthrightly. [3]

The disagreement among Lutherans that day was actually a three-way split. James Rongstad, pastor of the local white congregation in Selma, drafted a statement of his own opposing the demonstration led by Ellwanger, and read his statement to the assembled Concerned White Citizens group.

Both the administration and the students at ALAC also became involved in difficult decisions during this time of turmoil. Varnes Stringer, the Acting President of the school, together with the Board of Control, decided that since the students were minors, they should not participate in the demonstrations. One professor said, "Your parents didn't send you here to demonstrate."[4]

Nevertheless, the students on campus were keenly aware of what was going on in their community. The local newspaper carried an article

176

about Rongstad's opposition to the demonstrations. He taught a class in Old Testament at the school, and after the students learned of his viewpoint, they walked out of his class. That, in turn, led to a four-day walk-out for the entire student body. None of the students participated in the demonstrations, but during that walk-out they held a variety of discussion forums on the race issue as well as other problems.[5] Here perceptions differ somewhat. Despite disagreement by the students with their teacher over the race issue, Rongstad was a well-liked professor and at the end of the academic year was voted favorite teacher on campus.

Even though the students did not participate, the campus was not entirely removed from the community activities. Several pastors from the North who came to participate in the demonstrations stayed in the school's dormitory.[6]

Following the weekend of the Ellwanger-led demonstration , *The Lutheran Witness* carried a two-page article titled "Dilemma and Dedication" written by O.S. [Omar Stuenkel]. The article quoted Ellwanger as saying,

> The reason I felt that I as a Christian must participate was that it is one way in which the minority groups have an opportunity to show to authorities and the country their plight and to hold up injustice to the consciences of the nation for some kind of decision and action that will bring about a degree of justice.[7]

In conclusion Stuenkel wrote that, while methods differed, all apparently had the same goal. Homrighausen agreed, saying, "We had the same aim we differed on the method."[8]

It is not clear how much impact the visit of the white group to the court house had. But it did do this: It drew additional national media attention to Selma, and the next day came "Bloody Sunday." Ellwanger's efforts were definitely recognized at his congregation. When the Ellwangers returned to St. Paul's Saturday evening, the congregation had a celebration planned, with food and music. It was their way of affirming their pastor's strong stand in the campaign to gain voting rights.

March 7, 1965 - State troopers beat back marchers at Edmund Pettus Bridge, Selma, AL.

◊　◊　◊

On Sunday, marchers attempted to cross the Edmund Pettus Bridge, which crosses the Alabama River south of downtown Selma. This was intended to be the beginning of the march to Montgomery. But after the marchers had crossed the bridge, they were met at the foot of the bridge by State troopers on horseback, and were driven back with clubs, cattle prods, and tear gas. The brutal force employed by the troopers injured many, including women and children. The

"I Got One Of 'Em Just As She Almost Made It Back To The Church"

From *The Herblock Gallery*
© (Simon & Schuster, 1968)
Used with permission

encounter became known as "Bloody Sunday" and the scene was flashed on TV screens for all Americans to see. The nation was shocked by the violence used to halt the march, and within the next days many more protesters came to Selma. Martin Luther King, Jr., and many of the other leaders of the Southern Christian Leadership Conference were on the scene to organize the March.

Several additional attempts to cross the bridge were made in the days following "Bloody Sunday." For two weeks following Bloody Sunday, the protests in Selma continued and hundreds more protesters poured into the city to join the daily demonstrations. The tension increased markedly, which produced continuing concern for the safety of the students at ALAC. During this time, Homrighausen decided to pay a personal visit to Sheriff Clark. Here is how he recalls the visit:

> I went to the sheriff because of the threats. And I simply said to the sheriff, "You really need to pray. Your guys are not doing what's right. Let's get down on our knees." And he did. He took his tin hat off, and he got down on his knees and we prayed. I will never forget that. He put on his fedora, his little felt hat, and he said to his staff, "Call it off." Now what he was calling off, I don't know, but nothing happened that day.[9]

◊   ◊   ◊

March 11, 1965 - Rev. James Reed, white march volunteer, beaten to death, Selma, AL.

◊   ◊   ◊

The national outcry over the violence and bloodshed in Selma produced overwhelming support for the March, and now there was no holding it back. Two weeks after the bloody encounter, the actual March was underway. With U.S. flags waving and with TV cameras running, the marchers slowly made their way along U.S. Highway 80 to Montgomery.

Some Lutherans in the South participated at least in the final stages of the March. Among them were: Pastors - Joe Ellwanger, Will Herzfeld, and J. B. Marshall; James Gildersleeve and Ulysses Blackmon, both professors at ALAC; and John Davis who at that time was still a layman. Lutherans from the North, including some pastors, were also involved in the March.[10]

◊   ◊   ◊

179

March 25, 1965 - Civil Rights March from Selma to Montgomery completed.

March 25, 1965 - Viola Gregg Liuzzo killed by Klan while transporting marchers, Selma Highway, Alabama.

Ellwanger and A Measure of Fame

Joe Ellwanger and Joyce, his wife, were involved in the last leg of the three-day March when it arrived in Montgomery. At the conclusion of the March, King gave a speech, and at the end of the speech he named 18 pastors who were to go with him to Washington, D.C., to meet with President Johnson on the Voting Rights Act. Ellwanger was surprised to hear his name called to be one of that delegation. He was invited to join the group in recognition of his leadership in bringing the white delegation that protested on the Dallas County Court House steps on March 6.[11]

In connection with the visit to Washington, Homrighausen and Ellwanger clashed once again, because Homrighausen advised against participating; but Ellwanger insisted on going. In my interview with Ellwanger, he gave the following comments in response to Homrighausen:

> I have to follow my conscience and I really believe the very opposite of what you believe in terms of this not being the Church's [business]; I think that it *is* the Church's business to see that justice is done and that our brothers and sisters in the Lutheran Church, to say nothing of everybody else, have a chance to vote; and I think that it would be something you would be concerned about.[12]

Ellwanger and his wife made the trip to Washington. Here is how he described that experience:

> We walked into a church in Washington where people had gathered. They knew that King and 17 of us were meeting with Johnson, and so there was quite a gathering of leaders and judicatory heads and ordinary folks. I remember the church was packed with probably 1000 people; I mean, it was a big church

180

and it was packed. As we walked in, everybody stood and clapped and it was that kind of an electric, emotional moment in the movement, much of which you would have no sense of it if you were not actually there; but if you were there, you don't forget it.[13]

June 2, 1965 - Oneal Moore, black deputy, killed by nightriders in Varnado, Louisiana.

June 9, 1965 - Congress passes Voting Rights Act of 1965.

By his outspoken manner and intensive involvement in the racial issue, Ellwanger had gained a certain "celebrity status" in the Missouri Synod by this time. In 1964, he was invited to address the Southern California District Convention.[14] Prior to the 1965 Synodical Convention in Detroit, he was invited, along with others, by the editors of *The Lutheran Witness* to make his views known in print to the Convention. He wrote the following for the *Witness*:

> I am concerned about the entire life of the church - her worship and witness, her growth and service. But there is one area of her life that I should like to speak about specifically: the church's responsibility to speak and to live the radical Good News of Jesus Christ to racial injustices and discrimination.
>
> There have been and still are those who look upon the racial issue as such a "thorny problem." They feel the less the church has to say and do about it, the better. But we need to say to one another as Christian brother to brother at this convention that the racial issue and the current social change in our nation is not a problem for the church to avoid, but an opportunity for her to grasp.

We have been greatly responsible for the unjust patterns that necessitate the radical social revolution - by our segregated churches and by our justification of segregation by our silence.

We should look at this sweeping historic movement as an opportunity - perhaps our last - to make clear to the world that those who call Jesus Lord are concerned about lifting the foot of oppression and showing the love of Christ to our fellowman.

This is an opportunity for the church to ask itself probing questions about its own identity and purpose. This is an opportunity for the church to show that as a body of Christ she is not as concerned about her own institutional life nearly so much as she is in being the living presence of the serving Christ.

It is not a matter of whether there are any racial injustices. There are. It is not a matter of whether the current movement toward justice is American or significant or genuine. It is. It is not a matter of whether the church has any responsibility, as she demonstrates the love of Christ, to speak out against injustice and bring about justice. It has.

It is simply a question of whether the church will let other facets of our national life lead in this critical, moral, and theological issue, or whether the church will lead. It is a question of whether the church will speak and act with boldness and selflessness in the love of Christ.[15]

In the same issue of the *Witness*, Paul Simon, who was later to become a U. S. Senator, wrote these lines:

If the opportunity were mine to speak for five minutes to the decision makers at Detroit, I would give four of the five minutes to Rev. Joe Ellwanger, the Missouri Synod pastor in Alabama who stood so courageously - and so relatively alone among the white Southern clergy - for justice for all men.[16]

The Detroit Convention passed a total of ten resolutions pertaining to the race issue. One commended and encouraged both those who engaged

182

in lawful and peaceful demonstrations and those who use "other than direct-action methods for furthering social justice" and urged both sides not to judge the other. Another resolution declared that "no congregation is autonomous to decide whom it will serve." Obviously that was aimed at congregations which used their autonomy as the grounds to remain segregated.[17]

I was a delegate at the Detroit Convention, and when I gave my report to the pastors of the area, we met at St. Paul's in Birmingham. Ellwanger was not satisfied with my report because, in his single-minded approach to the race issue, he felt that I had not given enough emphasis to the racial resolutions passed at the convention.

July 18, 1965 - Willie Wallace Brewster killed by nightriders at Anniston, Alabama.

Visitors, or Interference, From the North

The South is well-known for its fierce sense of independence. Even the Civil War did not diminish that sense and, indeed, it may have intensified it. Northerners who sought to interfere in the ways of the South were considered carpet-baggers, scalawags, Damn Yankees, and a few other unprintable names.

As the racial changes took place in the South, the influx of Northerners was met in roughly three ways; and those three ways were also generally found among the Lutherans. Those who were pro-integration welcomed the support and encouragement which came from other sections of the country.[18] Those who were pro-segregation deeply resented the interference from outsiders, and sometimes that resentment flared up in physical violence.

183

August 20, 1965 - Jonathan Daniels, seminary student, killed by deputy, Hayneville, Alabama.

Three white protesters from the North – James Reed, Viola Liuzzo, and Jonathan Daniels — were murdered in 1965 as a direct result of the bitterness felt regarding the intrusion of outsiders.

Many Lutherans in the South found themselves in the third group, in the middle ground between two extremes.[19] They were the ones who emphasized preaching the Gospel and saving souls versus social action. The people in this group recognized that integration was coming, and were convinced that the change would come best gradually and slowly as the power of the Gospel changed the hearts of people. They considered the Northerners, sometimes called "Three-Day-Experts," as an interference because the outsiders had not lived in the area and did not really understand the nuances of relationships in the church as well as in the community. Often the Northerners demanded that integration move at a faster pace; and their very presence implied judgment regarding the methods being used. Those in that middle group did not find the influence of Northerners helpful.

For this survey, we will include the views of several who commented on the influx of Northerners. Ellwanger noted that several pastors came from Chicago to participate in the Selma March. In his case he was glad for their support and welcomed them.[20]

Jim Pape tells of an incident with a different twist. Norman Temme, from Synod's Public Relations Department in St. Louis, called to suggest that they make a movie of the turmoil in Birmingham. His aim was well-intentioned because he wanted to show how the Church was involved and how it makes decisions when it faces racial issues. Pape's response was, "If you come down here and bring your cameras, you're going to blow us right out of the water." The movie project was canceled.[21]

Ed Homrighausen recalled an episode with a Northern visitor, a pastor from Detroit, who stormed into the president's office in Cullman, AL, and charged, "Yeah, just like the hierarchy, sitting behind your desk while the rest of us are down there [in Selma!]" What the Detroit visitor did not know was that Homrighausen had just returned home after spending 72 hours in Selma dealing with Sheriff Clark and other officials.[22]

Regarding the influx of pastors from other areas, President Homrighausen was quoted in the *Birmingham Post-Herald*, saying,

> The men who are to occupy pulpits and are charged to feed their own flocks vacate this ministry to become engaged in a matter of which they have little or no understanding. Surely there must be enough work to keep these men busy in their own areas.

Two days later the newspaper endorsed Homrighausen's view in an editorial titled, "Meddling Does not Help."[23]

The two pastors in Jackson, MS, whom we met earlier in the Jackson Story, each tell of an experience they had with the same Californian. The first encounter involved Bernie Ansorge. We will let him give the account.

> I was invited during my second year in Jackson, in 1964, to write a reflective piece for the college newspaper at St. John's College in Winfield, Kansas - the *St. John's Reporter*. When I attended St. John's, I was editor of the *Reporter*, and so the current editor tracked me down and said, "As a former editor, what is your perspective of ministry in the South?" I wrote the piece, in which I said - I included myself now in the South - and I described how I got there. I was not called down there to change the social structure, I was called to do ministry of the Gospel. I was supported in that by a growing group of people in the black community, and this group was not receiving well all the others who were coming down just simply to change society. So my advice to those who would read my piece was, "Do the ministry of the Lord where you are called, where you are; don't think you can come halfway across the country and change things, because this is not conducive to the ministry of the Gospel at this point."

Well, I thought I had written it well, and submitted it, and it was printed. I got several responses, including one that surprised me, and blind-sided me. I got a few letters commenting about one or two things, and I appreciated those. But then a couple of issues later of the *Reporter* there was another article, about the same length as mine, that had come from another alumnus of St. John's College, who had considerable stature in The Lutheran Church - Missouri Synod at that time, but who was diametrically opposed to the point of view that I was espousing. And that was Ralph Moellering, who at that time was campus pastor at the University of California Lutheran Chapel at Berkeley.

He patronized me a little bit by referring to "Brother Ansorge" this and "Brother Ansorge" that. Well, there were different perspectives, and I've been around the block enough times now to know that everybody's got his own perspective, and you've arrived at your perspective by your experiences, and through an honest evaluation of what the situations are.[24]

About a year later, Moellering entered into the picture again, and this time it involved both Ansorge and Kuehnert. Before we get to that encounter, however, it is important to add some background information.

About a year after he arrived in Jackson, Kuehnert was asked to serve as Circuit Counselor for Circuit 7, which encompassed two-thirds of the State of Mississippi and included 22 congregations and preaching stations. The Circuit almost always had several pastoral vacancies, and it was a considerable challenge to get pastors to fill those spots. Kuehnert remembers that when Calls went out to men in the North some sent back the Call immediately by return mail. Others, when they were told on the phone that a Call had been issued, responded by saying, "You gotta be kidding! There is no way I am coming to Mississippi!"

In the Spring of 1965, Moellering traveled through Jackson on his way to the Selma March and contacted Ansorge to set up a meeting with him and Kuehnert on his return trip. Now Kuehnert tells the story.

Moellering stayed in a motel in Jackson and summoned us to meet with him in his room. And for three hours it was a

186

matter of his berating us, or us trying to defend ourselves and our ministry against his accusations that we were partners with Satan himself because, number one, my congregation had no blacks, and, number two, his [Ansorge's] congregation had no whites except him. And this was not the way the church was to be, or should be doing its ministry. "How can this be allowed to go on?" he insisted. And he worked me over because in the Circuit we had white congregations and we had black congregations, and they weren't getting together. About the three-hour point, I finally had all I could take, and I said, "Tell you what, Ralph; I've got four vacancies right now in this Circuit, and I am Circuit Counselor; I'll promise you that before you get back to Berkeley you've got a Call to the church of your choice here in Circuit 7." And that brought this whole thing to an end. He had nothing to say; he wouldn't have any part of it.[25]

Developments in the Youth Ministry in Those Years

In the 1950s and '60s, the Walther League was the official youth organization of the Missouri Synod which provided popular youth activities. Zone Rallies, Walther League camps, and joint meetings with other congregations were held in addition to regular local meetings. Since the pool of dateable Lutherans in the South was usually rather limited, the prevailing theory was that these gatherings provided opportunities where young Lutherans could meet other young Lutherans.

However, with the prospect of the black congregations looming on the horizon, the leaders of the District youth ministry were faced with a quandary. An argument widely used by white people against integration was, "You wouldn't want your daughter to marry one." As a result the District Youth Program was greatly curtailed for a few years.

The last segregated Dixie District Walther League Convention was held at Camp Sumatanga (near Lake Guntersville), August 16-18, 1963, with Grace Lutheran in Huntsville, AL, as the host. Even though the merger would not take place until the end of August, the Wheat Ridge Seals Campaign report in the Convention booklet listed a number of black congregations; however, the treasurer's report, which included only congregations which belonged to the Walther League, listed no black congregations.[26] (Wheat Ridge is social ministry originated in Colorado.)

In the middle 1960s, the Southern District Youth Committee was striving to bring about a merger on two fronts. As noted above, the Walther League provided most of the youth activities up until the middle "60s, and the Youth Committee's first aim was to work cooperatively with the leaders of the Dixie District of the Walther League. The second aim was to bring about the eventual racial integration of youth activities.

In New Orleans and Baton Rouge, regular Walther League activities continued while the issue of integrating youth activities was often hotly debated.[27] According to Bill Lieske, an abortive effort at an integrated youth event was made in 1964 in New Orleans. He recalls,

> An integrated meeting was scheduled at St. John [Lutheran Church]. It was well-attended, but did not go full term. Soon people from the neighborhood, and perhaps else-where, were creating a stir outside, which became so boisterous and belligerent there was fear for the safety of all in attendance. So, after prayer, the session was quickly terminated and all were dispersed quietly, and thankfully, without further incident or harm.[28]

Eldon Weisheit was appointed chairman of the Youth Committee after the 1963 Convention. On July 27, 1965, a one-day Youth Rally with an attendance of 60 was held at Trinity in McComb, MS, the congregation where Weisheit was pastor.[29] Apparently that was an all-white gathering.

In its report to the Convention in June 1966, the Youth Committee noted as follows:

> The Youth Committee has been especially concerned about the large number of youth in our District who have no available youth programs beyond the local level. To help fill these needs an LSV [Lutheran Service Volunteer] school will be held in Selma, Alabama this summer for the youth of the Negro congregations of our District and surrounding areas. This is not an approval of the "separate but equal" policy, but is a temporary solution to provided (sic) needed spiritual growth in a

188

meaningful way. The LSV School will have a dean from International Walther League. The remainder of the staff will come from our District.[30]

In addition, that summer the Youth Committee planned an integrated event which was held at Spring Hill College in Mobile, AL. Actually it was a triple-header event: The Dixie District Walther League Camp, July 24-29, with Ken Holdorf the dean; the Dixie District Walther League Convention, July 29-31, with Paul Elbrecht the speaker; and a Youth Encounter School, August 1-5, with Eldon Weisheit the dean.[31]

Since this was the first integrated youth event, the experiences of two men are worth noting. Bernie Ansorge was a member of the staff for the youth camp. He served a black congregation in Jackson, MS, and the following is his recollection,

> I drove to Mobile in my little red 1966 Volkswagen with two girls from my congregation in Jackson, Shelly Broadwater and Lillie Woods. Our trip to Mobile was through Laurel along the two-laned highways of Mississippi. At one point a car with several teenaged boys passed us. They did a double take when they saw a white man with two black girls. They slowed down and we passed them. They offered a few obscene gestures and tried to "caravan" with us for several miles. I tried to reassure the girls that nothing would happen. Thankfully, nothing did; but it was a little frightening for several minutes.[32]

According to Ansorge, during the camp the two black girls were mostly ignored by the other youth, and the staff talked to them a lot. Thus the first event took place without a serious problem other than that the black youth were left isolated and ignored.

According to Weisheit, no black youth attended the Convention since they were not yet members of the Walther League. But 10 to 15 black youth arrived on Sunday afternoon in order to participate in the Encounter School.[33] Some of the white youth, who also arrived early for the Encounter School were not pleased with the presence of black youngsters and proceeded to curse them and, according to Weisheit, "called them every dirty word in the book." As a result, some of the black youth packed and were ready to leave. Weisheit pleaded with them to stay at least through the evening devotion, and they agreed to do so.

He wasn't sure, however, what he was going to do for that devotion. He hurriedly worked out a devotion called "A Letter From Christ's Lawyer" in which he portrayed the church as the Bride who because of her conduct was being sued for divorce.[34] In the devotion he had this paragraph as the "Lawyer" speaks for Jesus:

> But did it ever occur to you that the evil you do to others is also done to Him? You have lied to your Husband. You have stolen from Him. You've sneered at Him, ridiculed Him, ignored His poverty, punctured His hopes. You've called Him obscene, foul-mouthed, abusive names: "Nigger! Wop! Kike! Dirty bastard!" "Inasmuch as you have done it unto one of the least of these My brethren, you have done it unto Me." Yes, Church, the charge of cruelty will stick. You have no defense.

Later the "Letter" continues with

> These are the charges against you. But the case will never come to court. There will be no divorce. No divorce, Church, because, you see, this was not Christ's idea but mine.... Only a sinner such as I could have even thought of it as a possibility....
>
> Nevertheless, your Husband, Jesus Christ, has asked me to give you a message. Unbelievable though it may be, upon your repentant confession of sin the message is this: I, by virtue of my office as a called and ordained servant of the Word, announce the grace of God unto all of you, and in the stead and by the command of my Lord Jesus Christ I forgive you all your sins in the name of the Father and of the Son and of the Holy Ghost.
>
> How will you respond to this amazing forgiveness?[35]

Weisheit happily reported that all the youth stayed for the entire gathering.

Accordingly, during the same summer and at the same location, two different groups came together at two different times; problems erupted at one, but not at the other. Such was the nature and challenge of the ministry in those transitional years. The Spirit was at work to bring about changed hearts, and peaceful mixed gatherings could take place. At the same time the prejudice of the past lingered in the old sinful nature and could flare up instantly without forewarning.

CHAPTER 10

REFLECTION AND EVALUATION

The Nature and Content of the Debate and Conflict

It was not easy for the South to accept the changes which obviously were coming during the 1950s and 60s. Wilfred Schrader summarized the feelings very simply, saying, "You can't educate people overnight, and say, 'This rule is going in, and we're going to do it different.' It takes time."[1]

Another faithful church-going white Lutheran said it more graphically.

> You think that you're going to come down and change things overnight. Things are going to change, and we all understand that. We're just trying to slow the speed down in which it happens. It's like you've put something into our mouth that's bitter, and it's hard to chew, and you want us to swallow that without chewing it. Well, we're going to have to chew it before we swallow it, and the more we chew it, the less we like it. But we know that we are going to have to swallow it anyhow.[2]

Therefore, the Lutheran Christians of the South had to chew on the matter. As noted earlier, the manner in which Lutherans "chewed" on the racial change fell into three categories — the pro-integrationists, the pro-segregationists and the middle-of-the-roaders (or moderates).

The middle group was primarily represented by President Homrighausen, who was called "a cautious leader" by one observer. Actually he was an interesting combination of outspokenness and caution. It was, he said, his "privilege to guide and lead."[3] His aim was to steer the ship of the

192

Church between the two extremes. At the Pensacola Convention he expressed an affinity with both sides, for a local news reporter wrote: "He [Homrighausen] said while the church's main function is to preach the Gospel of Christ, it must 'speak out' and 'speak clearly' on vital issues."[4]

Homrighausen claims that the District Board of Directors was fully in accord and supportive of the action he took during those nerve-wracking years. However, the Board also included members who were keenly in tune with the ways of the South, and their influence kept the District leadership from taking radical action too quickly.

The two extremes had very strongly-held views, and the debate often found them firing their artillery at one another while the moderate group stood on the sidelines and stayed comparatively quiet. It is important to take a closer look at the content and substance of the argument of the two vocal sides.

Joe Ellwanger most clearly represented the pro-integrationist view. Will Herzfeld and George Hrbek were in the same camp. Brockmann, Ellermann, Nau, and Reinboth also lent their support for this viewpoint. What was the substance of their argument? And how did they arrive at it? We will examine some sources and comments to seek an answer.

Writing in the March 1964 *Interaction,*[5] Ellwanger stated that five Scriptural doctrines have implications for the race question. Under the title "Christian Attitudes in Race Relations," he listed the following:

> 1) *Creation* — all men come from the same, loving, purposeful hand of God. 2) *Sin* — common failure to perfectly reflect God's glory binds all men together. 3) *Incarnation* — in taking on human form, Jesus identified Himself with every man. 4) *Redemption* — God's plan of redemption includes not only the uniting of man with God but also the uniting of man with man. 5) *The Church* — members of the body of Christ are one because of their one Baptism, their one Lord and Head, their receiving of the one Spirit, and their one hope of life with God.

After that list he added, "The Christian attitude in race relations is not a side issue which we can include or omit in our teaching of God's Word. It is essential to life in Christ."[6]

Herzfeld's theological thinking was stimulated largely by his anger and disappointment that "his sense of justice and fair play was violated, both by the Church and State authorities." His understanding of justice and fair play "came from the Word of God," he added. He explained his theological thinking further, as follows:

> I think that the biggest argument that we had, the one that kind of hung over us, was the two different understandings of what it meant to be Lutheran. This two-kingdom theory dogged most of us like the proverbial "Hound of Heaven" - both those who embraced it and those who could not embrace it, because there were some of us who said we just could not figure out which hand God used when God decided to do His work - whether it was God's left hand or right hand. We think that Luther was misunderstood. There were these arguments of whether or not it was the business of the Church to involve itself in civil rights...and the age-old problem that our job is to preach the Gospel.... We had a basic disagreement on what the Gospel is.[7]

Ellwanger elaborated on his experience by noting that his theological development involved two changes for which he was not well prepared as a Missouri Synod Lutheran; one, that he was led into political action and, two, that it was ecumenical in nature. By experience he came to believe that the Gospel calls us to be ecumenical because it is in the ecumenical setting that we give a fuller witness to our faith. Moving in that direction meant that he could not wait for approval from the Church hierarchy. In summary he stated, "It is part of our witness to the Gospel that we demonstrate a concern for the 'people at the edges,' which is basically what justice ministry is all about."

When Ellwanger was asked if he ever felt doubt about what he was doing, he admitted that he often felt that he was standing alone. While he had strong convictions about the rightness of his stand, he acknowledged that he often had uncertainties about timing and whether or not he should participate in specific demonstrations. Others, he noted, raised questions about demonstrations; one, because they were too risky and, two, because they were divisive.

194

Both Ellwanger and Herzfeld worked closely with Martin Luther King Jr. and were influenced both by King's methods and theology. Regarding King, Ellwanger said, "[He] had a very strong theology about the importance and necessity of non-violent resistance and demonstrations, and the more I did it the more I felt that there certainly is a validity in this methodology of 'doing justice.'"[8]

Ellwanger's approach was a radical departure from the classic Lutheran view; namely, that the Church is the right hand of God with the task of proclaiming the Gospel and saving souls, while the government is the left hand of God whereby the Lord keeps order in the civil realm. Lutherans were not pacifists, however, because they participated in just wars, but when it came to action in the Civil Rights Movements Lutherans for the most part were quietists. The commonly held belief was that each individual Christian could exercise his or her civic responsibility and involvement in social action, but the Church as such was not to engage in such activities.

This leads us to the other side of the spectrum — those who spoke most forcefully for the maintenance of the status quo both in Church and State. What was the substance of their view? We gain a clue about their thinking from a letter written in 1943 by L. A. Wisler, Executive of the Missionary Board for the Synodical Conference, to G. M. Kramer, Superintendent of the Louisiana Conference. In reaction to the book *My Neighbor of Another Color,* by Andrew Schulze, Wisler wrote:

> One bad feature about Schulze is this that he cannot distinguish between the local congregation or the visible church and the '*una sancta.* '... Just what it will do to the Mission - is hard to tell. We have our duty namely to preach the Gospel of salvation. We will abide by that."[9]

Thus, the pattern was of long standing: Preach the Gospel and keep the emphasis on the *Una Sancta*, the invisible Church. With that understanding, there was no need to interact with churches of another color.

This view was held by a number of pastors, especially some of the older ones; however, William Kennell most clearly represented this view. A number of people whom I interviewed had a variety of impressions of the content of his argument. Some felt that he did not want to get involved in social issues, while ironically others thought that he argued from a socio-logical view, maintaining that the races were best served on a separated basis. Unfortunately, I was unable to interview him for this study since he died shortly before the research began. However, he wrote a letter to *The Lutheran Witness,* that was printed two months after the Birmingham church bombing, which probably gives the best summary of his views. He wrote:

> We must recognize that there are difficulties in certain areas which could seriously disrupt the work of the Gospel should congregations immediately integrate. We have already witnessed some of these explosions — and how has anyone been helped? Which is the major point at issue — to see that the Negro receives the Gospel or that he is integrated with a congregation?
>
> For years Negroes under Lutheran pastors have received the Gospel within their own race and with many blessings. There have been other areas where they have received it within the same congregation of white brethren. The pattern cannot always be definitely set.
>
> But to close one's eyes to the real difficulties of this matter — to the harm it would needlessly do to some of our congregations and to our Christian outreach — when the same Gospel is available to the Negro in his own churches is neither proper nor Scriptural. Let not a senseless tragedy in Birmingham cause one to go to extremes and lose one's sense of balance in spiritual matters.[10]

Kennell's letter clearly reflected the same views which Wisler expressed; namely, the Gospel is available to the Negro and therefore his question: "Which is the major point at issue — to see that the Negro receives the Gospel or that he is integrated with a congregation?"

Furthermore, Kennell wrote of the importance of keeping a "balance in spiritual matters." That was the very crux of the matter. How were the leaders of the churches to keep such a balance? There were no quick and easy answers. Ron Reinhardt expressed the dilemma this way:

196

"We wanted to do the right thing, but do we have to be first? It was all new, and in all honesty we were a little bit afraid, and we didn't have anybody telling us the right way, or the best way."[11] That was precisely the struggle; the entire experience was new, and pastors and lay leaders were compelled to wrestle with the issue, and it is impossible to measure the personal agony which was experienced in deciding what action to take and what action to avoid.

As noted earlier, those who were in favor of integration and the merger often wrestled intensely with the application of Scripture: Just how did God's Word speak to this situation? On the other hand, those who favored the status quo apparently wrestled the least with the implications of Scripture. Instead, maintaining the status quo allowed for a spiritual "blind spot" with the result that they felt it was not necessary to examine the ramifications of Scripture.

In an article mentioned previously, Omar Stuenkel of *The Lutheran Witness* wrote a piece titled "Dilemma and Dedication" in which he sought to describe the conflict among Lutherans at the time of the Selma March. In the following paragraphs he caught the gist of the nature and content of the struggle among Southern Lutherans:

> Perhaps nothing illustrated better both the frequent dilemma and the continuing dedication of Christ's people in a time of crisis than the actions and expressions of Christian people in the South in recent months.

> All those interviewed made it clear and evident that their goal is one: the welfare of all people under God.

> Lonely battles of conscience necessarily involve Christian judgment based on many experiences and convictions established in the past. When applied to a given time and place, such judgments by Christians with the same goal will often vary on the method to reach the goal.

> It would be incorrect to assume that all that is necessary is a worthwhile Christian goal, important as that is. Methods are important, too, especially when they proceed out of principles thought to be Christian.

Wrong methods directed toward right goals may yield tragic results. But seldom is there only one altogether right way to act in a given situation. It is of the utmost importance that fellow Christians share their insights and discuss their plans. Often the lonely battle of conscience must still decide the specific action for each individual Christian in the time and circumstances before him.[12]

Did the Church Lead or Follow?

Did the Church affect the social change of the time, or did the social change move the Church into action? That was the question posed at the outset of this study. It was suggested earlier that a two-way street existed and each affected the other.

The Church, specifically the Southern District, had known since 1946 that the Synodical Conference recommended that the black work become incorporated into the local geographic Districts. It is said that Dr. Holls, who was District President in those years up until 1954, knew that something had to be done.[13]   Even in June of 1954 when the General Conference voted itself out of existence, First Vice President Hafner, who was in attendance at that meeting, said, "his district [Southern] is not opposed to taking over the supervision of the Negro missions...but it would take time and planning to work matters out...."[14]

Consequently, there was some pressure from within the Church body to take action. However, the specter of the isolated black Lutherans had already hung on the horizon for eight years, and apparently little was done during that period to bring them into the District.

Then, in May 1954, came the Supreme Court decisions to de-segregate all schools, and the wheels of the Federal Government began turning to implement that decision. Now the citizens of the South were forced to think about race issues in the community, if not in the Church.

At the Southern District Convention which was held five months after the Supreme Court decision, new leadership was elected and a few tentative overtures about race relationship were presented. At the 1955 Convention nothing more was done; the subject was barely mentioned in the Proceedings. Three years after the Supreme Court decision, and eleven years after the Synodical Conference recommendation, the four position papers were given at the Louisiana Pastors Conference. That Conference discussion prompted an overture for action which was presented to the District Convention in the fall of 1957. While the 1957 Convention proposed that the black congregations be received the following year,[15] it took three more years to hammer out the Guidelines for Discussion, another year before the black Lutherans were invited, and two more years before they were accepted into the District.

The process became a tension between speed and caution. At the 1958 Convention, the Special Synodical Conference Committee reported that they had worked "with due deliberate speed," and then in a resolution the Convention endorsed "the Committee's present philosophy of going forward with due, deliberate caution...."[16]

In all candor, it has to be said that the Southern District moved slowly. But was it too slow? Some thought it was too slow; others considered it much too fast.

In that same span of years, 1954 to 1963, the Montgomery bus boycott began (1955), the Supreme Court ordered buses to be integrated (1956); the U. S. Congress passed a Civil Rights Bill, (1957); Central High School in Little Rock was integrated (1957); sit-ins at lunch counters began (1960); the Supreme Court outlawed segregation in bus stations (1960); Freedom Riders tested the bus desegregation laws (1961); voter registration drives were started (1962); the University of Mississippi was integrated (1962); and the March on Washington for Civil Rights took place (1963). It is quite obvious that activities in government and society were moving forward with considerable speed, and Southern Lutherans were clearly aware of the changes taking place.

But who was influencing whom? Surely the Lutheran Church did not influence society, partly because it was inclined to stay out of social action and partly because it was a Germanic minority church in the South. The Baptist, Methodist, and Presbyterian Churches had the numerical strength, but they stayed out of the struggle almost totally. The Roman Catholic Church did take a firm stand for integration and exerted some positive influence, especially in New Orleans.

The Church that did affect society was the Black Church — those associated with the Southern Christian Leadership Conference under the direction of Martin Luther King, Jr. They were instrumental in the Montgomery bus boycott, the lunch counter sit-ins, the demonstrations in Birmingham, the voter registration drive, and the Selma-to-Montgomery March. In his *Letter from Birmingham City Jail,* King articulated their approach as follows: "Actually, we who engage in non-violent direct action are not the creators of tension. We merely bring to the surface the hidden tension that is already alive. We bring it out into the open where it can be seen and dealt with."[17]

Would the Federal Government have acted as quickly and as forthrightly to deal with Civil Rights matters if there had been no demonstrations and marches? Probably not. Politicians are ever attuned to the stirrings of the populace, and many of them were moved to take action after the Civil Rights problems were brought out into the open. So, in that sense the Church affected society; but in that process the Lutheran Church stood mostly on the sidelines.

However, what was taking place in the Black Church did spill over to the Lutherans of the South, mainly through people like Joe Ellwanger and Will Herzfeld. Both of them were members of SCLC and their activism led many of the moderates to support the changes which were under way. For instance, Herzfeld told me, "I felt you moderates were standing on the sidelines, and that you were at least cheering us on."[18]

Did the Church lead or follow? Speaking specifically of the Southern District, it followed. The District felt the pressure of the isolated black workers and congregations within its territory, and it felt the pressure of the social changes. It knew that things were going to change, but it had to chew on it a while, because fearful of social change, it went forward and followed "with due, deliberate caution."[19]

Experiences of Personal and Family Stress

The personal viewpoint and attitude also varied among individuals. Tom Noon exemplifies the wide swing of personal feelings. He has spent his entire ministry in the Black Church. From 1971 to 1976 he served Augustana Lutheran in Mansura, Louisiana, and since then he has served St. Paul's in Birmingham. When he arrived in Birmingham as a Prince of

Peace Volunteer in the summer of 1965, he experienced "a certain excitement...a kind of martyrdom about doing something right." No doubt, there was a sense of exhilaration for those who marched in demonstrations and stood in the front lines advocating justice. On the other side of the coin were threats and danger, and Noon also experienced those. He remembers the hateful stares, "looks that could kill" and the obscene gestures when he took black children to the city park.[20]

The threats and danger had a profound effect on pastors and their families. Two pastors spoke of the impact those times had on their personal spiritual life. Herzfeld said, "There was a lot of praying. I suppose our prayer life and our devotional life was much stronger in those days. That's where we got our strength."[21] Harold Woodworth, who went through the struggle at Concordia in Birmingham, reported, "We became a very, very close family, and we found our help in prayer and Scripture. We'd go around the house reading to one another [from Scripture]. Prayer was a powerful part of our life; it was a spontaneous thing - no canned prayer."[22]

Pastors' wives also experienced the difficulties of those turbulent years. Woodworth said, "It was no easy picnic for my wife."[23] Ellwanger's wife joined him in the Selma March and other activities. Herzfeld said "it was tough on a young wife [his] who was pregnant at that time," and "the women who were married to leaders in the movement developed their own ways of coping with the constant danger."[24] Fackler's wife suffered a miscarriage shortly after he was beaten by the Klan. One wife refused to be interviewed because her experiences in Birmingham over 30 years ago were still too painful. Elva Ellermann earlier shared her feelings of being isolated and censored during their first years in black ministry.

Likewise, personal support on a wider basis — family to family — was very important during the painful struggle of those years. While this support was provided by many and at many different levels, I will mention just two examples. In her recollections, Elva Ellermann expressed fond memories of the support that she and her husband received from Bill and Nancy Wedig. Their regular Sunday-evening bridge games gave them a forum for sharing both their professional and personal concerns.[25] Herzfeld spoke with grateful appreciation for Milton Popp, the white pastor in Tuscaloosa. The first time Herzfeld was arrested, Popp not only came to the jail to visit his colleague, but put up his own home in order to bail him out.[26] While differences and disagreements existed, the true nature of the Christian Church was also reflected in the care and bonds of fellowship which developed and sustained those in the struggle for unity.

Despite the struggle that took place in many congregations and with many individuals, sometimes there was no struggle at all. Eldon Weisheit shared one such happy example. In 1965 Pastor Kennell left Epiphany Lutheran in Montgomery, and Weisheit received the Call to that congregation. After receiving the Call, he decided to drive over from McComb, MS, and check out the race attitude at Epiphany. At the last minute he had second thoughts and concluded that, since they had not asked him about his views on race, he did not have the right to ask them about theirs. He made the visit but did not discuss the subject of race, and later accepted the Call.

Some months after he settled in at Epiphany, the members of the Church Council gathered at a restaurant after their meeting to socialize, and the question of race came up. It was revealed that during the call process the congregation leaders had decided that if a candidate came for a visit and made a big issue over the race question they were prepared to answer his questions in such a way that he would not accept the call. Upon hearing that, Weisheit added, "Since I didn't make a big issue of it, I really learned a lot about ministry — not to make problems that are not there. As it turned out, Epiphany was one of the joys of my ministry; and I would have missed that if I had gotten focused on that one thing rather than on what Christ had told us to do."

Weisheit reported another happy incident from his years at Epiphany which illustrates the power of the Gospel. A black lady asked to have her membership transferred to Epiphany and she was accepted without qualms, except for one difference. Henry Matthews, the chairman of the congregation, said, "Let the record show that salvation is still by the grace of God through faith in Jesus Christ, and not by integration."[27]

Thus, victories were won and changes took place as Southerners "chewed" on what was for many a bitter pill. By the power of the Gospel and the work of the Holy Spirit, that bitter pill was sweetened at least to some degree, and the walls of separation slowly and gradually came down. For a dozen years, starting in the middle 1950s, Lutherans of the South, both black and white, studied, debated, challenged one another, and took action — some quicker, some slower — and the concept of the merger eventually reached the congregational level. Dominick summarized the process beautifully by saying, "We took it as it came, in the name of the Lord."[28] At the 1964 District Convention, he had predicted that black people would not come in droves to white congregations, but now at least there was free access for them to worship with their white brothers and sisters.

Those years were a crucial phase in the history of Southern Lutherans. Will Herzfeld observed that "Some people could say that those were terrible times; but then they might have been the most creative moments in our ministry."[29] George Hrbek added, "Those years were my baptism into the ministry."[30]

At the core of the merger was a love that only the Gospel can produce. Many white people — Lutherans included — not only wanted to maintain the racial status quo, but some thought of black people as sub-human and their attitude toward them was nothing short of hatred. Such an ungodly attitude did not melt away suddenly. However, when I interviewed Arthur Bodley, a black man who grew up in Camden, AL, I was profoundly impressed by his remarks which expressed a radically different attitude. He said,

> I look at it from the perspective that I am thankful that I had parents to teach me to love. If I had not had that, I don't know where I would be...what kind of person I would be.... I was taught to love not in a particular racial situation, just to love all people. We were not taught to love blacks and hate whites, we said, "Love everybody." I have always taken the Bible seriously when it says, "Love all people."[31]

The Good News of God's love in Christ is radical in the face of typical human behavior, and in the struggle for unity it was this love which eventually manifested itself in healing the separation and bringing about the merger of the Lutheran Churches in the South.

April 4, 1968 - Dr. Martin Luther King, Jr., was assassinated in Memphis, Tennessee.

◊ ◊ ◊

An Era Ended

Students of the Civil Rights Movement consider the assassination of King as the end of that period which had its beginning with the Supreme Court's decision to desegregate schools. King's assassination sent shock waves through the nation and the relations between the races were put to a severe test. Riots occurred in various cities. Lutheran congregations also took note of the murder of King and, in varying degrees, observed the occasion along with the rest of the nation.

By the late 1960s, most of the merger process was completed and reasonably well established, even at the grass-roots level. Numerous personnel changes had taken place by then. Reinboth had left the District in 1964, and so had Hrbek. In 1965 Kennell accepted the call to Our Savior in New Orleans, and Weisheit moved to the parish which Kennell had vacated. In 1965, Homrighausen left Cullman, Alabama, to return to First English in New Orleans. Hermetz moved from Greenville, Mississippi, to St. Paul's in Cullman. We left Huntsville in 1966 for Good Shepherd in Shalimar in the Florida Panhandle, and Kuehnert became the second Richard to serve at Grace Lutheran in Huntsville.

In the summer of 1967, Ellwanger left St. Paul's in Birmingham and moved to Milwaukee; and in 1969 Homrighausen relinquished the office of District President in order to take another position in Miami. At the close of the 60s decade, two of the main players in the merger process had moved elsewhere, and the sound and fury turned to other concerns. By then, many of our people were far from home deep in the Viet Nam War, and at home the hippie movement had turned up the volume of protest against the war.

204

A Closing Word

How did the merger come out? How well did it succeed? What could have been done differently? The answer to those questions are still being debated, and individuals come to different conclusions. Here the words of Wilfred Schrader are worth noting: "We shouldn't judge people without realizing that it was difficult in those days. You weren't there."[32]

Indeed, those who were not there and did not live through those years will find it quite impossible to comprehend how deeply entrenched the social order of the Old South was and how bitter the struggle was to overcome the racial barrier. The mingling of black and white people today in society and in the Church, which seems so natural and taken for granted, did not come about easily. God's hand moved weak, sinful, and fearful people with love and courage to bring about change. While the unity is not yet perfect, nor will it ever be this side of heaven, nonetheless, the merger became a reality, and both races — and the Church — were enriched by it.

Every generation continues to face the challenge of reaching out to "people who aren't just like us." Jack Stewart, who weathered the storm as principal at McDonogh 19, in New Orleans, when it was integrated, offered the following formula with which to meet the challenge: "When you confront people, you don't do it with animosity, but you do it in love; in other words, you don't stop loving them, you let them grow, you give them space and time for the Holy Spirit to work."[33]

Thesis XIV of the Fourteen Articles adopted by Alabama/Upper Florida Conference expresses the same theological truth — the truth which provides both the goal and the power for the Church; namely,

> We firmly believe that the Holy Spirit is still operative in the Church today and that Christ is still Head of His Body and that therefore what may seem impossible to us, the complete unifying of Synodical Conference and Southern District churches, is quite possible with God. May we be enlightened and strengthened that the Word of the Holy Scripture be fulfilled in us, Phil. 1:27: "Stand fast in one spirit, with one mind striving together for the faith of the Gospel."[34]

APPENDIX A

GUIDELINES FOR DISCUSSION ADOPTED BY THE SOUTHERN DISTRICT

THESIS 1: All men, alike, have been born in sin and are under the judgment of God's condemnation. Romans 3:23.

THESIS 2: All men, alike, are the objects of God's loving concern. John 3:16.

THESIS 3: Jesus Christ, God's Son, made atonement for the sins of all men. 1 John 2:2.

THESIS 4: It is God's desire that His people be engaged, actively, in seeking the salvation of all people, regardless of any outward circumstances. Mark 16:15, Acts 1:8.

THESIS 5: It is God's will that His people exercise a spirit of humility both in respect to Him and in respect to their fellow men. 1 Peter 5:5-6, Romans 12:10, James 3:1-9.

THESIS 6: The purposes of the Christian congregation are twofold — a. To teach, strengthen, encourage and comfort its membership that all may remain faithful to the end. 1 Cor. 14:13, 2 Cor. 12:19, Ephesians 4:12. b. To reach out and win for Christ those who are still outside His kingdom. 1 Cor. 3:9.

THESIS 7: While it is true that in the physical arrangement of things on earth there are differences between people (education, social standing, language, race, etc.) nevertheless such things are neither advantages nor disadvantages in respect to man's standing before God. Gal. 3:26-29, Rom. 10:12-13.

THESIS 8:   The Christian congregation has the right to regulate its own affairs in keeping with its stated purposes (Thesis 6) so long as it violates no Word of God. However, it will always strive to be giving a **total living witness** which extends beyond the purely verbal sharing of the Gospel. Matt. 5:13-16, 1 John 3:18.

THESIS 9:   It is a natural thing that people in varying national, linguistic and cultural backgrounds will tend to associate with people of similar backgrounds when given the opportunity, and this applies also in church life. However, Christians will seek to rise above the inclinations of the flesh and under the Spirit's guidance strive to demonstrate their unity in Christ. James 2:1-9, Gal. 6:8-10, Col. 3:10-15.

THESIS 10:   It ought to be the sincere desire of every Christian that the time come when any individual will be privileged to attend any church of his choice, with full membership privileges. John 17:19-23, Romans 12:9-10.

THESIS 11:   It is Scripturally defensible for a congregation to practice segregation when the practice of integration would mean — a. the weakening or disrupting of their own congregation [and] b. the curtailment of their missionary outreach, provided no individual is thereby denied opportunity to receive the full ministry of the means of grace. 1 Cor. 6:12, Romans 15:1-7.

THESIS 12:   It is the Christian's chief aim to extend and preserve the Body of Christ and to accomplish this purpose he ought to be willing to forego privileges he might otherwise normally possess or experience hardship which might be necessary. Ephesians 4:1-6; 11-16.

THESIS 13:   Christians can not take lightly the problems within the church relating to discrimination, but will seek to lessen them and eventually solve them through sincere prayer and Christian love.

(Adopted at the Southern District Convention, New Orleans, LA, August 22-26, 1960.)

APPENDIX B

THESIS ON RACE RELATIONS AND SOUTHERN DISTRICT NEGOTIATIONS

THESIS I   In keeping with Christ's earnest prayer that all His followers be one so that the world might believe that the Father had sent Him, we deeply desire to be one in faith and fellowship with all those who recognize the lordship of Christ. We are convinced that the witness to Jesus Christ by the Lutheran Church in the South would be strengthened by the complete oneness of Synodical Conference and Southern District congregations in life, worship, and witness.

THESIS II   We testify that racial discrimination and segregation is sin, Acts 2:42, 1 John 1:7; 2:15-17, John 4, Acts 10 and all passages which prove that the barrier between Jew and Gentile is sin.

THESIS III   We believe that this sin requires repentance on the same Scriptural teaching which requires repentance of any and all sin. Matt. 3:2; 24:47.

THESIS IV   We therefore preach, teach, and witness against racial discrimination with the same earnestness and emphasis which we use against any other sin. James 2:1-10, Acts 20:27.

THESIS V   We hold that any sin and particularly a sin which is as prominent as racial discrimination should not be dealt with as an adiapharon but with that same firmness and candor which any article of faith should receive in its application. Matt. 28:18-20. "Observe all things."

THESIS VI   We believe that the fellowship within the communion of saints already confessed by virtue of membership in the Synodical Conference should be practised (sic). 1 John 1:7, Acts 2:42, Gal. 2:12.

THESIS VII   We believe that Christian fellowship (pulpit, altar, and communion) when practised (sic) under adverse worldly conditions will serve under God's blessings to strengthen unity in Kingdom building rather than harm the congregation's mission extension, since teaching and practising (sic) God's Word in fullness can never be antagonistic to the growth of the Kingdom. Acts 4:19-20; 5:29. Christians rejoicing in the unity which they have with the Father and with one another through Jesus Christ will gladly suffer to establish and maintain this unity and to extend it to a world dead in its separation from God and from man. Matt. 16:18, 1 Peter 1:7, Rom. 8:16-18.

THESIS VIII   We believe that all rights and privileges inherent in the Church are the possession, by grace through faith in Christ Jesus, of all Synodical Conference communicants and therefore should not be denied any of these members in requests for transfers or in the acceptance of transfers. (See the confirmation rite.)

THESIS IX   We believe that all rights and privileges as well as obligations and responsibilities given to a congregation by virtue of its membership in the one Body of Christ should not be denied any Synodical Conference congregation on the ground of racial origin or man-made discrimination patterns. 1 Peter 2:9, Rev. 1:6.

THESIS X   We believe that the Church should testify against all evils of racial discrimination and should not attempt to excuse or justify its silence on the ground of expediency. The Church does not seek to be at peace with the Christless

210

culture and world around it. The Church follows the example of our Lord who was nailed to a cross because He refused to make peace with it. John 18:36-37, Joshua 1:9, Acts 5:29.

THESIS XI We believe that an administration that does not seek to answer the above theses on the basis of Holy Scripture in following the example of Christ would not be blessed in Kingdom extension. Luke 10:25-37, John 8:31, John 13:35.

THESIS XII We believe that there would be no discrimination in ministerial and teacher training and therefore we maintain that not only existing Synodical Conference schools should be open to Negroes but that a school with adequate facilities and with full academic and professional advantages be built and maintained for the millions in the South (who would not be served by schools in the North). Mark 16:15-16, Matt. 28:18-20, Rom. 10:14,15.

THESIS XIII We humble ourselves in meekness, forbearance, and repentance, praying that we recognize our own sins and shortcomings in Kingdom building and that Christ the victorious and resurrected living Head of the Church, mercifully forgive us.

THESIS XIV We firmly believe that the Holy Spirit is still operative in the Church today and that Christ is still Head of His body and that therefore what may seem impossible to us, the complete unifying of Synodical Conference and Southern District churches, is quite possible with God. May we be enlightened and strengthened that the Word of the Holy Scripture be fulfilled in us, Phil. 1:27: "Stand fast in one spirit, with one mind striving together for the faith of the Gospel."

211

(Adopted by the Alabama/Upper Florida Pastor Conference of the Lutheran Synodical Conference, St. Phillip's Lutheran Church, Catherine, Alabama, June 30, 1961.)

APPENDIX C

Written in memory of O. H. "Sam" Reinboth
who died on January 13, 1971

OF SUCH IS THE KINGDOM

Of such is the Kingdom...
Of men like this:

He came our way
  and was with us
    only a few years.
Yet his influence
  was felt by many
And his followers
  were true.

Such a man was this:
  he was tough,
  and loving,
With lofty goals
  but down to earth.
He was a man
  of great piety
  but never pietistic.
He was upright
  but never
    holier-than-thou.
A man was he
  of high accomplishments
But always one
  who saw himself
    with humility
    under God.

He was a man
    of great intellect
Who felt at home
    with common people —
And more important,
    he made common people
    feel at home with him.

He was a man of
    great stature
        but did not
        look down
    on anyone.

He had a special way
    with people.
He knew you,
    remembered you;
    made you feel
    important and good.

He was warm
    and he drew you
    to him
With a handshake
    that quite literally
    pulled.

He had a special gift
    for meetings.
His timing was great —
    when to speak
    and when to wait.
And when he spoke
    he was precise -

Like an injection
   his words coursed
   through all the veins
      and the effect
      spread quickly,

To move
   and influence
      the whole body
         of assembled people.

Such a man was he...
Of such is the Kingdom.

— ROZ

Written in honor of Pastor Calvin P. Thompson (1883-1975)
who was granted an honorary Doctor of Divinity degree
at the 1972 District Convention

A MAN HONORED

He is a little man,
    the years have shrunken him
    and turned him gray
    and bent him slightly.

Though small, his love is large,
    his kindness evident,
    his face clearly written
    with gentleness.

With slow and slightly uncertain steps
    he moved to the front of the chamber.

Applause picked up,
    the assembly stood,
    smiling faces turned to him
    all around

To honor this man —
    who is not hard to honor
    and who was surprised
    to receive it.

His words are
    still full of life,
    speaking an eagerness —

after 89 years —
for more to come.

Brothers and sisters sang:
"For all the saints..."
and bathed this man with love
and hugged him warmly.

It was a very good
and happy moment!

— ROZ

President Homrighausen
welcomes C. P. Thompson
1963

SOURCES - Interviews and Correspondence (Identified: B - Black, W - White)

Allenstein, Verna, (W) Gadsden, AL, January 20, 1998, phone conversation.

Ansorge, Bernard, (W) Huntsville, AL, April 10, 1996, personal interview and numerous E-mail correspondences.

Benson, Sally, (W) Cape Canaveral, FL, April 28, 1997, personal correspondence.

Bodley, Arthur, (B) Pensacola, FL, February 10, 1999, personal interview.

Bomba, James, (W) Houston, TX, August 23, 1997, personal conversation.

Bretscher, Paul, (W) Valparaiso, IN, June 10, 1997, phone conversation, and correspondence.

Brockmann, James (W) Mesa, AZ, December 31, 1997 and January 12, 1998, phone conversations and correspondence.

Brockmann, Pat (W) Mesa, AZ, January 12, 1998, phone conversation.

Brown, James, (B) Pensacola, FL, November 5, 1997, phone conversation.

Brown, Johnny, (B) Camden, AL, May 2, 1995, personal interview, and correspondence April 30, 1997 and May 20, 1997..

Buerger, Martin, (W) Pittsburgh, PA, June 23, 1995, phone interview, correspondence and phone conversations August 30, 1996 and November 12, 1997.

Cameron, Ivory Carl, (B) Bessemer, AL, June 29, 1996, personal conversation.

Clark, Moses, (B) Atmore, AL, May 2, 1995, personal interview.

Coyner, Edwin, (W) Clinton, MS, August 22, 1996, phone conversation.

Davis, John, (B) Camden, AL, May 2, 1995, personal interview.

Davis, Warren, (B) Pensacola, FL, May 2, 1995, personal conversation, and numerous follow-ups.

Dean, Cynthia Green, (W) Pensacola, FL, July 9, 1996, personal interview and correspondence November 7, 1997.

Dickinson, Richard, (B) St. Louis, MO, April 22 & 25, 1997, phone conversations and correspondence.

Dittmann, Robert, (W) Mobile, AL, August 7, 1996, phone conversation.

Dominick, Albert,† (B) Baton Rouge, LA, May 3, 1995, personal interview.

Ellermann, Elva, (W) Slidell, LA, April 18, 1997, correspondence.

Ellermann, John, (W) Slidell, LA, April 30, 1995, personal interview, and numerous e-mail letters.

Ellwanger, Joseph, (W) Milwaukee, WS, March 21, 1996, phone interview, June 11, 1997, phone conversation and September 24, 1997, correspondence.

Fackler, James, (W) Vandalia, IL, May 5, 1996, phone interview.

Fisher, Anna, (B) Baton Rouge, LA, May 3, 1995, personal interview, and correspondence.

Gildersleeve, James, (B) Selma, AL, July 8, 1997, phone conversation.

Harders, Nancy, (W) Parker, FL, August 3, 1997, personal conversation.

Hermetz, Harold, (W) Cullman, AL, December 5, 1996, phone interview.

Herzfeld, Will, (B) Chicago, IL, March 11, 1996, phone interview.

Hoard, Samuel, (B) Orlando, FL, November 3 & 25, 1998, correspondence.

Holdorf, Kenneth, (W) San Angelo, TX, November 18, phone conversation.

Homrighausen, Edgar, (W) Lacombe, LA, May 1, 1995, personal interview, April 14, 1996, phone interview, September 7 & 8, 1997, phone calls and January 3, 1998 phone call.

Hrbek, George, (W) Cleveland, OH, July 6, 1997, phone interview and correspondence.

Johnson, Jeff G.,† (B) Los Angeles, CA, August 21, 1997, correspondence.

Kappeler, Eugene, (W) Monroe, LA, May 3, 1995, personal interview and correspondence.

Kieschnick, Harold, (W) New Orleans, LA, April 16, 1997, personal interview and phone conversation.

Kuehnert, J. Mark, (W) Houston, TX, phone conversations, September 20, and October 23, 1997.

Kuehnert, Richard Jr., (W) Danbury, CN, September 19, 1996, phone interview and correspondence.

Lieske, H. William, (W) Asheville, NC, Personal conversation and January 12 & 22, 1998 e-mail correspondence.

Marshall, James B., (B) Mobile, AL, August 7, 1996, phone interview.

McNair, Chris, (B) Birmingham, AL, September 9, 1996, personal interview.

Meyer, Richard "Pedo," (W) New Orleans, LA, January 14, 1998, personal conversation.

Moritz, Victor, (W) New Orleans, LA, April 10, 1996, personal interview.

Moss, John, (B) Sardis, AL, July 7, 1997, phone conversation.

Nau, John, (W) Hattisburg, MS, August 9, 1995, personal interview and correspondence.

Noon, Thomas, (W) Birmingham, AL, May 8, 1995, personal interview, and correspondence.

Pape, James, (W) Zimmerman, MN, January 31, 1996, phone interview and correspondence.

Pflieger, Richard, (W) Albuquerque, NM, September 18, 1995, personal conversation.

Pieplow, Charles, (W) Birmingham, AL, November 5, 1997, phone conversation.

Prellop, Alfred, (W) Baton Rouge, LA, April 16, 1997, personal interview.

Quiram, Gerald, (W) Midwest City, OK, August 20, 1996, phone conversation.

Reinhardt, Ronald, (W) Decatur, AL, December 12, 1996, phone interview.

Schrader, Wilfred, (W) Pensacola, FL, July 9, 1996, personal interview and phone conversations.

Schuetz, Thomas, (W) St. Rose, LA, September 11, 1996, phone conversation.

Schultz, Kurtis, (W) Birmingham, AL, September 9, 1996, personal conversation, and phone calls.

Schulz, Victor, (W) Pensacola, FL, July 9, 1995, personal interview and correspondence.

Skinner, John, (B) New Orleans, LA, May 2, 1995, personal interview and correspondence..

Stewart, Jack, (W) New Orleans, LA, January 31, 1996, phone interview and September 9, 1997 phone conversations.

Strelow, Theodore, (W) Burlington, NC, August 4, 1997, phone conversation and September 10, 1997, correspondence.

Tellis, Glenn,† (B) Crestview, FL, August 16, 1996, personal conversation.

Thompson, Edwin, (B) New Orleans, LA, May 2, 1995, personal interview.

Veit, Ben, (W) Lawton, OK, June 28, 1996, personal conversation.

Wedig, William† & Nancy, (W) New Orleans, LA, May 2, 1995, personal interview.

Weisheit, Eldon,†(W) Tucson, AZ, March 4, 1997, phone interview, March 7, 1997, October 2, 1997 and December 11, 1997, correspondence.

Whitney, Verena, (W) Pensacola, FL, December 11, 1997, correspondence.

Wiggins, James, (B) Montgomery, AL, April 11, 1996, personal interview.

Windhorst, John, (W) Birmingham, AL, June 6, 1996, phone conversation.

Witthaur, Herb, (W) Jamestown, ND, May 26, 1995, personal correspondence.

Woodworth, Harold, (W) Jacksonville, IL, July 2, 1996, phone interview and July 2, 1996 and August 21, 1996, correspondence.

NOTES

Preface

1. Personal interview with Albert Dominick, May 3, 1995.

Introduction

1. Conference Papers delivered at Percy Quinn State Park, MS, April 29-May 2, 1957. Carbon copies in Southern District Archives. Photo copy in my possession.

2. *Proceedings, 53rd Convention of the Southern District,* pp. 44,45. Note: The Florida Panhandle is in the Southern District.

3. According to *Free At Last,* A History of the Civil Rights Movement, published in 1989 by Teaching Tolerance, 400 Washington Ave., Montgomery, AL, 36104. Used with permission.

4. Based on information in *Free At Last,* pp. 100-102.

Chapter 1 - Background of the Old South

1. Quoted from *The South And The Southerner,* by Ralph McGill, (Boston: Little Brown and Company, 1963), p. 24.

2. Several years after the Public Accommodation Law opened eating places to all races, I saw a sign in a public eatery in Scottsboro, Alabama, with the words: "We Still Reserve The Right to Refuse Service to Anyone."

3. Personal interview with William Wedig, May 2, 1995. Bill Lieske recalls that upon seeing the "Colored" sign at a water fountain, he wondered how they colored the water, and why anyone would want colored water. E-mail letter from Lieske, January 12, 1998.

4. From a book titled *Black Monday* by Brady.

5. *TIME,* March 25, 1956, p. 26. Used with permission.

6. Personal interview with John Nau, August 9, 1995.

7. Personal interview with Moses Clark, May 2, 1995.

8. From *Jesus Breaks Down Barriers,* a story written about John Davis, by Ray M. Rogers, n.d.

9. Personal interview with John Davis, May 2, 1995.

10. Information based on a letter from Walter H. Ellwanger to Thomas Noon, February 2, 1978. Original in the archives of Concordia Historical Institute, photo copy in my files.

11. Personal conversation with Ben Veit, June 28, 1996.

12. Personal interview with Gene Kappeler, May 3, 1995.

13. New Orleans has two St. Paul Lutheran congregations. The other, a black congregation, is located on Annette Street.

14. Nau.

15. Ibid.

16. Conversation with Richard "Pedo" Meyer, January 14, 1998.

17. Personal interview with Albert Dominick, May 3, 1995.

18. Conversation with Anna Fisher, May 3, 1995.

19. Dominick.

20. Ibid.

21. Personal interview with John Skinner, May 2, 1995.

22. Ibid.

23. Personal letter from Elva Ellermann, April 18, 1997.

24. Phone conversation with Pat Brockmann, January 12, 1998.

Chapter 2 - Movement Toward Merger

1. *Proceedings of the 47ᵗʰ Convention of the Southern District,* pp. 32,33.

2. The decision to disband the General Conference was by a margin of one vote. See *Black Christians - The Untold Lutheran Story,* by Jeff G. Johnson, (St. Louis: Concordia Publishing House, 1991), p. 199. According to Johnny Brown, when the vote was taken he and Teacher Rivers had left the meeting to visit someone "down in the country." Had they stayed, they both would have voted to retain the General Conference. Thus the history of Black Lutheranism turned on such a narrow margin. Personal correspondence from Johnny Brown, May 20, 1997.

3. *The Missionary Lutheran,* Vol. 32, No. 8, August 1954, p. 63.

4. Cf. *The Transition of Negro Missions from The Synodical Conference Missionary Board to the Southern District of the Lutheran Church - Missouri*

Synod, by James E. Brockmann, July 1, 1969, p. 4. The paper is in Brockmann's file, a photo copy in my files.

5. *Proceedings,* p. 41.

6. Ibid

7. *Proceedings,* p. 37.

8. Ibid, p. 84.

9. Ibid, p. 82.

10. Ibid, pp. 84,85.

11. In the Southeastern District 19 of 137 congregations were black, in the Southern District 55 of 157 congregations were black.

12. See *Roses and Thorns,* by Richard C. Dickinson, (St. Louis: Concordia Publishing House, 1973), p. 114.

13. Letter from Del Borcherding to John Ellermann, June 6, 1954. Original in Southern District Archives. Photocopy in my files.

14. Mimeograph copy in Southern District Archives. Photocopy in my file.

15. *Proceedings of 48ᵗʰ Convention of the Southern District,* p. 18.

16. Robert S. Graetz, *Montgomery: A White Preacher's Memoir,* (Minneapolis: Fortress Press, 1991), p. 53.

17. Personal interview with John Nau, August 9, 1995.

18. Phone conversation with Paul Bretscher, June 10, 1997, and correspondence October 2, 1997.

19. Graetz, p. 118.

20. *Proceedings of the 1956 Convention of the Lutheran Church - Missouri Synod,* St. Paul, MN, p. 759. The Lutheran Human Relations Association of America (LHRAA) was instrumental in bringing the race issue to the convention; see *Race Against Time* by Andrew Schulze, (Valparaiso: Lutheran Human Relations Association of America, 1972), pp. 88-92.

21. Dickinson, pp. 110,112, 204.

22. *Proceedings, 1956 LC-MS Convention.*

23. Carbon copies of the originals are in the Southern District Archives. Photocopies of the copies are in my files.

24. James Eastland, Mississippi's Senator at the time stated, "[Mississippi will] maintain control of our own elections and...will protect and maintain white supremacy throughout eternity." (*TIME,* March 26, 1956, p. 26. Used with permission.)

25. *Proceedings of the 49ᵗʰ Convention of the Southern District,* p. 94.

1. *Proceedings of the 49ᵗʰ Convention of the Southern District,* pp. 94,95.
2. Ibid, p. 16.
3. Ibid, p. 1.
4. Ibid, pp. 11,12.
5. Ibid, p. 94.
6. Other members of the floor committee were: Pastors - Ahrendt, Eller-mann and Zucker; Teachers - Lillian Stewart of Gethsemane, New Orleans and Edwin Bode of St. Paul/First English, New Orleans; and laymen - Fox, Trinity, Birmingham, Dubina, Our Savior, Columbus, MS, Fasse, Our Savior, Crestview, FL, and Christian, Our Savior, New Orleans. Also on the committee as advisory mem-bers were: Walter Ellwanger, Superintendent of the Alabama/Upper Florida Con-ference and Gotthilf Kramer (retired) the former Superintendent of the Louisiana Conference of the Synodical Conference.
7. *Proceedings,* p. 95.
8. Convention Workbook.
9. Ibid.
10. Personal notes.
11. *Proceedings,* p. 94.
12. Ibid, p. 95.
13. *Proceedings of the 50ᵗʰ Convention of the Southern District,* p. 91.
14. Ibid, p. 91.
15. Ibid.
16. Ibid, pp. 91,92.
17. *Proceedings of the 51ˢᵗ Convention of the Southern District,* p. 83.
18. *Proceedings of the 50ᵗʰ Convention,* p. 93.
19. *Proceedings of the 12ᵗʰ Annual Valparaiso University Institute of Human Relations,* July 28-30, 1961, pp. 39,40.
20. Phone interview with Joe Ellwanger, March 21, 1996.
21. Phone interview with George Hrbek, July 6, 1997.
22. *Proceedings of the 51ˢᵗ Convention,* p. 87.
23. Ibid, p. 88.
24. Ibid.
25. Ibid, pp. 85 & 91. Note: The Theses, as presented, are given on page 85, and the revised Theses are on page 91.
26. Ibid.
27. Ibid.
28. Ibid.
29. Ibid.

30. Ibid, p. 83.

31. Ibid, p. 84.

32. Ibid, p. 90.

Chapter 4 - Social Turmoil and Reaction

1. Cf. *Free At Last,* (Montgomery: Teaching Tolerance, 1989), pp. 46,47.

2. *TIME,* December 12, 19960, p. 21. Used with permission.

3. Phone interview with Jack Stewart, January 31, 1996.

4. Ibid.

5. Phone conversation with Tom Schuetz, September 11, 1996.

6. The source for the Selma account was a phone interview with George Hrbek, July 6, 1997 and information supplied by Sally Benson, April 28, 1997.

7. This account is based on a personal interview with Eugene Kappeler, May 3, 1995.

8. Unless otherwise noted, this account is based on a phone interview with James Fackler, May 5, 1996.

9. *The Cresset,* Publication of Valparaiso University, Valparaiso, IN, June 1961, pp. 16,17. Used with permission.

10. Phone interview with Edgar Homrighausen, April 14, 1996.

11. Ibid.

12. Phone interview with Joe Ellwanger, March 21, 1996.

Chapter 5 - Steps Leading to an Invitation

1. A carbon copy of the Pastors Conference minutes is in the Southern District Archives. A photocopy is in my files.

2. Personal interview with Albert Dominick, May 3, 1995.

3. *The Missionary Lutheran,* Vol. 39, No. 8, September 1961, pp. 69,72.

4. Phone conversation with Joe Ellwanger, June 11, 1997.

5. Personal interview with Eugene Kappeler, May 3, 1995.

6. Personal interview with Edgar Homrighausen, May 1, 1995.

7. *The Lutheran Witness,* February 7, 1961, p. 11. Used with permission throughout this mongraph.

8. Ibid.

9. Homrighausen.

10. *The Lutheran Witness,* June 13, 1961, p. 20.

11. Ibid, p. 3

12. *The Lutheran Witness,* September 19, 1961, p. 16.

13. *The Lutheran Witness,* Southern District Supplement, October 3, 1961.

14. *Proceedings of the 52nd Convention of the Southern District,* p. 52.

15. Ibid, p. 122.

16. Ibid.

17. Ibid, pp. 122,123.

18. *The Lutheran Witness,* Southern District Edition, Convention Report, October 3, 1961.

Chapter 6 - Adjusting to a New Reality

1. *The Lutheran Witness,* February 6, 1962, p. 20.

2. Minutes of the Church Council of Immanuel Lutheran Church, Penacola, FL, February 15, 1962.

3. Ibid, April 12, 1962.

4. Ibid.

5. Ibid, April 20, 1961.

6. See also World Book Encyclopedia.

7. Personal interview with Wilfred Schrader, July 9, 1996.

8. *The Lutheran Witness,* Southern District Edition, May 29, 1962.

9. Personal interview with Edgar Homrighausen, May 1, 1995.

10. Phone interview with James Pape, January 31, 1996.

11. Homrighausen.

12. Personal interview with Bernard Ansorge, April 10, 1996.

13. Phone interview with Eldon Weisheit, March 4, 1997.

14. *The Lutheran Witness,* Southern District Edition, October 15, 1963.

15. Phone interview with Will Herzfeld, March 11, 1996.

16. *TIME,* May 19, 1997, p. 27. Used with permission.

17. *The Lutheran Witness,* April 3, 1962, p. 23.

18. This account is based on a phone interview with James Pape.

19. *The Lutheran Witness,* Southern District Edition, November 13, 1962.

20. Phone interview with Joe Ellwanger, March 21, 1996.

21. Personal interview with Arthur Bodley, February 10, 1999.

22. Phone interview with James B. Marshall, August 7, 1996.

23. Personal interview with John Davis, May 2, 1995.

24. Ellwanger.

25. Personal interview with James Wiggins, April 11, 1996.

26. Personal interview with Johnny Brown, May 2, 1995.

27. Wiggins.

28. Bodley.

29. Marshall.

30. As shown on the front-cover photo of *The Lutheran Witness, September 17,1963.*

31. Bodley.

Chapter 7 - 1963, An Unforgettable Year

1. *The Lutheran Witness,* Southern District Edition, February 5, 1963.

2. John Davis grew up in a very large family; he is one of 34 children. His father had 4 children by his first wife and 15 each by his second and third wife. At the time of his father's death, there were 117 grandchildren, and the 39th great-grandchild was born on the day of his funeral.

3. Phone interview with Joe Ellwanger, March 21, 1996.

4. See *A TESTAMENT OF HOPE, The Essential Writings of Martin Luther King, Jr.,* edited by James Melvin Washington, (New York: Writers House, Copyright 1968 by Martin Luther King, Jr., copyright renewed 1996 by The Estate of Martin Luther King, Jr.), pp. 289-302. Used with permission.

5. Phone interview with James Pape, January 31, 1996

6. Ellwanger.

7. Pape.

8. *The Lutheran Witness,* May 28, 1963, p. 10.

9. Ibid, July 9, 1963, p. 3.

10. Ibid, September 17, 1963, p. 21.

11. From a phone conversation with James Brockmann, on January 12, 1998.

12. Letter to Albert (Tony) Lehenbauer from Homrighausen. Copy in the Southern District Archives.

13. Personal correspondence from Bernard Ansorge, December 12, 1997.

14. Personal interview with Albert Dominick, May 3, 1995, and personal interview with Edgar Homrighausen, May 1, 1995.

15. Phone interview with Will Herzfeld, March 11, 1996.

16. Brockmann.

17. Phone interview with Harold Hermetz, December 5, 1997.

18. Phone interview with Eldon Weisheit, May 4, 1997.

19. Personal interview with Wilfred Schrader, July 9, 1996, and Minutes of Voters' Meeting, Immanuel Lutheran, Pensacola, FL, January 27, 1963.

20. Minutes of Church Council Meeting at Immanuel, April 18, 1963

21. Ibid, June 6, 1963. See also *The Lutheran Witness,* Southern District Edition, September 17, 1963. It was reported at the time that special permission for the use of the NAS chapel had to be granted by U. S. Attorney General, Robert Kennedy.

22. Schrader.

23. *The Lutheran Witness,* Southern District Edition, July 23, 1963.

24. Pastor Dominick did not get to serve at the altar for Holy Communion as Homrighausen had proposed. The September 17, 1963, Southern District *Supplement* records: "Dr. Edgar Homrighausen, District President, was the Communion celebrant; Rev. Luther Loesch, pastor of Immanuel, the host congregation was the officiant. They were assisted by Rev. Fred Zucker, Biloxi, Miss., Rev. O. H. Reinboth, and Wm. F. Wedig of New Orleans [all white men]. Over 460 were strengthened at the Lord's Table...."

25. *The Lutheran Witness,* September 17, 1963, p. 8.

26. Southern District Edition, September 17, 1963.

27. *Proceedings of the 53rd Convention of the Southern District,* p. 24. A reporter for the *Pensacola News Journal* picked up on the word "quiet" and in the next day's edition wrote: "Lutherans...quietly admitted Negro congregations for the first time...."

28. Ibid, p. 44.

29. Ibid, p. 45.

30. Ibid, p. 109.

31. Southern District Edition, September 17, 1963.

Chapter 8 - Reaction To The Merger

1. Phone interview with Martin Buerger, June 23, 1995.

2. Phone interview with James Pape, January 31, 1996.

3. Personal interview with Thomas Noon, May 8, 1995.

4. Pape.

5. According to *Free At Last,* (Montgomery: Teaching Tolerance, 1989), Virgil Ware was riding on the handlebars on a bike with his brother and "they were approached by two white boys riding a red motor scooter decorated with Confederate stickers. The boy riding on the back of the motor scooter pulled out a .22-caliber pistol and fired twice without saying a word.... [They] killed Virgil Ware casually, as if they were shooting at an animal." (p. 60) Such was the atmosphere and racial turmoil in Birmingham following the church bombing.

6. Cf. *Free At Last,* p. 58. The following is found on page 59 of *Free At Last:* "September 15, 1963 was remembered as a day of victory for the Klan.

Shortly after the church bombing, white supremacist leader Connie Lynch told a group of Klansmen that those responsible for the bombing deserved 'medals.' Lynch said the four young girls who died 'weren't children. Children are little people, little human beings and that means white people.... They're just little niggers...and if there's four less niggers tonight, then I say, 'Good for whoever planted that bomb!'"

7. Ibid, p. 61.

8. Personal interview with Chris McNair, September 9, 1996.

9. *The Lutheran Witness,* October 15, 1963, p. 19.

10. McNair.

11. *The Lutheran Witness,* p. 19.

12. Ibid.

13. *The Lutheran Witness,* October 1, 1963, pp. 3,4.

14. Phone interview with Joe Ellwanger, March 21, 1996

15. Buerger.

16. Phone interview with Edgar Homrighausen, September 7, 1997 and Ellwanger, see above.

17. Unless otherwise noted, the sources for this account are as follows:
Buerger, also phone conversation November 12, 1997.
Ellwanger.
Phone interview with Harold Hermetz, December 5, 1996.
Homrighausen.
Phone interview with J. Mark Kuehnert, September 20, 1997.
Personal interview with John Nau, August 9, 1995.
Personal interview with Thomas Noon, May 8, 1995.
Pape.
Phone interview with Gerald Quiram, August 20, 1996.
Phone interview with Ronald Reinhardt, December 12, 1996.
Personal conversation with Kurtis Schultz, September 9, 1996, and phone conversations.
Phone conversation with John Windhorst, June 6, 1996.
Phone interview with Harold Woodworth, July 2, 1996.

18. Some felt he was up-staging Pastor Reuter who had long been a leader in the District.

19. *Southern District Summary,* January 29, 1964, p. 3.

20. Ibid, p. 4.

21. In a phone interview on January 3, 1998, Homrighausen told me that he was pressured by a number of pastors into saying something. Furthermore in the *Southern Official Summary,* he explained: "I know that rumors have been spread concerning my action to suspend First Lutheran Congregation of

Birmingham and Reverend Hans Reuter from the Lutheran Church - Missouri Synod." (page 3)

22. *Proceedings of the 54th Convention of the Southern District,* pp. 29-31.

23. In about 1990, First Lutheran held a joint Reformation Rally with Prince of Peace Lutheran, a black congregation. However, only 3 or 4 from Prince of Peace attended. Phone conversation with Charles Pieplow, November 4, 1997.

24. See Note #11 above.

25. Unless otherwise noted this account is from the following sources:
   Ellwanger.
   Personal interview with Victor Schulz, July 9, 1996.
   Woodworth interview plus a copy of his diary.

26. Mimeographed History of Concordia Congregation. Photocopy in my files.

27. *The Lutheran Witness,* Southern District Edition, February 18, 1964.

28. This account is based on the following sources:
   Homrighausen.
   Phone interview with George Hrbek, July 6, 1997.
   Personal interview with Harold Kieschnick, April 16, 1998.

29. Phone conversation with James Brockmann, January 12, 1998.

30. This account is based on a personal interview with Bernard Ansorge, April 10, 1996, and phone interview with Richard Kuehnert, Jr., September 19, 1996.

31. The two pastors met with limited success in reaching city officials. Ansorge, however, adds an ironic twist: "Five years later the mayor appointed me to a subcommittee for the dedication of a new civic center in Jackson. By that time I was a member of the Jackson Choral Society and had been elected as its president. So, in the capacity of president I was invited to participate in the ribbon cutting ceremony of the new civic center. I attended several parties and receptions with the mayor then, but he never really knew that I was a pastor of black church." (Correspondence, November 15, 1997)

32. Personal interview with Wilfred Schrader, July 9, 1996. According to Warren Davis, Jehovah Lutheran (a black congregation) used Immanuel's facilities when they organized in 1924. (Personal correspondence, November 5, 1997. Also personal correspondence with Verena Whitney, December 10, 1997.)

33. Nau.

34. Ansorge.

35. Hermetz.

36. Phone interview with Eldon Weisheit, March 4, 1997.

37. Reinhardt.

38. Weisheit.

39. Letter from John Ellermann, October 25, 1997. According to my findings, Good Shepherd Lutheran - Shalimar, FL, was the first congregation in the Southern District to have integrated membership. Good Shepherd received four black adults by confirmation on December 19, 1965. Ascension Lutheran - Huntsville, AL, was a very close second. They received a black family by transfer from St. Paul's Birmingham, AL, on December 21, 1965.

40. Cf. *The Lutheran Witness,* Southern District Edition, June 1965.

41. Personal conversation with Nancy Harders (Pastor Storm's daughter), August 3, 1997.

42. Phone conversation with Theodore Strelow, August 4, 1997.

43. Homrighausen.

44. In that time period, the number of congregations grew from 67 to 167.

45. Herzfeld, Ellwanger and phone interview with James B. Marshall, August 7, 1996.

46. Letter from Reinboth to Brockmann, April 28, 1961. Copy in my file.

47. Personal interview with James Wiggins, April 11, 1996.

48. See *The Lutheran Witness,* Southern District Edition, August 6, 1963.

49. Kieschnick.

50. *The Lutheran Witness,* Southern District Edition, January 19, 1965.

51. Ibid.

52. Personal interview with John Davis, May 2, 1995; personal conversation with Warren Davis, May 2, 1995 and Wiggins.

53. The Lutheran Witness, Southern District Edition, June 23, 1964.

54. Les Allenstein helped in the negotiations. Conversation with Verna Allenstein, January 21, 1998.

55. Homrighausen.

56. A recollection of Bernard Ansorge.

57. *Proceedings of the 54th Convention of the Southern District,* pp, 29-31.

59. Ibid, pp. 27,28.

Chapter 9 - Continuing Protests

1. Personal interview with Edgar Homrighausen, May 1, 1995

2. *The Lutheran Witness,* March 30, 1965, p. 13.

3. Ibid.

4. Personal conversation with Warren Davis, November 7, 1997. According to Davis, both Dominick, a member of the Board of Control, and Hunt, a member of the faculty, did not approve of the demonstrations or the March.

5. Warren Davis, and conversation with James Brown, November 6, 1997.

6. Warren Davis.

7. *The Lutheran Witness,* March 30, 1965, p. 13.

8. Ibid, p. 14.

9. Homrighausen.

10. Phone interview with James B. Marshall, August 7, 1996.

11. Phone interview with Joe Ellwanger, March 21, 1996.

12. Ibid.

13. Ibid.

14. Personal correspondence with Joe Ellwanger, September 24, 1997.

15. *The Lutheran Witness,* June 1965, pp. 15,16.

16. Ibid, p. 18.

17. *Proceedings of the 49th Convention of The Lutheran Church - Missouri Synod,* Resolutions 9-21 and 9-22, p. 171.

18. Martin Luther King, Jr., did not consider outsiders as interference. Instead, his rationale was: "Injustice anywhere is a threat to justice everywhere. We are caught in an inescapable network of mutuality, tied in single garment of destiny. Whatever affects one directly affects all indirectly. Never again can we afford to live with the narrow provincial 'outside agitator' idea. Anyone who lives in the United States can never be considered and outsider anywhere in this country." See *A TESTAMENT OF HOPE, The Essential Writings of Martin Luther King, Jr.,* edited by James Melvin Washington, (New York: Writers House, copyright 1968 by Martin Luther King, Jr., copyright renewed 1996 by The Estate of Martin Luther King, Jr.), p. 290. Used with permission.

19. In an article he wrote for the Valparaiso University Institute of Human Relations, Joe Ellwanger identified four groups, namely; 1) The Violent Segregationist, 2) The Committed, Non-Violent Segregationist, 3) The Fearful Status Quoers (Moderates) and 4) The Committed Integrationist. See *Proceedings of the 12th Annual Valparaiso Institute of Human Relations,* Julys 28-30, 1961, pp. 35-40.

20. Ellwanger.

21. Phone interview with James Pape, January 31, 1996.

22. Homrighausen, May 1, 1995.

23. *Birmingham Post-Herald,* August 30 and September 1, 1962. Used with permission.

24. Personal interview with Bernard Ansorge, April 10, 1996.

25. Phone interview with Richard Kuehnert, Jr., September 19, 1996.

26. Dixie District Walther League Convention Handbook, pp. 19,25-29.

27. E-mail correspondence with H. William Lieske, January 28, 1998.

28. Ibid, January 12, 1998.

29. *The Lutheran Witness,* Southern District Edition, August 1965.

30. *Proceedings of the 55th Convention of the Southern District,* p. 51.

31. *The Lutheran Witness,* Southern District Edition, July 1966.

32. Personal correspondence with Bernard Ansorge, December 11, 1997.

33. Personal correspondence with Eldon Weisheit, November 28, 1997.

34. Personal interview with Eldon Weisheit, March 4, 1997.

35. *The Lutheran Witness,* November 1966, p. 25.

Chapter 10 - Reflections and Evaluation

1. Personal interview with Wilfred Schrader, July 9, 1996.

2. A recollection of Bernard Ansorge.

3. *Proceedings of the 52nd Convention of the Southern District,* p. 49.

4. News article in the *Pensacola News-Journal,* August 28, 1963.

5. A Journal for Sunday School workers published by Concordia Publising House.

6. *The Lutheran Witness,* April 14, 1964, p. 5.

7. Phone interview with Will Herzfeld, March 11, 1996.

8. Phone interview with Joe Ellwanger, March 21, 1996.

9. Letter from Rev. L. A. Wisler, St. Louis, MO, to Rev. G. M. Kramer, New Orleans, LA, dated Feb. 18, 1943. Quoted from *The Transition of Negro Missions from the Synodical Conference Missionary Board to the Southern District of the Lutheran Church - Missouri Synod,* by James Brockmann, p. 2.

10. *The Lutheran Witness,* November 12, 1963, p. 22.

11. Phone interview with Ronald Reinhardt, December 12, 1996.

12. *The Lutheran Witness,* March 3, 1965, p. 14.

13. According to a recollection of Edgar Homrighausen.

14. *The Missionary Lutheran,* August 1954, p. 63.

15. *Proceedings of the 49th Convention of the Southern District,* p. 95.

16. *Proceedings of the 50th Convention of the Southern District,* pp. 91,93.

17. *A TESTAMENT OF HOPE, The Essential Writings of Martin Luther King, Jr.,* edited by James Melvin Washington, (New York: Writers House, Copyright 1968 by Martin Luther King, Jr., copyright renewed 1996 by The Estate of Martin Luther King, Jr.) p. 295. Used with permission.

18. Phone interview with Will Herzfeld, March 11, 1996.

19. *Proceedings of the 50th Convention,* p. 93.

20. Personal interview with Thomas Noon, May 8, 1995.

21. Herzfeld.

22. Phone interview with Harold Woodworth, July 2, 1996.

23. Ibid.

24. Herzfeld.

25. Personal letter from Elva Ellermann, April 18, 1997.

26. Herzfeld.

27. Phone interview with Eldon Weisheit, March 4, 1997.

28. Personal interview with Albert Dominick, May 3, 1995.

29. Herzfeld.

30. Phone interview with George Hrbek, July 6, 1997.

31. Personal interview with Arthur Bodley, February 10, 1999.

32. Schrader.

33. Phone Interview with Jack Stewart, January 31, 1996.

34. *The Missionary Lutheran,* September 1961, p. 72.

AUTHOR RICHARD ZIEHR'S BOOK
MAY BE ORDERED
BY MAIL OR TELEPHONE

TO ORDER:

Mailing Address: ELAHAR ENTERPRISES
803 Bradford Drive
Ft. Walton Beach, FL 32547-3208

Telephone: (850) 862-2630

e-mail: ELAHAR@AOL.com

Yes, please send the number of books indicated below:

Title	Unit Price	Quantity	Subtotal
The Struggle For Unity	$15.95		

TOTAL:_____
+ Postage & Handling:_____
GRAND TOTAL:_____

Postage and Handling Charges	
1 – 4 books	$3.00 per book
5 or more	$2.00 per book

Make checks payable to: ELAHAR Enterprises

Ship to:

Your Name _____

Address _____

City_____ State ____ Zip_____